Astrology
The Inner Eye

Elaine Smith

Astrology
The Inner Eye

©1997 Elaine Smith

ISBN 1 86163 003 4

Cover design by Paul Mason

Published by:

Capall Bann Publishing
Freshfields
Chieveley
Berks
RG20 8TF

Acknowledgements

My warmest thanks to Ann Claydon and Joy McGilvray for their continued support during the writing of this book. Ann for her word-processing skills, patience and valuable criticism and Joy for her 'Red Pen' and excellent command of the English Language. To all my students for without you and your endless questions this book would never have materialised.

Forthcoming Titles

Book 2 A Student's guide to Astrological Techniques
Book 3 A Student's guide to Psychological Astrology

Contents

Introduction

This book is a collection of notes and ideas that materialised through many years of teaching and listening to students. When they said how much easier it is to understand the principles of calculation and interpretation when it is explained to them, I wondered how this could be made clearer for those unable to attend classes. The general opinion being that it was almost impossible to learn from books as some authors infer that the students have some knowledge, so quite often important factors are missed out or not clearly explained. This handbook is my attempt to simplify calculation and interpretation and take some of the mystery away with a glossary of Astrological Terms. In this way Astrology can become accessible to everyone.

At first everything may seem complicated and difficult to understand, like learning a new language for the first time. The most important tool you need to understand Astrology is perseverance and time for the language to become more familiar and perhaps more books that help to simplify the language so that everyone can understand.

Astrology is a language of time and symbolism, so give yourself time for these features to become familiar. I have taken classes where I have been aware that some students experience disappointment because they have not been able to grasp enough knowledge in one session to be able to work with Astrology. "I didn't realise there was so much in it" was the familiar cry. There is as little or as much in it as you want, depending upon whether it is just a passing interest for you, or the beginning of a life time study. For many people it is a life time study where you will be forever learning something new or experiencing an old concept in a different way. However, you should after six months of serious study be able to attempt some chart interpretation for your family or friends. A well structured basic course would be an excellent foundation for your studies. It is important to find others who are also interested in Astrology, make good use of the Associations that exist to pass on knowledge of workshops and meetings that may be local enough for you to attend.

Astrology can be a journey for a lifetime which will bring you in touch with many new ideas and concepts that will enhance your awareness, and bring you a deep spiritual experience as you respond to the ancient patterns of wisdom that have inspired mankind for centuries.

Chapter 1

A Basic Framework

This first chapter contains some simple data on astronomy which needs to be read in conjunction with diagrams 1 and 2. The earth revolves around the sun making one complete circuit in a period which we call one year. In this revolution around the sun, the solar orb is successively seen from the earth through each one of the twelve signs of the zodiac. The astrological year commences about the 21st of March, which is the vernal or spring equinox. At this time the sun is said to enter the sign of Aries, the first sign of the zodiac, and during the year it passes through the whole twelve signs or 360* of the circle. This journey of the Sun or of the Earth around the Sun, (causing the Sun to appear to pass through these signs) takes a little under 365 and a quarter days. Every 30* marks off one distinct division so far as the zodiac is concerned and by this we judge the internal or individual characteristics of the person born in that particular month. These divisions give us twelve clear and definite types that stand out distinctly.

The earth also revolves once upon its own axis, every 24 hours and this causes the whole 12 signs of the zodiac in turn to pass round the earth once each day of 24 hours, a fresh sign rising over the horizon at any place approximately every 2 hours, and one separate degree of the zodiac about every 4 minutes. Hence we may have two very different individuals born within 5 minutes of time. It should be remembered that every 4 minutes of time equals approximately one degree of the zodiac so every hour equals 15*, or the whole sign of the zodiac equals 2 hours in time. From this it will be seen that a given point on the earth will take 2 hours more or less in passing through one sign of the zodiac, thus the ascendant passes through the whole of the circle of the zodiac in one day owing to the rotation of the earth on its axis, or as by the earth's

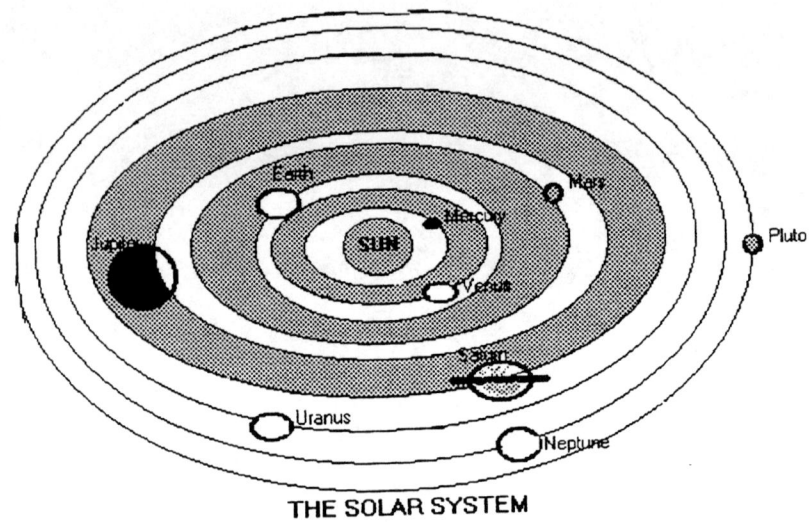

THE SOLAR SYSTEM

Diagram No. 1

revolution in its orbit the sun is made to appear to pass through the 12 signs in one year, or one sign for each month.

The sign occupying the east point is known as the rising sign or the ascendant. It is very important to clearly distinguish between this and the sign occupied by the Sun, as this can cause some confusion for new students. These two separate motions must be clearly thought out and the astronomical fact of these two revolutions of the earth constantly borne in mind. Once around the Sun and once upon its own axis. The former takes the year of 12 months and the latter a day of 24 hours. If you are still not clear about this please look at the diagrams one and two.

There is still another motion through the zodiac which we must consider and that is the motion of the Moon around the Earth. Once every lunar month of 28 days the Moon appears to pass through each sign, and in 2.5 days making a complete circuit. (Please refer to lunar diagram 9). To sum up we have learnt that

6

there are three very important considerations with regard to the signs of the zodiac. First the position of the sun each month caused by the yearly revolution of the earth around the sun, secondly the Moon's place in the zodiac each day, and thirdly the position of the east point or ascendant caused by the earth's daily revolution upon its own axis.

The zodiac is an important element of astrology to become thoroughly acquainted with. It is the track or belt through which all planets pass. It lies approximately 8^0 either side of the ecliptic. (The ecliptic is the apparent path of the sun around the earth or in reality the earth's orbit). The ecliptic meets the equator at a spot which is called the First Point of Aries or the vernal equinox. The signs of the zodiac should never be confused with the 12 constellations bearing the same names, for although at certain periods of the world evolution the signs and the constellations coincided and will do so again, this is not now the case. (Please see Precession of the Equinoxes in the glossary at the back of this book.)

The astrological signs are not bodies but spaces of 30^0 each that divide the ecliptic into 12 equal parts, the measurement both of the ecliptic and of the equator begins where they intersect each other as the sun ascends northwards. We measure this distance from the First Point of Aries (vernal equinox) on the ecliptic and call it (celestial) longitude. If a planet lies a little north or south of the ecliptic we call this distance latitude. The longitude of a planet is measured on the ecliptic by signs and degrees, but on the equator by degrees only and this is called its Right Ascension. While its distance north or south of the equator is the Declination. For further clarification of some of these terms please see the glossary at the back of this handbook.

Astrology is a technique for gaining wisdom and understanding through learning to identify our consciousness with celestial patterns and rhythms. The zodiac represents the basic realisation that the quality of life on earth perpetually, rhythmically and seasonally changes. The yearly series of relationships between the Sun and Earth cause the seasons and our experience of seasonal changes in weather, plant life and animal activity form the foundation of the most ancient concepts of the zodiac.

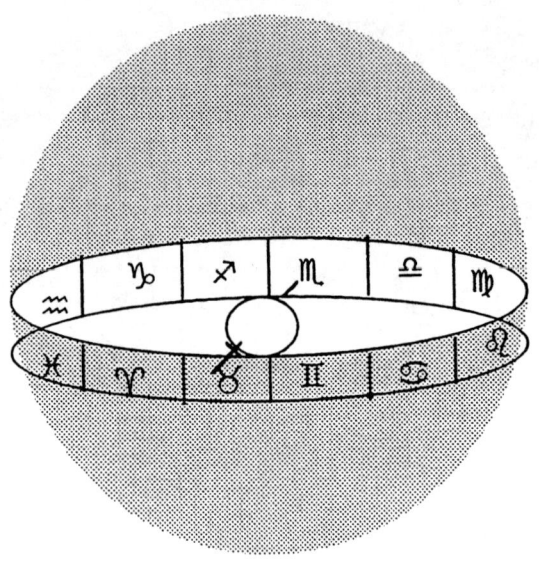

Diagram No. 2

The zodiac is divided into four quadrants. Each quadrant or season begins with an equinox or solstice. An equinox is the day the sun on the ecliptic, its apparent path around the earth, crosses the equator and moves towards the earth's north or south poles; days and nights are of equal length at both equinoxes. The solstice is the day the sun reaches its greatest distance north, the summer solstice, or south the winter solstice, of the terrestrial equator. At the summer solstice days are longest and nights are shortest in the northern hemisphere. At the winter solstice in the northern hemisphere the longest night meets the shortest day of the year. (The reverse occurs at the solstices in the southern hemisphere).

The Qualities
Equinoctial and solsticial signs are called Cardinal signs because when the sun enters them a new season begins. This indicates that

8

much work has to be done to adjust to the new season, so cardinal people tend to be active hard workers. Signs following cardinal signs are called fixed signs because when the sun passes through them the quality of the season becomes set or fixed. The same applies to people with a fixed sign emphasis, they may dislike change and have a lazy attitude to new ideas preferring to remain fixed to their old patterns of thought. Signs following fixed signs and preceding cardinal signs are called mutable signs because when the sun passes through them there is a transition from one season to the next. Here people know the season is coming to an end and are anxious for change, they have learned to be flexible and adapt more easily to a changing environment. So seasonal conditions on Earth challenge human beings to initiate - cardinal. A new set of seasonal appropriate activities - fixed. And to making transition - mutable, to a new set of seasonal conditions.

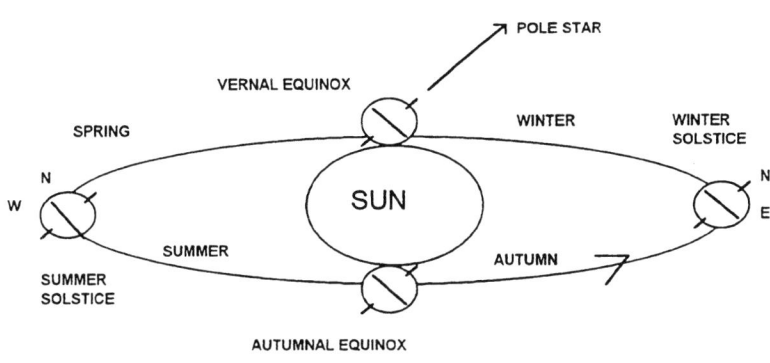

Diagram No. 3 Shows the inclination of the earth's axis which is the main cause of the earth's seasons.

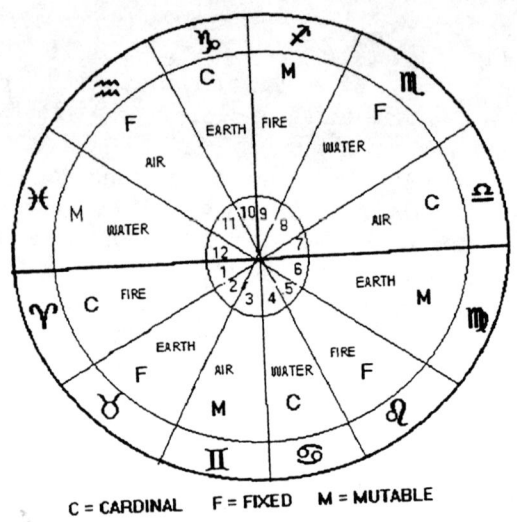

C = CARDINAL   F = FIXED   M = MUTABLE

Diagram No. 4

	FIRE	EARTH	AIR	WATER
CARDINAL	♈	♑	♎	♋
FIXED	♌	♉	♒	♏
MUTABLE	♐	♍	♊	♓

Diagram No. 5

To summarise the Qualities; Cardinal people are ambitious rather than adaptable and tend to desire excitement and activity. There can be opportunities to give situations and issues more time than people.

Fixed people are strong willed and fairly resilient to eternal influences and may consider values and ideals to be more important than the individual.

Mutable people can be personal and sentimental rather than idealistic or ambitious, showing concern with people and relationships than personal ambitions.

Our experience of the sky evokes a deep spiritual response which involves our body, mind and feelings. It can be a moving experience and something that we need to integrate into our daily lives. To do this we must be able to understand it in a coherent and significant way. To explore astrology, the journey must take us to seek a coherent order to our lives but to search for a meaning and our place within it. Which means we should search for answers, not only amongst the stars but from the depths of our being, and to understand our relationship to what we see and experience.

Chapter 2

The Elements

The pattern of the zodiac is divided according to the ancient scheme of four elements. FIRE, EARTH, AIR and WATER, of which all life on Earth was thought to be composed. Fire signs are dynamic and active. Earth signs productive and practical. Air signs relational and mental. Water signs emotional and assimilative.

If you look at diagrams 4 and 5, on page 10 paying particular attention to the table of qualities, you will see that with the four Elements and the three Qualities, each sign emerges as a unique combination.

The elements are divided into 2 groups, fire and air being positive/masculine and earth and water being negative/feminine. The fire and air are considered to be self expressive and active and dynamic, and the water and earth to be slower and repressive, passive and receptive. They resemble the Chinese philosophy of yin and yang, water and earth being yin and fire and air being yang.

It must also be remembered that an astrological chart contains all four elements, but the position of the planets emphasises the ele-

ments that we are more consciously aware of. If we have more planets in Fire and Air we will be more positive and active naturally, but need to work on our more emotional and compassionate side. But, if we have more Earth and Water in our natal chart then we may be emotional, practical and considerate but need to incorporate some assertive action into our lives.

An Imbalance of Elements

There are twelve signs of the zodiac and these twelve signs are broken up into four groups, Fire, Earth, Air and Water, and each member of the group is given a different quality. They have the cardinal quality - these are the people who respond to challenge and hard work. The fixed quality - these have fixed opinions and ideas and are likely to be settled rather than keep changing. And finally the mutable signs - these tend to be very adaptable with a restless quality, they flow with life accepting changes when they come.

Your birthchart is in effect made up of all the twelve astrological signs, but wherever the planets are placed shows where their sign or element is emphasised, as is shown in diagram 6.

As you can see in diagram 6, Venus, Mars, Mercury, Sun, Uranus and Neptune are all in Capricorn. The Moon is in Virgo which gives us seven planets in Earth, so here we have a definite emphasis on Earth especially as the Ascendant is Taurus and the MC is in Capricorn also. The rest of the chart is made up of two planets in the Water sign of Scorpio (Jupiter and Pluto) and only one planet in Air (Saturn) which is a very earthy planet and the ruler of Capricorn and the ultimate dispositor of all the Capricorn planets. However, there are no planets emphasised in the element of Fire so you would say that this chart lacks Fire. But what we really mean is that this person is not aware of Fire on a conscious level. Because of this there may be many ways in which they endeavour to bring this fire to their consciousness. Therefore it may feel as though you have a void where the Fire element should be and you continue to attract Fire lessons until you learn to integrate it into your daily life.

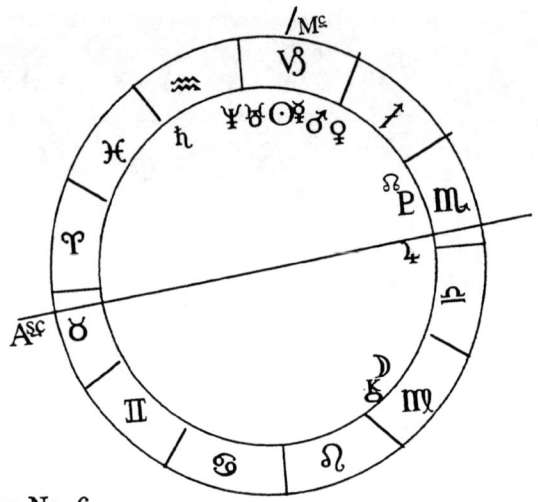

Diagram No. 6

Too much emphasis on an element is described more fully in the next chapter but whenever there is an abundance of planets in one element it is an indication of a lack elsewhere.

It may be more important to understand what is operating on an unconscious level as it is less likely to be under our control than an element that is operating consciously.

As you can see Diagram 6 shows an over-emphasis on Earth. This subject may experience depression, or be unimaginative and dull. These qualities are already obvious to them, they need to be more concerned about the less obvious elements. Lack of Air and Fire means they must learn to be more assertive about their needs and to develop imagination and broaden their interests; the empty houses will show in what areas of life they may accomplish this. Even people who have a strong emphasis on a certain element in their charts - may if they have been repressed in childhood - act as if this element is missing. This energy can be more disruptive and less easy to recognise. For example a really strong and aggressive parent may produce a very submissive child even though that child has several planets in Fire.

Fire

If you lack Fire or have only one planet emphasised in this element the experience of that element is working mainly unconsciously and sooner or later will come to the surface. There can be a feeling of intensity surrounding an element that is lacking, so when we begin to experience it, it can be somewhat difficult to deal with. Lacking Fire could make us lack warmth, independence and personal vitality. You may have difficulty asserting yourself or acting independently of others. If you lack Fire you may experience it as anger, violence or domination and strength of character coming from someone else. On an extreme level you may even suffer fires, burglaries or violence.

Fire people are very organised and do especially well dealing with chaos so lack of Fire may mean fear of chaos because you know that you cannot handle it. You sometimes lack the ability to assert yourself. You need also to look in your chart to where that one planet or the empty space falls, in what house? This house or area of life may show you where you are going to experience the fire element in your life. It may be a difficult area of life where you always meet opposition or someone who over-powers you, until at some point you learn to deal with it.

Air

The lack of Air in a chart can indicate an inability to think or reason clearly, particularly if there is also a strong emphasis on Water. It can also mean that you are unable to detach yourself from your own point of view as Air gives the ability to see someone else's viewpoint. It is sometimes difficult to communicate with and relate to others, or there may be a lack of education, so we can attract things of an airy nature. You may spend your whole life studying in order to compensate. Sometimes you may find yourself the subject of slander or gossiping and being acutely sensitive to what other people say, or more often find people talking about you behind your back. You can get involved with obsessive ideas and ideologies; ideologies that could take you over.

Earth

A person who lacks Earth may be rather impractical although this is not always the case. It is not always easy to define, it can sometimes be a strange sense of not being rooted in the physical universe, finding it hard to keep your sense of reality straight, losing all sense of proportion in a stressful situation. It can also bring embarrassment about your own body, about sexuality, money or the need for stability.

Sometimes lack of Earth has to do with stability and money and you can be dogged by financial troubles or sometimes it is purely an attitude to money. It can be a symbol that you dislike, feeling that you don't deserve it or in some way it is unspiritual, or that you cannot be spiritual and have money. You need to learn to avoid situations in which people behave in an unreal way with no thought for practical concerns. You need to keep your sense of reality by being outdoors with nature, to deal with situations that are real and where you are able to feel your feet firmly planted in the ground.

Water

A lack of Water may indicate that you have difficulty empathising with others. This does not mean that you are unemotional but it means that your feelings may not be central to your consciousness, even though your emotions may be active. You may neglect your own inner needs in favour of practical or intellectual considerations to the extent that inner needs cry out for expression. Such people may begin to act coldly and without feeling until they finally realise that something is wrong. Lack of Water can produce an emotional partner. A partner who makes scenes or a child that constantly wants attention, or a mother who uses emotions and guilt feelings to force you to do things for her and against your will, means you may have a lack of Water. Water in dreams is usually of an emotional nature and about the unconscious, it filters into dreams in an uncontrollable way, like a tidal wave which floods conscious thought - it could make you irritable, moody, lacking in feelings or could produce an emotional breakdown.

Chapter 3

Fire

Action and energy

The signs associated with the element of Fire are *Aries, Leo* and *Sagittarius*. Those whose charts contain the strong Fire element have great enthusiasm for life, almost bursting full of energy and vitality. They need to be free to express themselves in a way that is natural to them. Warmth, spirit and freedom are represented by fire. It is a desire for life and a will to be. Although these tremendous high spirits can be thought of as exciting to some, it can be irritating and difficult for others to live with.

Fire signs rarely hurt others through deliberate action, but more through lack of self control or lack of sensitivity. The cautious and emotional qualities of earth and water may be aggravated by the high spirited action of Fire and by reciprocal reaction, a Fire sign may well feel smothered by earth, and feel that water can generally be a wet blanket. Air signs can gently fan the flames of Fire and push them into further action, although with too much Air Fire can quickly become bored with all ideas and no action. In general, Fire people can be very emotional but more in a passionate or high spirited way, they are not inclined to brood quietly like Water people, everything has to be out in the open. When they are angry there is no use at all to try and reason with them, they lose their tempers easily and only the very bravest are likely to approach them before their energies have calmed down.

For the very young, the Fire element can have its own difficulties which are aggressiveness and bullying, rebelliousness, a tendency to dominate other children, finding it difficult to cry or show their emotions. If any of these traits are spotted then careful guidance and understanding will be needed if the young Fire child is not to

17

experience difficulties in later relationships. Fire children are not usually concerned with anything practical. They like to be allowed to do exactly what they want whether it is useful or not. They find school life more difficult because of the sedentary nature of studying. They are restless children who are keener to get out in the sports field than they are to sit down for long periods at their desks.

Zodiacal Fire Signs

Aries

The first Fire sign and the first sign of the zodiac is ARIES, which is a positive sign and its quality is cardinal and it is ruled by Mars.

Aries responds to the cardinal challenge by spinning into action frequently. An Aries person has drive and enthusiasm and when their enthusiasm is burning fiercely they can wear everyone out with their endless energy. But when the enthusiasm dies down then so does the energy and all the unfinished work is left, probably never to be touched again. Aries always takes on more than they can ever possibly hope to finish and it needs the more persistent efforts of Taurus to complete their unfinished tasks. All this fiery enthusiasm of Aries does not just fizzle out or disappear out of the window, the reason for it diminishing is because it has already gone on to another project.

A true Aries can be a weaver of beautiful dreams; he has the energy to create them and begin them, but needs someone around who will complete all the boring bits when he tires of them and goes off onto a new idea. So like a child Aries wants mother around to tidy up when he has finished all the exciting work, hence the male Aries is often attracted to the Cancerian female, the mother and the child.

Aries people can be vibrant, energetic and exciting but beware, if you are a sensitive flower, they don't mean to be selfish, they simply don't think. Their minds are always on the next dream.

We all know the Aries who bursts through the door with an enormous grin on his face, isn't everyone pleased to see him, then he notices the startled silence and slightly shocked looks. At least they are looking at him! Then he notices someone lying flat on his back on the floor. Well, what was he doing behind the door, didn't he know someone would come though it? It is always someone else's fault, they should have known and anticipated what he would do. Whoever was standing behind the door should have known he would burst through it like the building was on fire. So as Aries are ready to shrug off the blame for anything they may have caused, they are also ready to jump into action and save anyone from another's action.

The Aries female is not always as ready as the Aries male to spring into action and rescue others from their fate. She is more inclined to await the knight in shining armour to gallop to her rescue, to fulfil her destiny. However this rarely happens and if she is really honest, does she really want anyone else to have the glory of her success. She ultimately finds that she has to rescue herself to be mistress of her own destiny. And although she still dreams of her knight his performance would be only on her terms. In some ways she is so idealistic that in reality her dream could not exist.

The positive energy of Aries is a fearless, courageous spirit whose mission in life is to inspire and lead. They make very loyal friends and are not inclined to seek revenge. Their most difficult faults tend to be their thoughtlessness, rarely thinking of others before themselves. Their difficulty in seeing a task through to the end and their naiveté in believing that everyone else is waiting just to finish all their unwanted tasks.

The Aries aggressiveness may come from their fear of being attacked so they attack first. To an Aries, identity is important and they may spend their whole lifetime trying to discover who they are until they finally discover that they have become the person they most wanted to be.

Leo

The second Fire sign and the fifth sign of the zodiac is LEO, which is also a positive sign and its quality is fixed and it is ruled by the Sun.

Fire signs tend to represent identity and expression of that identity. Where Aries is the child then Leo represents the father and there is always some difficulty with the father in his destiny. It can be very important for Leo to develop his own creative outlet as he desperately needs recognition for his own abilities, Leo should be prepared to put plenty of time and energy into making sure he produces something that will make him feel that any praise has been earned.

When immature and still developing confidence he may be too sensitive to anything which seems to affront his personal pride. Leo truly meets his challenge when his pride and the aura of authority he loves to project are based on accomplishment. So he certainly comes into his own when he is head of something, either a company or in his own household. It is not that important what it is as long as it contains his adoring subjects.

Leo's have an abundance of vitality radiating from their centre, or the warmth of the Sun which is the ruler of their sign. A Leo who is secure in his sense of worth is genuinely kind, warm hearted and loving. They feel secure with success and the admiration of others. They are not particularly interested in the Aries dream unless they can make it a reality. Success to them is sticking at it and making it work and winning the admiration of all their contemporaries. And if they can make a dream work, then it was their dream to begin with. Some Leos seem to be born with a sense of failure, then can feel misunderstood and unloved. They need to get over this completely if they are ever going to find their creative source.

A Leo who is unsure of himself compensates for his feelings of inferiority by becoming arrogant and boastful. His uncertainty lies in the fact that perhaps he is not quite so wonderful as he thought, so he has to keep up this pretence by flattering himself and telling everyone how wonderful he is in case they have not quite noticed.

His other faults lie in his tendency to be arrogant, overbearing and too pushy, although this often seems to be how others see them rather than as they truly are.

A side not often seen is that they can be very vulnerable, they need lots of encouragement and can be easily put down which can be quite disastrous for young Leos, as a blow to their fragile egos can take a long time to heal.

Those who don't understand the Leo personality seem to make it a lifetime's task to put down this sign which can be quite devastating if they happen to be the parent of a young Leo. An ego that takes constant battering may never recover, so it is sometimes said that the weakest and the strongest individuals come out of this sign.

Sagittarius

The third Fire sign and the ninth sign of the zodiac is SAGITTARIUS whose quality is mutable and is ruled by Jupiter.

If Aries is the child and Leo the father, then Sagittarius must surely be the grandfather or the sage and the teacher. The sign of Sagittarius is linked to the Centaur and the most famous centaur in ancient mythology was Chiron. So Sagittarius is the sign of the philosopher and the teacher and of religious pursuits. Generally Sagittarians have a clear conception of the image they wish to achieve and they often set out to work hard to put into practice their ideals.

They have a great restlessness which seems to drive them on, so that when they reach a goal they immediately begin to pursue another. This is because it is the journey towards the goal that is important to them and not the arrival or the reward at the end. Boredom can be a big problem for Sagittarians. They hate doing anything more than once and long before anything becomes repetitive, they are already treading the path towards another goal.

Travel is also a favourite pursuit but they are not the kind that will buy a package tour and spend a fortnight laying on some distant beach. They need to be mobile, they need a city to explore, a ruin, a castle or a place where no one else has been, and the more alien the culture, the more his interest is held. Sagittarians seek to explore all new possibilities, either physically to travel or in highly competitive sport or philosophically by exploring new dimensions of thought.

They seek adventure, they are freedom loving, future oriented and optimistic. But when they are more mature they no longer seek freedom from restriction but use their freedom to obtain to their higher ideals. They can be very frank and outspoken and lack tact, but their tactlessness stems from their frankness or their lack of thought. There is rarely any malicious feelings behind what they say. They can be very hurt when people take offence because they truly haven't meant to cause any. Sometimes this sign can produce drifters and uninteresting characters who are quite content to let others do everything for them, but whoever they are they become fretful, irritable and rebellious when placed anywhere where they are restricted or restrained.

At the heart of Sagittarius there is a great need to explore and understand life. Like Leo they can be a deeply religious sign, always seeking to enlarge their consciousness. They have intuition and vision and say that life is to be explored and enjoyed, but ultimately to be understood. With young Sagittarians there is always an element of 'risk taking' and they rarely see danger as they throw themselves wholeheartedly into what they do. Because of this it can be quite a traumatic experience bringing up one of these youngsters. However, the other side of the coin is that some of these youngsters can be extremely studious putting all their energy into mental applications and sometimes these people are the eternal students never wanting to grow up and take a responsible position in the outer world.

Chapter 4

Air

Intellect and communication

The signs associated with the element of Air are Gemini, Libra and Aquarius. Air in the chart is a persons ability to think and reason clearly and objectively and to not let emotions take control or distort thinking. Air people have the ability to detach themselves and stand back from daily life experiences. This enables them to see life in perspective and take a rational approach to everything they do.

Air signs do not get heavily involved in an emotional way with other people's worries. They are able to remain detached which enables them to work more effectively with all sorts of people. They are in fact the most social of all signs in the sense they can appreciate the other persons thoughts, seeing them objectively regardless of whether they agree with them.

Air signs can become too involved with abstract ideals and theories, and if this happens they can become out of touch with reality leading them to become fairly eccentric and fanatical. The difficulties that this element can have is the fact that they may not be in touch with their own and other people's feelings and emotions. They can lack an understanding of their own deep emotions as well as an acceptance of the limitation of the physical body. They may simply think that emotional considerations are unimportant and find it difficult to understand why other people are always showing their feelings and emotions. In this way Air people can have an insensitivity that is somehow different from the insensitivity of Fire signs.

With Fire signs their insensitivity results from the need to exert their will without any interference from other, whereas the Air signs insensitivity comes from not understanding emotions or that what they say could actually hurt others. There is often a tendency to intellectualise everything, and as academic life often has a very strong Air flavour, this can make some forms of studying a rather sterile occupation for the other more vibrant signs who seek to experience life as well as understand it. Education these days is entering into a more experiential mode, probably brought about by the signs who are more in touch with their senses.

Often Air signs feel that if something cannot be understood according to an intellectual rationale then it must be unimportant. They tend to seek knowledge and the gaining of wisdom as their ultimate goal. Air people are very good at communicating with others because their ability to understand matters logically makes them good at explaining it back to others. They are also able to influence other people's opinions.

Parents should be aware of an Air child's ability to sway people and influence them because they can make their point of view seem so convincing. Air people are usually liked by others. They know how to create a favourable impression and are usually willing to make compromises in order to seem more attractive to others.

Zodiacal Air Signs

Gemini

The first Air sign and the third sign of the zodiac is Gemini. All the air signs are masculine, positive signs and Gemini is ruled by Mercury, and its quality is mutable.

Gemini is the sign of the twins and their drive is to communicate, to gather information and experiences at the mental level. They catalogue data and communicate with others, and contact with mentally stimulating people always makes them feel alive. They enjoy any form of communication through writing, talking or being involved in fairly volatile discussion groups.

Gemini's are versatile and quickly adapt themselves to their surroundings. They love variety and take pleasure in all mental pursuits which they sometimes can take to extremes. Like their opposite sign of Sagittarius they are restless and get bored easily although their restlessness is often more mental than physical. Unpredictable is another word you could apply to Gemini because they are so changeable. They have mood swings from dark to light moods, sometimes introvert, sometimes extrovert. Generally, their behaviour is pretty inconsistent. They become bored very quickly and need to move on to something new.

They often do more than one thing at a time and express their desire to be in more than one place at a time. They seem unable to cope with worry or stress which often unnerves them. They can display a nervous image by rushing everywhere and if made to sit still they fidget and tap their fingers. Their moods are very swift in changing so that it is sometimes like dealing with two separate people. A young Gemini may have a tendency to be spiteful, this may be an effort to get attention or to gain a reaction, but whatever the reason they are difficult to ignore. The Gemini's task seems to be to gather information and pass it on to others, and they are always searching for intellectual security.

Líbra

The second Air sign and the seventh sign of the zodiac is LIBRA. It's quality is cardinal and is ruled by Venus.

Librans have remarkable powers of comparison. They like to balance all things mentally but they can, of course, go to extremes like all cardinal signs. They need to judge and are given the opportunity in life to experience both opposites, to make reasoned and fair conclusions from their experiences. They work hard to come up with the right answer and are sometimes then shown that life is not fair. They try to express justice, equilibrium, balance, order and dispassionate judgement.

They have kind and amenable natures from the rulership of Venus. They can be courteous, agreeable and very pleasant, diplomatic and charming but when insecure they are easily influenced by others, this will lead them to do almost anything to stay in a relationship. You rarely find a Libran leaving a relationship unless they have another one lined up, because they hate being alone so much. Librans love to have everything balanced and in a state of harmony and get confused and irritated if things are out of harmony. This can be so important to them that they bend over backwards to restore any balance in a relationship, so eventually they run the danger of making themselves into doormats.

A Libran home is frequently a very pleasant and beautiful place to be in. If conditions are right they make excellent home makers, but they are not made for heavy work and dislike getting themselves dirty, so if conditions are not right they often do nothing at all in the home and soon become disheartened. They have a reputation for being indecisive from their ability to see a point from every angle. They take so long weighing up the pros and cons of a situation which is why they take such a long time to make a decision. They are at their best at social gatherings. They are able to circulate so everyone has a share of their charms. Finding it difficult to be on their own, and their dislike of living on their own makes this the sign most likely to be married more than once.

Aquarius

The third air sign and the eleventh sign of the zodiac is AQUARIUS. It is a fixed sign and is ruled by Saturn and Uranus.

Aquarians project a cool detached nature. They find close emotional relationships difficult and they are so idealistic that they may try to change people rather than accept them as they are. Aquarius has often been called the sign who loves humanity but hates people.

They rise above Libran's preoccupation with relationships and concentrate more on the kind of impersonal relationships that links all humanity. An Aquarian is able to think fairly objectively without consulting their feelings. They are able to absorb all their practical experiences including the emotional ones and think them over. In a relationship they can be very faithful but they need the freedom to mix with friends of both sexes, because friendship, exchanges of thoughts and ideas are important to them, and love only seems to last if it is based on similar outlooks. Aquarians are often seen as eccentric, unconventional, resourceful and progressive. They can be depended upon and trusted.

They have a remarkable ability to study human nature and are often involved in political movements or protection of animal leagues. They are usually the organisers as they are great planners of campaigns, although they leave the fighting and the aggressiveness to the more passionate signs, such as Aries or Scorpio. They do, however, approach everything with great originality which is where they get their reputation of being called different or strange.

An Aquarian can steal from others without looking at the consequences in the way perhaps of Robin Hood. So he may begin something for others but he underestimates or overestimates human nature and things get out of hand, and at some point he has to face the consequences that he began. So a less well developed Aquarian could be tricky and deceptive and clever in the achievements of his own ends, or a rebel without a cause.

Chapter 5

Earth

Cautious and practical

The signs associated with the element of earth are Taurus, virgo and Capricorn.

People with a strong emphasis in Earth show that they are in touch with the reality of the material world as well as their physical senses. Earth people tend to rely more on their senses and their practical reasoning than upon the inspiration or intuition of the other elements. It is instinctive to them to fit into the world of making a living. They are able to supply basic needs and persist until they reach their goals. All of these qualities come naturally to those of the Earth element. Earth people tend to be cautious, premeditative, rather conventional and unusually dependable. They are generally fairly suspicious and can be dubious about the lively, far more agile minded people, although they may be fascinated by them. They could find Air signs frustrating with their impractical and unworkable schemes. They sometimes feel that Fire signs storm through their life much too quickly and too forcefully to do anything worthwhile or be trusted.

They are usually quieter and more placid than Fire and Air. They are practical and need to know what good something is before they take it up. However if they could learn to get on with the more intuitive and inspirational signs they would be very good at making other people's idealistic dreams come true. And if it can be done at all they are the ones to do it. But they can be very conservative, much preferring to deal with the tried and the true. Earth people need order in their lives or else they feel very insecure, and one of their greatest strengths is their ability to stay in control of themselves no matter how strange or difficult their environment is.

At a very early age they develop a strong sense of reality and do not easily loose track of what is important. They certainly need to be encouraged to develop their imagination because the combination of imagination and their solid practicality can be extremely effective, and it will counter their tendency to become dull and unimaginative which does sometimes result from an over emphasis on the Earth qualities.

The self esteem of an Earth person is strongly focused on being able to do something well. They are often able to make objects of considerable beauty and craftsmanship because they have the patience to do the job. Children with a great deal of earth need to be encouraged to be imaginative and to develop their own sense of self worth.

Zodiacal Earth Signs

Taurus
TAURUS is the first Earth sign and the second sign of the zodiac and is a fixed sign and like all the other Earth signs is feminine and negative, and security is their priority. It is ruled by Venus.

Taurus is patient, enduring and persistent and able to conserve energy, rarely wasting it like Aries people do. Taurus people are usually methodical and devoted to their endeavours and this is where the root of some of the difficulties that they have to face may lie.

Methods or routines that are stubbornly applied can become rigid or dogmatic and a devotion that is exclusive to any one person could lead them to become demanding and possessive. They are fond of the good things in life and like to be surrounded by their possessions. They are happiest with a steady job, a comfortable home and good food, but if this sign is very strong these people can get very stodgy, lack imagination and get stuck in a rut throughout life.

When Taurus becomes obsessed with something that they desire there is no holding them, so desire is a dominant force in Taurus whether it is sexual satisfaction, food, drink, money, status or anything else you can think of. One of the faults of this sign is greed and desire. Their better nature can easily be over shadowed by their rampant desires. They would find it difficult to keep to a bargain if something better was offered, they would not see this as disloyal but sensible.

Taureans can be very stubborn sometimes sticking rigidly to an attitude that they have really outgrown. Their possessiveness and jealously can be very destructive in relationships as they find it difficult to give their partners sufficient freedom (or love and trust) to develop naturally. They need to work on controlling their desire nature and develop more understanding not only of the needs of others but that others needs can be and often are different to theirs.

Vírgo

VIRGO is the second Earth sign and the sixth sign of the zodiac. It is mutable and is ruled by the planet Mercury.

Virgo can represent naiveté and innocence. Innocence in its refusal to be penetrated or violated. Life's experiences are not taken in, so many with Virgo ascendants are virginal in that they allow nothing to touch them deeply. An inward childlike simplicity accounts for their black and white judgement. The Virgo searches for the perfection which may be spurred on by their inner dissatisfaction or discontent. Virgo's have either the kind of divine discontent which spurs them onward or the kind of petty restlessness that blames others. Generally they are constructive and able to make the most of their situation or condition.
They are very discriminating, have great reasoning power and very ingenious methods of working. They are the most critical of all individuals but they are able to turn this criticism upon themselves as well as others, for they seem to be always taking them-

selves to pieces. Virgos have the most problems with relationships out of all the signs, especially if Venus is also in this sign. Their partners have a lot of trouble living up to their ideas of perfection and love often does not last under constant criticism.

Virgos are very industrious and persistent, tending towards more practical things than ideas. They are precise in detail and can readily put right any errors or defects in their own character. They can also be more selfish at times than most of the other signs as they are always aware of their own interests. They can be extremely sensitive and sometimes rather timid. When insecure Virgo can be harping, when mature they are discerning and efficient. Virgo's needs are fulfilled when they are able to apply themselves diligently with self discipline to any matter they have in hand.

They have a naive belief that as long as you know the name of everything it will stay in its place. If it is filed it can't go wrong and everything is safe. So Virgo is inclined to have everything in its place and a place for everything and find it hard to cope when things are out of order. This sign is one that is most unable to cope with chaos unless it is putting someone else's chaos back into order.

CapRicoRn

Capricorn is the third Earth sign and the tenth sign of the zodiac. It is cardinal and is ruled by the planet Saturn.

Capricorn is always linked with the symbol of the father. It does not matter what kind of father the Capricorn has, but the relationship is nearly always complicated and the early years of their life is often difficult. Sometimes it can mean that the loss of the father has forced them to take on responsibilities early in life. In other cases the father may have been stern or aloof or weak or unstable, and sometimes over idealised.

With Capricorn females the father is more likely to be idealised as the girl may spend a long time looking for someone to play the fatherly role before deciding to marry. With a Capricorn male the father may be one with whom they feel they have to compete or whose love seems hard to obtain. So the father is often a mystery and a challenge or a problem to be solved, and often the first half of a Capricorns life can be difficult. So many Capricorns are busy rebelling against the father during this period or trying to live up to his expectations or competing with him in some way.

Capricorns fair well with responsibility, in fact they seek it out. They are ambitious enough to want to attain a position of authority. Capricorns often like to be in a position of power as this fulfils their need for security. They are often able to make the most of their talents and are capable of attaining great heights as they possess both ambition and endurance, though they can be limited by their fear of taking risks.

They need security and a regular salary, though like Scorpio they can be quite ruthless in their ambitions. They are frequently found at the top of some institution or structure, such as the civil service or police force, and more often than not they are attracted to politics.

Capricorn can be quite a powerful sign and can accomplish a great deal in the world but there is a fanatical streak in them. Tolerance is often hard for them to understand because they have had to discipline themselves in a ruthless way to gain the goals that they are after, and they cannot understand why others cannot achieve the same goals or why they are not interested in the same discipline. They need to learn to understand that others may not have goals in the same sense that he does, or that people have different type of goals.

Capricorn has as much capacity to love as any other sign but they must remember that to love someone is to give them recognition as an equal, not just to guide them in a fatherly way, as they are likely to be the kind of father who may withhold love if there is no obedience. The more Capricorns allow themselves to relax the more they are able to see that less disciplined souls are no less worthy, that they may actually hold a key to happiness that somehow Capricorns have missed. They are, however, just as capable of enjoying themselves as the next sign, they have a very rye sense of humour that is not always recognised.

Chapter 6

Water

Sensitive and emotional

The signs associated with Water are CANCER, SCORPIO and PISCES. They are all feminine and negative. Water is thought to be the element of the soul, it is feeling, emotion and compassion. Water signs are in touch with their feelings and in tune with the shades and subtleties that many others don't even notice. It represents the realms of deep emotion and feeling responses ranging from compulsive passions to overwhelming fears to an all encompassing acceptance and love of creation.

Since feelings by their very nature are partly unconscious the Water signs are often aware of the power of the unconscious mind and are themselves often unconscious of much of what really motivates them. Water signs have no solidity or form of their own, and are therefore often content when their flexible nature is given structure by others, particularly Earth signs who have the solidity and practical application that is trusted and relied upon by Water. Water signs often shy away from those who are more boisterous or who have strong personalities. They feel more comfortable with those who are rather secretive and more self contained, which gives them a greater feeling of protection and security.

Water signs may get lost in dreams and idealism even if they do not show it outwardly. Their logical and rational intellect needs to be developed, so they can at least communicate their feelings to others and thereby get some release from emotional tension. Emotions dominate their thinking so much that it is hard to reason with them.

As children the water element is sensitive and needs an emotionally secure childhood. It is never necessary to reprimand them too strongly as they always know when they have done wrong because they can sense the anger coming from others. They are particularly sensitive to the negative vibrations, so should not spend too much time around negative people. Their emotional impressions of childhood do not fade as they tend to hold on to their past with a great tenacity. Even Scorpio which is the toughest of the three signs would find deep wounds still in the unconscious through an emotionally insecure childhood and may spend their whole adult life looking for the peace and serenity that they lacked, and in doing so avoids anything that reminds them of the past.

They may make friends slowly and appear withdrawn. It is important to help water children to get away from themselves because they tend to get very involved in their own internal worlds. Yet on the positive side this can result in a vivid and creative imagination, but negatively may cause them to lose touch with reality.

Zoðiacal Water Signs

Cancer
CANCER is the first Water sign and the fourth sign of the zodiac. It is cardinal and is ruled by the Moon. The very sensitive nature of Cancer makes them feel very keenly everything that affects other members of their family and for them, domestic affairs can become a break on their own individual progress. They can be reserved and shy as they fear ridicule and dis-  approval. When emotionally secure the Cancerian is protective and nurturing, hospitable and attentive to the needs of the others. When uncertain or insecure they become overly maternal, clinging or possessive. They feel most comfortable at home and in their most insecure moments they may find themselves travelling homewards where they always find security and solace.

They are likely to be very economical, and fond of saving, feeling insecure without money behind them or put safely away for a rainy day. Cancerians are often very good with money and can accumulate wealth, but will never show it off, so often giving the impression they are hard up. There is a tendency to save everything, letters, books, stamps, and all types of curios and odds and ends. They have a very retentive memory and assimilate information by intuitively feeling things out.

Although others may have difficulty in penetrating the Cancerian depth, the Cancer type often guards its inner life closely. They have a fondness for power and having gained it they have the ability to hold on to it whether it is their family or in their job. They can be perpetual wanderers always seeking roots somewhere else. Sometimes they are running away from the past, from their childhood.

The mother is a particular significant and powerful figure for the Cancerian. It represents feelings of the past and the security that he longs for intensely. Family life can sometimes be so important for the Cancerian that it begins to become suffocating and he may have to leave to find himself again, thus leaving a broken home or marriage - even though family and parenthood are tremendously important.

Scorpio

SCORPIO is the second Water sign and the eighth sign of the zodiac. It is fixed and is ruled by Mars and Pluto.

The nature of Scorpio can be either intense and passionate or cruel and distant, as it can be a sign of extremes. When insecure they are often jealous and competitive. They have the ruthlessness required to succeed in a difficult world of business. Scorpios love a challenge and is the only Water sign that will fight and enjoy it, mainly because they like to experience everything at peak. They thrive on mysteries and rise to the challenge of discovering the reason behind something. They can be very persistent. Like the other Water signs Scorpio is sensitive and easily hurt, which is often forgotten due to their tough image. Scorpios can be magnetically attractive or repellingly vindictive.

They have a charismatic quality that the more timid signs will back away from. Some Scorpios can give the impression that they see into the depths of your soul. Scorpios search for security in both the heights and depths of life as it is a sign of intense desire. They are reserved and inscrutable, stubborn and passionate, clinging tenaciously to the things they value and will fight for them to death.

They have the ability to spot weakness in others and know how to go straight to that weakness if they are seeking revenge. Scorpios have the ability to penetrate deeply beneath the surface and understand more what is going on inside others than they understand about what is going on inside themselves. They are natural psychologists and like to psychoanalyse everything, they can be extremely suspicious of other people's motives rarely believing that anyone will do something for nothing. There is a jealous vindictive side to the insecure Scorpio who believes others are out to put him down. They can hold on to hurt for years until the opportunity for revenge arises. Like Cancer they enjoy power in the form of control and may use any emotional means to get their own way.

Pisces

Pisces is the third Water sign and twelfth and last sign of the zodiac. It is mutable and is ruled by the planets Jupiter and Neptune.

As a Water sign Pisces is very sensitive, often emotional and very impressionable. Pisces have a great ability for tuning in to the thoughts of others and finding himself immersed in their thoughts and feelings, and can have difficulty in separating himself.

Pisceans are elusive and difficult to understand as they seem to have a peculiar understanding all of their own. They are nearly all drawn in to spiritualism or investigation of the unseen.

They are very changeable, imaginative and fanciful and love to live in a world of romance and fantasy. Great daydreamers, Pisces are often locked in a world of their own that is hard for anyone else to enter. They nearly always pretend to be something other than they are and can appear over-restless, over-anxious, lacking life energy and purpose and are often fairly undecided how to act. Always waiting for an opportunity, they may be seen as drifters.

Pisces is often linked with the legend of the mermaid that falls in love with a mortal. The fish is also the symbol of Christ and the soul, so at some point Pisces have to face and meet and deal with their vision of God. Under this sign you find the lowest of humanity, the alcoholics, the junkies and the hopeless and yet in other Pisceans we find poets, musicians, great actors, visionaries and mystics who attempt to bring to ordinary life a glimpse of something more magical. This can be from a work of art to human love.

The insecure Pisces type is impressionable, prone to a sense of guilt and easily victimised and an inveterate rescuer, even of people who don't want to be saved. In the role of Saviour it is possible for some Pisces to also become the victim as their compassionate nature is so easily taken advantage of.

There is a tendency towards low self esteem and they may sacrifice their own needs for the sake of others. They can be taken in by sob stories and any other forms of emotional blackmail, often believing others needs to be greater than their own.

When mature, Pisces is psychically sensitive, loving, deeply religious or committed to a spiritual path. The fulfilled Pisces sees all of human suffering and is transfigured by being a caring, helpful friend to all who seek their aid.

Chapter 7

The Planets

In astrology planets provide the power, the energy and the principles, whereas the signs are the circumstances and conditions through which they operate. A good analogy may help your understanding if you think of the planets as the actors, the signs as parts they play and the houses as the stage where they act out their parts. The Table on page 42 shows the strengths and weakness of the planets. What this really means is that in certain signs where the planet is exalted or in dignity it is easier to express the energies of that particular planet; therefore if a planet is in detriment or fall it is not as you may have read that the influence is evil, it is simply that it is more difficult to express the qualities of the planet because they conflict with the sign. However, there is some conflict of opinion as Astrologers disagree as to whether Mercury actually is exalted in its own sign of Virgo or the more technical sign of Aquarius. The outer planets having been more recently discovered give more room for argument, we may need to experience all the planets through the signs before we come to an agreement.

The planets are also divided into two main groups we have the "inner planets" or personal planets, these are the planets that move quickly in their orbit around the zodiac.

The Sun, Mercury and Venus, as seen from the earth all complete their orbit in about one year, and Mars takes about two years and the Moon, of course, takes about one month. This is quite a short orbiting period when compared to the outer planets which are Jupiter, Saturn, Uranus, Neptune and Pluto. Jupiter takes about twelve years, spending about a year in each sign, whereas Pluto the slowest moving planet takes about two hundred and forty eight

Sign	Ruler	Part of Body	Bodily System
♈	♂	Head	Motor centres of Brain
♉	♀	Throat	Thyroid Gland
♊	☿	Hands, Arms, Lungs.	Nervous System
♋	☽	The Breasts Stomach	Alimentary Digestion
♌	☉	Heart Back	Cardiac system
♍	☿	Intestines	Pancreas Metabolism
♎	♀	Kidneys	Elimination of Waste
♏	♂♇	Sexual Organs	Reproductive System
♐	♃	Hips, thighs, Liver.	Sciatic nerve expiration
♑	♄	Knee	Digestive system gall bladder.
♒	♄♅	Calf, ankles	Circulatory System
♓	♃♆	Feet	Lymphatic System

Diagram No. 7 Table showing Signs and Planets in relation to Parts of the Body.

years. The last three planets are often referred to as the transcendental planets as they have a more profound or mystical message for us to understand.

The inner planets will move position from one day to the next so that each individual born will have quite different placements unless born on the same day and time. The outer planets however, can belong to a whole generation. A teacher for example could expect to see in her classroom a whole class of pupils with Jupiter to Pluto in the same signs, although they will of course be in different houses. The only planet she may notice that changes every year would be Jupiter so she will experience different Jupiter types as each year her class changes.

The Sun

The sun's diameter is 109 times that of earth. It rotates on its axis in about 25 days.

The Sun represents your spirit. It is the energy which enables you to exist. The sign that the Sun occupies will be strongly emphasised, it is the unfoldment of the self and the development of the ego. It represents individuality, will, striving for significance. It activates the characteristic desire of ambition, urge for power, leadership, creativeness, constructiveness, self-reliance, organisation, administration and individuality.

Through developing the qualities of the sign in which the Sun lies and through encountering the sphere of life designated by its house placement, you gain a greater sense of power, purpose and direction in life. The position of the Sun indicates where you need to distinguish yourself in some way, to radiate your influence and shine forth, to stand out and be special. The Sun in the chart shows where you develop the power to be self-generating and active rather than merely reactive.

The Sun represents your path in life, the Sun in its own sign of Leo will be emphasised strongly and will give you all the qualities of leadership, good organising ability, creativity, and although it is

PLANET	DIGNITY	DETRIMENT	EXALTATION	FALL
SUN	Leo	Aquarius	Aries	Libra
MOON	Cancer	Capricorn	Taurus	Scorpio
MERCURY	Gemini Virgo	Sagittarius Pisces	Aquarius* Virgo*	Leo* Pisces*
VENUS	Taurus Libra	Scorpio Aries	Pisces	Virgo
MARS	Aries Scorpio	Libra Taurus	Capricorn	Cancer
JUPITER	Sagittarius Pisces	Gemini Virgo	Cancer	Capricorn
SATURN	Capricorn Aquarius	Cancer Leo	Libra	Aries
URANUS	Aquarius	Leo	Scorpio*	Taurus*
NEPTUNE	Pisces	Virgo	Leo*	Aquarius*
PLUTO	Scorpio	Taurus	Aquarius*	Leo*

Diagram 8 Planetary Table Showing Strengths and Weaknesses
* The asterisks show where there is some conflict of opinion amongst Astrologers.

warm hearted and generous it can be pompous. In Aquarius, the Sun's opposite sign, the solar traits will not be so strong and although Aquarians are kind and friendly, they are far more detached and aloof and quite difficult to get close to.

Planets in aspect to the Sun are greatly energised and infused with creative force. The Sun is the centre or heart of the solar system and symbolically represents your centre from which everything is activated.

The Sun is important to our everyday bodily function. It is of vital importance as it is the energy of the persons entire well being. It is our heart chakra through which all emotions flow, the centre of life, the life giver to our physical bodies. It rules the sign of Leo which medically rules the heart. If the heart is sluggish or impaired the whole body suffers. We need a sufficient supply of vitamin A which is gained from the Sun to prevent a variety of heart ailments.

The symbol of the Sun is a circle with a dot in the centre and this represents the outpouring of the force of life through its centre. The dot also represents the creative spark of Divine Consciousness which is in each and every one of us.

The Moon

The Moon is the earth's satellite, it orbits the earth in just over 27 days and rotates on its axis once in each revolution, so the same face is always presented to the earth. It has no atmosphere. The Moon moves about 12 or 13 times faster than the sun. It travels through the zodiac approximately once every 28 days. It conjuncts the Sun once each month in the Suns zodiacal sign. In their subsequent cycle together the Moon waxes and wanes. As it waxes it symbolically gathers in the harvest of experience and stores it as memory, precedence and tradition. As the Moon waxes and wanes it also regulates the tides on earth and as feelings are symbolised by water, the Moon's motion represents the rhythmic flow of public moods.

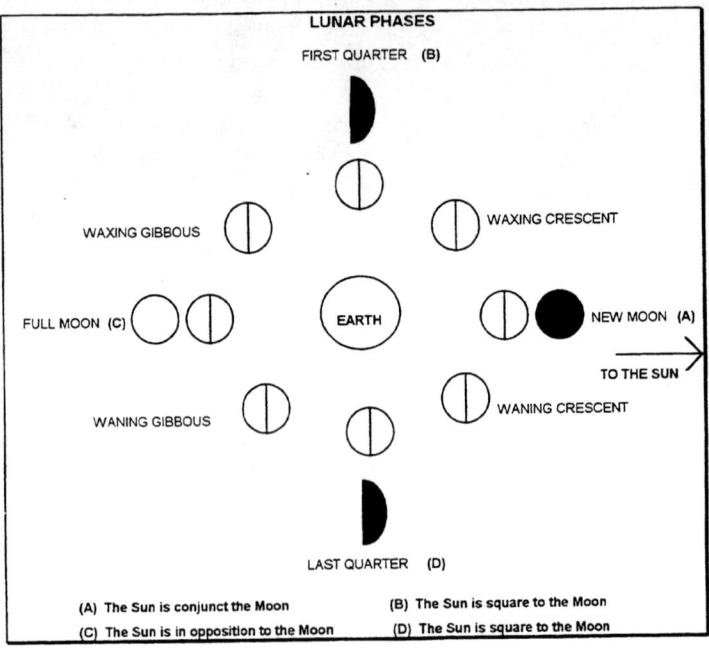

LUNAR PHASES

FIRST QUARTER (B)

WAXING GIBBOUS

WAXING CRESCENT

FULL MOON (C)

EARTH

NEW MOON (A)

TO THE SUN

WANING GIBBOUS

WANING CRESCENT

LAST QUARTER (D)

(A) The Sun is conjunct the Moon   (B) The Sun is square to the Moon

(C) The Sun is in opposition to the Moon   (D) The Sun is square to the Moon

Diagram 9

We can approximately tell the position of the Moon by observing its phase in the sky, for example a new Moon is conjunct the Sun so wherever the Sun is on the day of the new Moon is also the Moon's position. A full Moon is opposite the Sun so it would not be too difficult to work out its zodiacal position once you get used to observing the phases in this manner. (See diagram 9).

The Moon represents our capacity to respond to life in a rhythmic way, our day to day capacity to flow with what life brings. It represents the unconscious side of the personality, our set of habits and instincts. It is the constantly changing personality that responds and acts to external stimuli.

After the Sun the Moon is the most important body in your birth chart. The characteristics of the sign it occupies form an integral part of your personality. It has a bearing on your emotions, your habits and all your actions in a given environment, and on a person's instinctive behaviour.

The Moon is also associated with birth, motherhood, emotional disturbances and personal habits, the home and the family. Lunar traits are passive, patient, receptive, sympathetic, moody, changeable and sensitive. Outward mannerisms and general behaviour and habits depend largely on your lunar characteristics, for example when the Moon is in it's own sign of Cancer then Cancerian traits are emphasised, there is a powerful need to cherish and protect and the family instinct is prominent. If the Moon is in an Air sign like Gemini, it will lack stability and there is a likelihood of much indecision, because it represents emotional security. The Moon is maternal love rather than romantic love.

Whereas the Sun shows the constitutional quality of the body, the Moon can tell the conditions of health. A prominent Moon in a natal chart can generally indicate a drug sensitive person. Also the position of the Moon will help establish a person's emotional needs. Good health is not just a matter of eating the correct foods, it's a combination of diet, emotions and mental attitudes. If emotions are misdirected, suppressed or repressed they can build up and fester in the subconscious mind, so if emotions such as guilt, anger and jealousy are not properly dealt with, they too can cause illness. The Moon also rules the body fluids. At a New Moon our fluids are at their lowest level and there is a resultant weight loss, so if there is a need for an operation the best time is five days before or after the New Moon when there is least chance of swelling, bruising or bleeding.

There has been some research by Doctors who are sympathetic to astrology which has shown that a person should endeavour not to undergo surgery five days before or after a Full Moon when the body fluids are at their highest, as this could cause excessive swelling or haemorrhaging or seepage from wounds. It has also been realised for sometime that it is not wise to undergo an operation on the part of the body ruled by the sign in which the Moon is transiting, and some astrologers believe this is also the case when the Moon is transiting the opposite sign, so if you were to have an operation on your kidneys you would not do so if the Moon at the present time was in Libra or in Aries.

The symbol of the Moon is the crescent which are two semi-circles joined. One semi-circle represents Divine Consciousness and the other human consciousness. These two forces represent the personality. The Moon represents all that is receptive in our personality, our intuition, emotions and daily experiences.

Mercury

Mercury is the nearest planet to the Sun, and revolves around it in 87.97 days. It rotates on its axis once as it goes round the Sun, hence it nearly always shows the same face to the Sun as the Moon does to the Earth.

As Mercury is the nearest planet to the Sun its placement in the birthchart is always within 28 degrees of the placement of the Sun, so it is either in the same sign as the Sun or in the previous sign or the sign ahead. It is associated with the intellect, mental perception and with the nervous system, and also day to day travel. Mercurial traits are the desire for knowledge and the ability to communicate it to others, your reasoning power and your perception. Mercury in Aries is quick thinking and outspoken, showing a quick wit but in Taurus it shows a practical and steady mind which needs time to assimilate facts.

Mercury also rules your co-ordination, so that someone awkward or clumsy could have a difficult aspect to Mercury. Mercury represents the intellectual faculties, it indicates curiosity and wanting to know all there is to know. Its realm is also the sphere of perceptions and ideas, and although Mercury is the gateway to understanding, it is not necessarily profound in itself. It indicates thought but not thoughtfulness, eagerness for knowledge but not the application of knowledge. Mercury symbolises gathering data and information, knowing, formulating at the verbal level, communicating, listening and rationalising. Mercury's functional activities can be misapplied. Negative applications of what Mercury represents include equivocating, rationalising, intellectual superficiality, senseless chatter, and belonging to different schools of thought yet without any real drive or knowledge.

Mercury also rules the nervous system. Mercury the messenger of the gods is also the messenger of the nervous system relaying split second commands throughout the body. The placement of Mercury in the natal chart can indicate mental attitudes and sometimes inflexible attitudes which can stress the body. Although mental exhaustion is not normally manifested through a badly aspected Mercury, the nervous system may take a severe buffeting perhaps resulting in nervousness, tension and an inability to relax. People with this placement need to control their worrying and learn to relax as proper mental attitudes are also important to our well being.

The symbol of Mercury, the circle, represents the source of energy flowing to the mind, the cross stands for Earth energies flowing to the mind and the semi-circle are impulses received from the higher mind.

Venus

Venus is only slightly smaller than the Earth. It takes 224.7 days to orbit the Sun. It's rotation period is calculated to be 243 days. It has an extensive atmosphere.

Venus is also close to the Sun as seen from the Earth, and is never more than 48 degrees from it along the ecliptic. Venus therefore occupies the same sign as the Sun or falls within two signs either side of it on your birthchart.

Venus is associated with the power to love and relate and the ability to make close relationships with others, and depending on its aspects the powers of attraction. Venus shows how we make adjustments to encourage a relationship. It is the desire for companionship which can be satisfied either through personal relationships or social contacts.

Venus is the urge for harmonious relationships. A gentle, kind and friendly manner, the appreciation of beauty and the arts, but it can be lazy, indecisive and weak willed, this depends on its placement. Venus is at it's sexiest in Scorpio and will create a deeply passionate and emotional nature, whilst Venus in Capricorn tends to be rather chilly, and often indicates considerable sacrifice or loneliness through the affections, as love is expressed rather coolly. Most of our outer feelings are expressions of what we feel inside.

While Mercury represents experience encountered through the level of the mind, Venus refers to the inner value we give experience at the feeling level. It is often said that Venus is the planet of love and attraction, but it can just as well be the planet of hate and repulsion according to the inner value we give to certain experiences.

Venus can be love and aversion and can draw us into some experiences and away from others. Those we enter into, provide the substance for our inner growth and fulfilment. Ideally Venus represents harmony, for if we are attuned with our inner self we naturally attract that which will help develop and fulfil us. This meshing of a need with what will answer it is the true harmony Venus symbolises. Venus can be a symbol of all harmonious relationships of beauty and of our need to give and receive appreciation. It can also negatively refer to self indulgence, narcissism, emotional superficiality and unrealistic demands for love or luxury, but it indicates active participation in social affairs because this satisfies the need to be amongst people.

Venus through its rulership of Taurus and Libra helps regulate the throat, thyroid and kidneys. This planet also has dominion over half the circulatory system, the venous supply, and it is sometimes concerned with skin texture - its beauty and flawless character. Venus as well as Jupiter controls what one likes in terms of food, the texture, taste and quality, since wrong foods can damage a person just as fast in bodily terms as wrong emotions can. Venus must be carefully looked at for its placement can indicate a person with a sweet tooth or one who tends towards obesity. An individual with a prominent Venus may go on binges, gorging on sweets and gaining weight. Since Venus also deals with a need for love, a person

48

with a poorly aspected Venus may eat an inordinate amount of sweets to achieve a sense of affection he or she feels is not supplied by others. However, the reverse can be true, these people can also deny themselves as they feel unworthy. Venus dictates how we feel about ourselves. If we like ourselves we will probably have a good diet, if we dislike ourselves we tend to abuse our bodies with less nutritious foods.

Venus symbol is the combination of a circle and a cross, the circle is spirit and an indication that we aspire to perfection over the more material and sensual desires of Earth.

Mars

Mars is smaller than Earth, its diameter being about half of that of the Earth. It orbits the Sun in 637 days and rotates on its own axis in about 24.5 hours, the atmosphere is less dense than the Earth. The orbit of Mars falls outside the Earth and its position in the birthchart is not closely linked with that of the Sun, for Mars takes about two and a half years to travel through all the signs, remaining for about two months in each sign.

Martian characteristics are the drive to be energetic, to become heated either in illness or temper. It is associated with aggression, heat, action, decisiveness, directness in approach, a defender of the weak and can indicate strong sexual motivations. In Capricorn its sign of exaltation, energy is used in obtaining objectives in life, ambition could dominate to the exclusion of all else and energy would be carefully and constructively employed. Whereas in Libra the sign of its detriment, there is often a fluctuation of energy being sometimes languid and sometimes passionate, and those with this placement can fall in love hastily and often.

As we go through life we develop a sense of self, this sense of self has to express itself through action. This action is what Mars symbolises. It represents the mobilisation of energy, the capacity to do and to assert oneself. Mars is the fuel that operates the ego as ruled by the sun. When Mars' capacity to do is activated there may also develop a tendency to force issues and overdo, especially when doing compensates for insecurity or frustration. In such cases the negative aspects of Mars operate as recklessness, argumentativeness, vindictiveness or even open hostility.

Mars rules over the muscles and adrenal glands. Mars is the energiser and stimulator of all aspects of our bodies. Whereas the Sun is our basic engine, Mars is the fuel that energises it. It is the key planet associated with our physical get up and go, our energy levels.

The placement of Mars in the natal chart can indicate how active each of us is. For instance; Mars in a fire sign may produce athletes or aggressive people. Mars in air signs may mean great mental energies, but must be on guard against mental exhaustion and nerve related breakdowns. Mars in an earth sign may produce people who prefer to sit in a comfortable chair and watch sport rather than play it. Mars seems the least happy in water signs, as energy may be in short supply. Since everyone needs exercise Mars will help evaluate how much and what kind each person needs. Mars is also very important in indicating how quickly an individual can bounce back to health. It works best in fire and air, but in earth and water there is a tendency to slow recuperation.

Mars has rulership over the red blood cells and is an indicator of anaemia, and in terms of health problems an activated Mars can mean inflammation, rapid temperature increase and any acute onset of an ailment.

The symbol of Mars was originally the polarity to Venus, it used to be the reverse symbol, so with the cross over the symbol of spirit, sensual and material desires succeed over higher aspirations. However, the balance of spirit and matter is the highest expression of this energy.

Jupiter

Jupiter is the largest and most massive of the planets. Its diameter is 11 times that of the Earth. It orbits the Sun in 11.86 years. It rotates in a little less than 10 hours. It has 12 satellites (Moons), some are as far as twenty million miles distant from it and two of them go round in orbit the opposite way to the rest. Jupiter takes about 12 years to make its way through all the signs. Its orbit being a bit erratic it spends a disproportionate amount of time in each sign. Jupiter has always been associated with growth and expansion and is the largest planet in the solar system. It is linked with deeper knowledge, advanced studies, philosophical outlook, religion, foreign countries, travel, book publication and good fortune. Although Jupiter is thought to be a favourable omen it does have its difficult side which tends towards over indulgence, wastefulness and extravagance.

Jupiter is the higher expectation that the future will reveal one's best hopes, or to put it another way the expectations of reward without having to make a contribution. It is also the higher mental faculty that seeks meaning in the deepest issues of life. The function of Jupiter is to integrate according to spiritual principles, whatever is or has become scattered and unrelated. Jupiter operates most positively when it organises the actions and accomplishments of an individual into a meaningful, self sustaining whole.

The keywords usually associated with Jupiter are expansion and free ranging. Expansion can be either of the mind or the body for example Jupiter in Cancer is prolific, preservative and harmonious, it tends towards kindness, good humour and generosity, with strong charitable and compassionate and protective instincts. Whereas in Sagittarius its positive traits are emphasised and the intellectual capacity can be developed to the full. It is favourable for literature, travel, residence overseas and the study of profound subjects. So with Jupiter every process that urges growth and expansion of the consciousness is given a spiritual value and a distinction between right and wrong is established. It is the eagerness to replace the harshness of physical survival with immortality. The word expansion is applied to Jupiter so it could well indicate overeating and lack of control, so Jupiter ruled people tend to eat rich foods that are high in acid. Jupiter is also connected with the liver and the fats of the body. Cholesterol and glucose metabolism are also Jupiter related functions.

The symbol of Jupiter is the half circle on the cross of matter. This represents the soul triumphant over the earthly (material) experiences.

Saturn

Saturn is the second largest planet, it's diameter nine times that of Earth. It has the most extensive atmosphere of all and it takes 29.5 years to orbit the Sun, and rotates on its axis in 10.38 hours. It has three rings lying in a plane inclined to the ecliptic at about 28 degrees, they consist of a large number of small particles, Saturn also has 10 satellites (Moons) lying outside the rings.

As mentioned, Saturn takes approximately 29.5 years to orbit the sun and the return of Saturn to its natal position marks an important time in your life when one cycle of experience has come to a close and great changes are about to take place.

Saturn has traditionally been associated with limitation, frustration and delays. These, however, are all by products of Saturn's concern for the rightness of things, for seeing that all is in order according to cosmic laws and truths. Under Saturn it is better to be delayed and right than early and misguided. As it follows the sphere of Jupiter's social participation, Saturn's is the realm of social responsibility. Saturn represents the process of finding your place in society and fulfilling your responsibilities there. This requires self discipline and a realistic sense of limitations and priorities. Saturn represents the necessity and capacity to tie up loose ends, to be logical and forthright. When you deal with Saturn you deal with authority and with either or both your capacity to weld authority and to teach others, and with your capacity to learn from others who have the authority of longer experience than you.

Negative aspects of Saturn include self righteousness when in authority and reactive depression when you must unwillingly yield to the authority of others.

In ancient astrology Saturn was known as the malefic planet for even his virtues can be rather dismal; such as self control, tact, thrift, caution. But his vices are particularly unpleasant as they operate through fear. Saturn defines the fear of what is unknown, which too often inhibits your progress through lack of confidence. Saturn holds none of the glamour associated with the outer planets and none of the humaneness of the personal planets. Saturn is usually considered to be the bringer of limitation, frustration, hard work and self denial and even the bright side is associated with wisdom and self discipline in hard work, and one who does not very easily laugh at life.

By it's sign and house position Saturn denotes those areas of life where the individual is likely to feel thwarted in self expression, where he is most likely to meet with frustration and difficulties. However it is possible to bring out the best in yourself by learning through your contacts with Saturn as he is a great teacher and can bring you good self control and knowledge of your limitations.

Saturn is the wisdom that results from the thoughtful application of knowledge. It has been observed that wherever another persons Saturn falls in your birthchart you will learn from that person in that area of life, for example if someone's Saturn falls in your 7th house you will learn the true meaning of a close relationship from that person.

Whatever sign Saturn is found in at birth might determine what organ or area of the body is potentially sluggish or not working up to normal expectation, and if Saturn is found retrograde then the chances of that body malfunctioning is then thought to be increased.

Saturn rules the bone structure of the body, teeth and ears. It rules the mineral calcium, fluoride and sulphur and it is well known that bones and teeth need adequate amounts of calcium to keep our frames strong enough to carry us around. Proper amounts of fluoride are necessary to combat tooth decay and bone damage. Arthritis is also a Saturn disease, due to the rigidity of its nature. The symbol of Saturn is composed of the same two elements as Jupiter, the semi-circle and the cross which shows that until we have mastery over material and earthly conditions we cannot enter the realm of the soul.

Uranus

Uranus has a diameter four times larger than earth. It orbits the sun in 84 years and rotates on its axis in 10.7 hours. It has five satellites, the four most important revolve in a retrograde action. Uranus is a slow moving planet and takes about 84 years to orbit the Sun. A person's life span is said to be one orbit of Uranus or three orbits of Saturn. Unlike the inner planets Uranus takes about seven years to pass through one sign and therefore marks the style of a whole age group, each group every seven years showing its own distinctive Uranian characteristics.

It is associated with modern science, physical changes, sexual perversion and sudden nervous breakdowns. Positively it is humanitarian, friendly, kind, independent, original, strong willed, inventive and versatile. It is said to be a higher vibration of Mercury and you can get pure genius under this sign. Negatively it is cranky, eccentric, perverse and rebellious, and the inventor of unrealistic schemes or of objects that never work.

Uranus beckons us to go beyond the relative safety of the well worn paths of Saturn, to spiral upwards into the realms of imagination to project us away from the ruts, in search of excitement. It is the need to be free from the bonds of responsibility. When Saturn's responsibilities are fulfilled, opportunities for innovation, originality and transformation may appear. These may come in the form of crisis for Uranus is often associated with sudden disasters and accidents.

If calling a crisis an opportunity does not help at first, we can endeavour to make it so at least by opening ourselves to the changes it brings by allowing the changes to deepen and broaden our range of understanding and responses to life. The main problem with meeting crisis is that we tend to do so with the intent of returning everything to normal as soon as we can. Convention and tradition are rejected as being too binding to allow the full expression of the individuality, so a Uranian crisis has been truthfully worth while only when we don't return to normal afterwards, but have somehow been permanently transformed by the experience.

People with Uranus in a strong position are likely to buckle under stress or to react to it more strongly than other people as they may be in a state of nervousness, unable to relax. They need to learn to unwind through exercise or meditation as quietening of the mind will quieten the nerves.

The type of ailment that is Uranian is likely to be brought on by shock, - emotional, physical or mental, or by any other unexpected circumstances such as surgery or an accident. Since Uranus indicates quick release of any situation, gives the person hope of a complete and swift recovery.

The symbol of Uranus is the spirit and aids development on earth with two semi-circles that represent the soul or collective unconscious to raise personal consciousness.

Neptune

Neptune has a diameter nearly four times that of earth. It orbits the Sun in 164.79 years and rotates on its axis in 15.8 hours. It has two satellites, one of which moves in a retrograde action. It stays approximately 14.5 years in a sign.

Neptune is associated with all that is mysterious and intangible, and anything to do with the seas is distinctly Neptunian. It is linked with artistic and spiritual inspiration, anaesthetics, drugs and poisons. Poetry and dancing come under its rulership. It also aids spiritual imagination and sensitivity.

Negative Neptunian traits can lead to deceit, carelessness, being impractical and unworldly, escapism literature, and often alcoholism and drug addiction is attributed to a badly placed or weak Neptune. So Neptune represents all that is illusive, mystical, magical and intangible.

If we try to rationally explain that which cannot be seen, touched or contained, then it may result in a case of Neptunian confusion. While Uranus may represent an opportunity to go beyond convention, Neptune refers to the almost bewildering array of new possibilities we encounter once we have. Neptune is the sphere where non ordinary consciousness operates, a realm of psychic phenomena or of altered states of consciousness. These states may be spontaneous, sought after by years of preparation or merely induced by hallucinogenic drugs. In contrast to daily reality the realms of Neptune may seem either unreal and illusionary or more real than real. This is the source of Neptune's association with confusion and deception. Of course one may be confused when experiencing an utterly new and unfamiliar realm in which things may not be what they seem. The real danger with Neptune is self deception, of seeing and believing what we desperately want it to be.

Neptune operates most positively when we allow experiences it brings to de-condition our minds and habitual responses especially when taking things for granted, then in a new light we may use our intuition to gain a more compelling transcendent sense of truths, and experience ourselves more fully as manifestations of universal love.

Neptune rules the lymphatic system, the pineal gland, the sinus gland, and the spleen and it is involved with infections and poisons in the body. Any mysterious, inexplicable confusing element that is toxic is in Neptune's domain. A prominent Neptune may also indicate a potentially drug sensitive individual, one who should be given lower than average dosage of any medication. Whereas Mars implies strength, virility and energy, Neptune signifies the opposite. An undefined sense of tiredness or lethargy may be Neptune based. There is a chance of general weakness or laziness in the organ or part of the body ruled by the sign in which Neptune is found. Neptune's symbol is the three pronged trident of Neptune. It is the semi-circle of the soul pierced by the cross of matter.

Pluto

Pluto was discovered in 1930 and is a very slow moving planet. Its diameter is a little under half of the earth and it orbits the sun in 248. years, so that its affect will be on a generation as a whole unless it is in a strong position conjunct the Ascendant, MC or in its own house, and strongly aspected in your natal chart. Due to its erratic orbit it spends a disproportionate amount of time in each sign.

Pluto is associated with the creative and regenerative forces of the body, enforced change with eruptions, volcanoes and earthquakes, the beginnings and endings of phases in life.

Plutonian people are those who seek to change, transform and take control of everything around them. It rules the energies inside you and will lead inexorably to change. It rules death and regeneration of the self as old aspects of your life pass away and are replaced by new ones that could not otherwise have come into being.

Pluto also has to do with the secretive and subversive elements of society, revolutionary groups, organised crime and the like. Pluto reminds us that the last phase of any process is also the beginning of a new cycle, that death is a gateway to rebirth and that we reach furthest beyond ourselves when we go deepest within. With Pluto all things tend to turn into their opposites when carried far enough. Pluto represents all that is paradoxical. It is said both to breed secrecy and intrigue and to force hidden matters out into the open.

With Pluto we must never be satisfied with surface appearances, but must probe deeply into the heart of things as Pluto may symbolise especially forceful and penetrating insights and persuasive communications.

Negatively intimate communications may be tainted by deliberately obscuring the truth. Festering repressed feelings may be at the root of such negative Plutonian drives. Yet true to it's paradoxical nature, Pluto also represents catharsis and purity. Catharsis is the result of a death/rebirth regeneration. Purity is the expression of being what one essentially is. The message of Pluto is that we need not go anywhere to find a source of light, it is within us. Pluto rules life and death and the enzymes production as well as the size and shape of red and white blood corpuscles, the basis of our health concerns.

Pluto's most important function is rulership of the endocrine system. Without the glands functioning more with one another the rest of the body is going to feel out of sorts. A strongly aspected Pluto or one near the ascendant or midheaven, can indicate potential endocrine related ailments. You then need to look for which gland is malfunctioning for example if Pluto is found in Aries then the pineal gland may be affected, in Taurus the thyroid and in Cancer the pituitary.

Finally Pluto rules the subconscious depths of our mind. If we keep a lot of negative emotions hidden in our subconscious mind then sooner or later it will alter our physical health in the same way as an afflicted Moon will.

Chiron

Chiron is a very recent discovery. It was first observed in November 1977 by Charles Kowal of Hales Observatory. At first he was uncertain whether it was a comet or a minor planet. Compared to the smallest of our major planets Mercury, Chiron is very small indeed, but as a minor planet it is relatively large. There is yet to be a confirmed agreement as to whether Chiron is a minor planet, an asteroid or a comet. The most recent speculation is that it is a comet but yet does not obey all the rules of a typical comet. It's orbit around the Sun is approximately 50 years and one of it's distinctions is an extremely eccentric orbit. It lies between Saturn and Uranus but it wanders over Saturn's orbit so that at times it is nearer to the Sun than Saturn is.

Chiron's orbit is thought to be unstable, so there is a possibility that it may be cast out of our solar system. At its closest point to the Sun when it wanders over Saturn's orbit, it is closer to Earth during that time, and at its point in orbit farthest from the Sun it wanders over Uranus' orbit, so it appears to form a bridge between these two extremes. Therefore one interpretation is that it shows us where we can best tap Saturn and Uranus energies. It shows the area of life where we can turn to get out of a rut, or where one searches for others with similar interests.

Chiron is also associated with healing. In mythology Chiron had an earthly wisdom and healed with herbs and nature. He also had a lot of sadness. He was accidentally wounded with an arrow by Hercules which produced a wound that could not be healed. So his archetype is of a wounded healer - the wound being the gap between the real and the unreal, or between heaven and earth. Chiron is caught between Saturn and Uranus and it is thought that there is some connection between Chiron and the sign of Sagittarius, because Chiron was a Centaur, a sage, a philosopher and a teacher of the children of the gods.

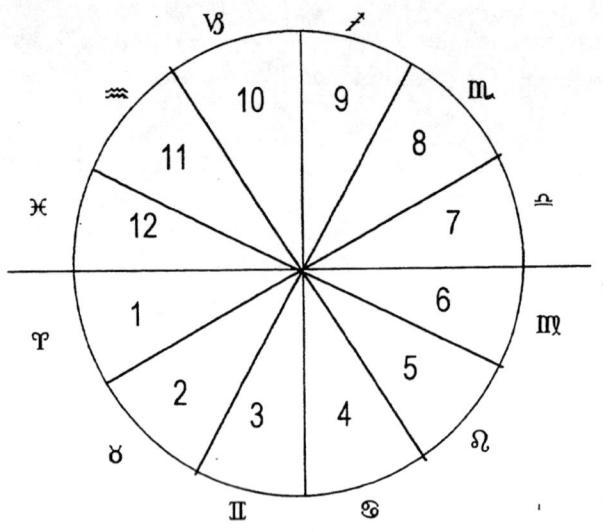

Quick Summary of House Meanings

1. Personality or the image presented to others. How others see you. Your persona.	2. Personal Resources Attitude to Possessions Your Value system Material possessions.	3. Brothers and sisters Neighbours and relatives Short journeys Communication
4. The nurturing parent Your support system Roots and family history Domestic life/home.	5. Creativity, leisure. Children and pleasure. Games and Sport Love affairs, Uniqueness	6. Attitude to work. Relationship with co-workers. Health. Being of service to others.
7. One to one relation-ships. Business or marriage partners. Enemies or competitors.	8. Intense relationships Sexual relationships. Unearned income Insurances, inheritances.	9. Further education. Religious pursuits Foreign travel and culture. Philosophy, teachers.
10. Those in authority over you. Father image. Experience of external world. Outer self.	11. Friendships and group membership. Hopes and wishes. Shared identity.	12. Institutions, hostels, prisons etc. Unconscious mind. Clandestine relation-ships. Spiritual awareness.

Top: Diagram 10, bottom: Diagram 11

Chapter 8

The Houses

A birthchart is divided into twelve sections which we call houses. The sizes of these sections depend upon the house system that we have used. For example if we use the equal house system the twelve sections are divided equally, each containing 30 degrees. With all other house systems the sections are not equal and some of the more popular will be explained at the end of this chapter. The houses are traditionally counted anti-clockwise from the ascendant. The earth rotates once every twenty-four hours and during that time the twelve signs and ten planets pass through the twelve houses.

The personal houses are ONE, FIVE and NINE. This is where we realise our creative energy and make our mark on the world.

The practical houses are TWO, SIX AND TEN. They are concerned with practical matters, our values and money and how we go about working to achieve them.

The social houses are THREE, SEVEN and ELEVEN and these are concerned with personal relationships, one-to-one and casual to groups.

The unconscious houses are FOUR, EIGHT and TWELVE. These are to do with our unconscious memories, thoughts or emotions as they all operate beneath the surface.

As you have probably noticed these houses correspond to the four elements, Fire, Earth, Air and Water respectively, which means the personal houses are fire, the practical are earth, the social houses are air, and the unconscious houses are water.

The First House

Our first house which begins with the ascendant shows us something of the atmosphere in our early environment, but also shows how we were innately prepared to deal with it. It is our perception of the world and colours our view. The first house is the house of Aries and is associated with the personality and self image, our potential means of self expression and sometimes the physical body, health and vitality. If this is what we are projecting onto the world then this is how others see us. Whatever behaviour patterns we have are put out and coloured by our first house sign. It is the sign on this house that shows our personality and the face we present to the world. It is important that this is a true expression of who we are, but this is not always the case, and this seems to be especially true if the Ascendant is in a different element to your Sun. It is an incomplete image of the rest of the chart, so whatever energies we are putting out in the first we draw back in the form of relationships in our seventh. Our Ascendant also shows how we are predisposed to deal with experiences in every new phase of life. It is through the ascendant that we express the rest of the behaviour patterns that unfold through life in our chart.

We can begin to see that different signs on the Ascendant will show us how different people begin to view life. For example a person with Sagittarius on the Ascendant would see the world as a place full of adventure and opportunities, they will have enthusiasm and eagerness to begin to explore life's possibilities. The person with Capricorn rising, or Saturn in the first house, may see the world as a cold and gloomy place, expecting it to be full of fears and doubts and heavy responsibilities. And those with Gemini rising, or Mercury in the first house, may see the world by understanding that knowledge, especially of their environment, is necessary to their survival. So the way we meet life is shown by the sign in the first house.

Planets close to the Ascendant can also show us something about our birth. For instance Pluto close to the Ascendant could show a life/death struggle with the mother, or the infant in danger during delivery. With the Moon it may show a late birth, with the child not wanting to leave the womb, or with Neptune perhaps a child not wanting to be born at all. Whereas Mars may show a quick or easy birth or sometimes surgery is necessary for the child to be born. Whereas Uranus may show that the birth of the child caused some disruption. One example of a birth with Uranus closely conjunct the ascendant was during the war years when the baby was born in a caravan and kicked over a kerosene lamp causing a fire and total disruption within the birth environment.

Our Ascendant shows the qualities that we use in order to fully express our Sun, so there does come a time when we appear to be growing more like our Ascendant but it is in fact our effort to use these qualities so that we can truly express the innate quality of the Sun that give this image. As we move through life and expand our awareness, the first house is the area of the chart crucial to our self discovery and as we meet these energies very early in life they are deeply ingrained by the time we are adults.

The Seconò House

The second house, a practical house and the house of Taurus, represents values, possessions, money and resources. In the first house we searched for identity and in the second we need to find our own personal talents, our sense of worth and what we value in life, and more importantly what makes us feel secure.

The second house is associated with wealth and this is where we look to find our own personal wealth or personal talents. For example with Venus or Libra in the second we have natural good taste, artistic qualities, or overall physical attractiveness that draws people to us. Mars or Aries in the second may show natural courage, leadership qualities and honesty or directness, and being very clear in what we want out of life.

It is knowledge of our natural abilities that helps to make us feel secure in our own identity. For example Pisces or Neptune in the second may find security in their religious or spiritual philosophy whereas Saturn or Capricorn may have good business sense and only feel secure if they can use it working for a large establishment.

So our second house can show what we value and what we hope to gain in life, therefore it is what we strive for. This is where we discover what it is in life that supports us through the good and bad times. It is here we see our personal resources, land and material values, what our attitudes towards wealth and property are. For example Neptune here may feel it is unspiritual to be concerned with material things, because his financial affairs are not likely to be very clear, but those I have known with Neptune in this position, although they may never be materially wealthy, money always seems to turn up exactly when they need it. A large number of planets in this house can indicate a very talented person, or it may increase their possessiveness and strengthen the desire to increase their material possessions or wealth.

The Third House

The third house is the house of Gemini and is the first of the social houses. It deals with the communications, personal ideas and their ways of expression, short journeys and relatives - but this does not include parents. The sign on this house may well colour your thinking and show how you make yourself understood as well as show something about your local environment.

So for example if you have Aquarius or Uranus in the third then it may show that your personal environment may be unusual in some way, or that you may communicate to others not so much in an unusual way but about different subjects such as astrology or humanistic and psychological studies. Whereas Saturn or Capricorn in the third may show that it is fairly difficult to express your thoughts and, your environment may be very structured and secure. Alternatively Scorpio or Pluto in the third could mean that not only do you dominate your surroundings and the conversation but you could also be rather sarcastic.

This house not only governs your everyday mental activities and how well you manage your everyday affairs, it is also associated with brothers and sisters, and the planets and sign in this house may show how they affected you. Again Saturn or Capricorn may have been someone who had the responsibility of the other siblings, or if Mars or Aries is in the third then there may have been many arguments and fights during your early childhood. If the Moon or Cancer was in the third then you may have mothered the other children in the family.

This position does not only show our responsibilities to our brothers and sisters but it also shows how we were affected by our interaction with them. For example Saturn may have shown that it was rather difficult to get close to a particular brother or sister and that they appeared to be rather cold and unfeeling, which may have made us discover that cold and unfeeling part of ourselves.

Neptune here may have shown how another sibling could have been rather illusive and mysterious and again difficult to get close to. But there would not be the same feeling of being cold and unloving, you would feel loving but somehow rather remote. Mars here would not have just meant arguments and fights but it would mean that brothers or sisters may have had the ability to bring out the anger in yourself so that you felt angry or irritated most of the time.

The third house is the house of the lower mind, that deals with our day to day existence and for most of the time this operates unconsciously and deals with life in a rather routine manner. Many planets here could show a busy personal environment, with many people in your life or could show many changes in your early environment, such as changes of residence which consequently may have made you rather restless finding it difficult to settle down. In some people it could make them more flexible and able to adjust to any environment, and perhaps they get too restless if the environment becomes too rigid or restricting. In another it could manifest as seeking a more stable and secure environment, having tired of all the moving around as a child.

The first house is how we perceive our environment, the second is how we feel secure in it and the third is how we relate to it.

The Fourth House

The fourth house is the house of Cancer and it is associated with the home, domestic issues, endings, parents and ones past and relationship to tradition. This house can form the basis of our identity. It is the inner self, your soul and the roots of your being. The tenth house is how you project yourself in the outside world, so the fourth house, the opposite, is how we are when we are entirely on our own and there is no one else around. It is what we are really like when there is no one else watching.

It is often where we retire to after confronting our outer social world. It can be our family and those we share our roots with and who will provide emotional support for us. So the fourth house can represent the environment we were brought up in, and the planets or the sign can signify the atmosphere we felt in the home.

For example Saturn or Capricorn can sometimes describe a home atmosphere that is cold and unloving or austere and strict. Whereas Venus will describe it as warm and harmonious with pleasant surroundings. Mercury and Gemini or Virgo may describe home as a place where learning went on, where there were many books around and it became a place of education. Aquarius or Uranus in the fourth can sometimes show that your home was a meeting place where people got together to discuss their ideas and beliefs, so you may have learnt your own personal philosophy fairly early on in life.

Your fourth house can also show your perception of the nurturing parent, so again if Saturn was here your home may have been a secure and well structured environment, but it may have been difficult to extract the love and warmth that you needed. If the Moon was there you would have managed to get the love and caring and nurturing that you needed, regardless of whether the parent was there or not most of the time, when they were there you would have been able to get what you needed. With Mercury there you may have seen your parents as being easy to talk to. Someone you could discuss your thoughts and ideas with, but not necessarily on an emotional level unless there was an easy aspect to the Moon.

Any really difficult aspects to this house could well need to be worked out in therapy if they are neglected during the early years. So it is in the fourth house that we discover our own inner identity.

The Fifth House

The fifth house is the house of Leo and is associated with children, self expression, personal creativity, romance, gambling, speculation and investments. In the fifth house, unlike the first, we are not content just to be someone, we need to be someone special. It is the house of the ego. The Sun, its ruling planet, is the centre of our solar system which gives out heat and light. A chart with strong fifth house placements shows a person who needs to shine and be special and to feel that others are moving around them. This can mean that they need to be the centre of attention, and some perhaps crave being worshipped. So it is the fifth house where we need to be recognised for our specialness.

This is the area of the chart which is given to creative expression, and the sign and the planets here may show us possible outlets for our creativity. Mercury or Gemini may show a talent for public speaking, or Mercury and Virgo a talent for writing. Neptune and Pisces can be absorbed with music and dance, poetry or photography, or display a very artistic flair. Cancer or the Moon, Taurus or Venus may have a flair for cooking and nurturing others. In Aries there are leadership qualities and the ability to put their own identity onto whatever they are doing.

The creative outlet here in the fifth also includes sport and recreation and gambling and speculation. They have the need to test their wit against fate, to take chances that may come off. When we look at our personal creativity, gambling and speculation. This brings us into understanding the fifth houses expression in children, for children are our greatest creative expression, which also is a gamble and a bit of a risk. For when we create a child have no idea how they are going to turn out. They can also become part of our creative expression for we inflict on our children all our own desires and needs and understanding and experience of the world.

We can see something about the type of children we would have by fifth house placements. For instance Jupiter in the fifth or Sagittarius may simply produce Jupitarian children, or we may produce children who are very adventurous and have a hunger for exploring life. With Pisces or Neptune there we may have just Piscean children or they may be very artistic and creative with a flair for music or dance.

Finally the fifth house is always said to deal with pleasures and enjoyment and this includes love affairs that are joyful and lovers that are fun to be with. This can enhance your self expression for through the eyes of your lover you find new aspects of yourself through the appreciation of another. This is where we find romance and it is where we become the main focus of attention for someone else's feelings. It can show our sexual expression and the power to enchant and hold the attention of another. Generally love affairs in the fifth are people that we love to be with but not necessarily the person that we commit ourselves to. The planets and their aspects in the fifth will show the type of relationships we are likely to encounter, whether we take them seriously or whether they are just for fun.

The Sixth House

The sixth house is the house of Virgo and this is associated with jobs, personal service, health, employees, small pets and techniques. The sixth house is known primarily as the house of work. The fifth house is where we have had our fun and the sixth is where we get down to some organised work. Work can be anything from our daily tasks that we have to do to support our daily existence, which can be rather routine and sometimes tedious, up to our normal employment where we may have to go out every day and perform tasks for someone else.

Planets and signs in the sixth can describe issues relating to work and employment. Signs and planets here not only show our attitude to our work but can sometimes show the nature of our work, as well as relationship with co-workers. For example Jupiter or Sagittarius could be involved in travel, they could be agents, couriers or explorers. But they bring to their work the element of growth, to do everything they can in a progressive or expansive way. The Moon or Cancer could be involved with cooking, caring or looking after children, but in whatever job they do they manage to perform the nurturing role to most of their co-workers. So here we also see our attitude to work, it is where we have to face certain boundaries, for daily employment implies a daily routine as we have to arrive there more or less on time and we are not as free as we might like to be. While Saturn or Capricorn would like a stable structured job with a regular salary where they can work steadily and surely through out their life, Uranus or Aquarius would hate to clock in and would prefer to work without a boss overlooking them.

We also look to the sixth house to see the nature of relationships with co-workers. For Venus or Libra may fall in love with someone at work while Pluto or Scorpio may be involved in intrigue or rather complex encounters. Whereas Mars and Aries may have leadership conflict or stir up arguments. The sixth house is square to the third so unfinished business in early relationships with brothers or sisters may resurface with co-workers.

Planets in the sixth show energies we bring to our work areas, and how we co-operate. Uranus would have invented new ways of doing things, while Neptune may still be trying to remember what they did yesterday. The relationship in employment is one of inequality so it can also show how we cope with authority and how we cope with being in a subservient position. Again Pluto or Mars in this position is not going to cope very well with being in a subservient placement, whereas Venus is happy to fit in with what any one else wants them to do.

The sixth house is also the house of health, and health can be affected by tension or difficult conditions at work. For instance anyone with Uranus in the sixth will have an underlying restlessness and nervous tension if they are restricted and not free to move around in their work. This can be solved by seeking work that is not fixed in routine and where they are given the freedom to use their own personal originality, then they would find the tension disappears.

Whilst overwork can strain the health, also too little work will leave you feeling listless with little purpose in life, as it is shown that where there is high unemployment there is also a higher level of illness. Working gives us a sense of purpose but it is also true that people can use illness as a way of escaping from work that they find suffocating and restricting.

The sixth house could reveal some psychological reasoning behind certain illnesses. Saturn could show a certain fixedness and an inability to adapt in the working life which can show up as certain arthritic diseases. Uranus could show problems with the circulation if they remain too fixed and in routine. Many planets in the sixth may show an especial interest in health and fitness, also Mercury and Virgo may show a complete interest in diet and health foods as well. Those who are interested in healing others may have a heavy sixth house emphasis.

The Seventh House

The seventh house is the house of Libra and is associated with partners, marriage or business, open enemies, open conflicts, law suits and counselling relationships. The seventh house can be understood in conjunction with the first. The kind of energies that we give out in the first house are received back in the seventh. The seventh is to do with our one to one relationships. Sometimes the qualities that we attract in our seventh belong to us but are unconscious and we try to live them out through the partner or sometimes through the experiences that the partner brings. Sometimes it is part of ourselves that we are not happy with and it is easier for us to live it out through someone else than internalise it in ourselves.

For example if we have Saturn in the seventh we may attract someone with Saturn in the first house and so we may end up looking after the Saturn side of life for them. If we have Venus in the seventh we may attract someone with Venus in the first or Libra on the ascendant. So with Venus in the seventh we may end up always being the one who gives in or gives way, as Venus in the first can be more selfish and more concerned with their own needs within the relationship. Mars in the seventh may attract a partner who is assertive, courageous or argumentative and we live with this until we find the assertion within ourselves.

So the seventh house can represent the type of relationship that is common both to marriage or between two people locked in combat. It deals with all one to one relationships whether it is marriage or a counselling situation. It is an aspect of confrontation and awareness. These relationships are opportunities to experience part of ourselves that we don't wish to experience internally, so if we repeat relationships or patterns in relationships over and over again it could be that it is telling you something about yourself that you may have to confront or come to terms with.

Planets in the seventh often signify the kind of energies that we experience either through our partners or though situations in life. So that whenever an inner situation is not made conscious it happens outside as fate, and what we are not aware of in ourselves we may attract to us within other people so that in a way we are trying to make ourselves whole, even if it is difficult for us to own the image of ourselves that we see within another. It does seem that many people with an emphasis in the seventh house are in helping or caring professions.

The Eighth House

The eighth house is the house of Scorpio and is associated with other peoples legacies, death, sex and regenerative influences. This again is the opposite house to the second and has to do with finances, resources and values of other people. So it is always in a way a relationship house and is to do with the values of your partner or one to one relationships.

The eighth house may hold unresolved issues that have developed from childhood, so a person with Pluto in the eighth who had a mother who was powerful and manipulative may see all people as powerful and manipulative or perhaps just all women. There may be a tendency for the person to attract those that are powerful and manipulative into their lives so that their expectations are obliged.

This is the area where we can cleanse and regenerate by trying to bring to the surface unresolved issues from previous relationships. It is the house of psychological insight or where we have psychological blocks.

It is also the house of death which is generally the death of a situation, an old order passes away before a new one can begin, so there is renewal as well as destruction. If you find things removed from your life it may be an indication that it has outgrown its usefulness. So where the second house is to do with personal values and personal resources, the eighth house teaches us how to share. So these are to do with joint resources and joint experiences. We can share our experiences so another can learn by them.

The eighth house can sometimes show the type of energies in the air to which we are sensitive, so that again someone with Pluto in the eighth will sense when changes are about to happen, whereas someone with Venus in the eighth may sense when love is in the air.

Difficult aspects to planets in the eighth can warn of difficult separations, messy divorce settlements and crises in your life where it is difficult to find support so that you are unable to share. We all need support from someone to help us through the most difficult times of our life. The eighth house can sometimes imply degrees of pain, crisis and suffering, where we can come through it renewed or cleansed and perhaps wiser about ourselves.

Understanding your eighth house could also be a key to your own sexual nature. Your difficulties or your attitudes towards sex, and to find a way in which you can regenerate yourself. For instance Gemini or Mercury on the eighth may find it helpful to talk to others, whereas Mars or Aries on the eighth may find it helpful to get involved in some sort of sport which would release some of the frustration or energy. Whereas Taurus on the eighth may find it refreshing to do some gardening. So perhaps studying the eighth may be an indication how you can regenerate yourself.

One final point is that the predicting of someones death is taboo, largely because astrology runs the risk of scaring someone to death with fear. Modern researchers have found that the expectation of death can be a major factor in bringing it about.

The Ninth House

The ninth house is the house of Sagittarius and is associated with higher education, philosophy and religion, long distance travels, the higher mind and in-laws. It is concerned with the search for wisdom and knowledge. It is opposite the third and deals with whatever is not day to day routine. It is the abstract mind versus the concrete. Whenever you consciously think about something this belongs to the ninth, instinctive thought belongs to the third.

The ninth house is where we seek the truth. It is the higher mind and is linked to abstract theories and intuitive processes. It shows how we pursue religious or philosophical issues. It can show our god image. We need meaning in our lives and it is the ninth house where we strive to find that meaning, otherwise we may feel that we have nothing to live for. Depression or other forms of neurosis can be related to a lack of purpose or meaning in life or that a belief structure has been shattered in some way.

Anyone with many planets in the ninth will be unwilling to accept the limits of their everyday existence, they want to reach out and experience anything that is new and unfamiliar, to discover things about the world, seek out the truth. They are interested in any type of consciousness-expansion such as philosophy. They seek out ways to raise their level of awareness.

Jupiter and Sagittarius in the ninth is also linked to travel, the seeking out of new knowledge around the world. Travelling can be done physically or mentally and the planets here may show what we encounter on our travels. With Saturn you may experience delays or difficulties on journeys, or more specifically travel for practical purposes such as work or study. Pluto or Scorpio in the ninth may attract experiences abroad which profoundly transform us in some way.

The ninth house can also describe our relationship with our partner's relatives, our in-laws. So whether the relationship is pleasant or stormy will be shown here. Strong placements in this house also give an unusual degree of intuition and foresight. The ability to sense the direction in which something or someone is heading.

The Tenth House

The tenth house is the house of Capricorn, and is associated with our public image, social contribution or status, profession and parents or government officials, or people in power over us. The tenth house is the opposite to the fourth. Whereas the fourth house is the parent who nurtures and cares for you, the tenth is the parent who prepares you for the outside world. He or she may be an authority figure and in certain cases such as single parent families, the parent may correspond to both of these angles.

The midheaven is the highest point in the chart and correlates to the tenth house, though in the equal house system does not always fall in the tenth house. The qualities of any sign or planet in these position corresponds to what to us is most visible to others, what stands out in us. Whereas the IC and the fourth house represent what we are like privately and how we behave at home behind closed doors.

The tenth house indicates the way we behave publicly, the image we wish to present to the world, how we would like to be seen by others, how we would describe ourselves to them by status. It is the qualities that we want to be admired and respected for and what we strive hardest to be like.

It is the tenth house that helps us decide what contribution we would like to make to the world and what we would like to be most remembered for. It can sometimes be called the house of ambition as this house can certainly describe our career or vocation. But it is more likely to suggest the approach one has to the career rather than the actual profession.

A large number of planets in the tenth may come out as a need to achieve something and to be a person of importance, and there may be a strong identity link to one of the parents, and with this there could be a tendency to live out the parents dream especially in cases where the parents dream is frustrated in some way and they were not able to fulfil their potential.

It can also signify how we play the parental role. How we assert our authority to our own children and those around us. Why we have a sense of discipline. It can signify all relationships where there is an inequality and one is in authority over the other.

The Eleventh House

The eleventh house is the house of Aquarius and is associated with social values, aspirations and ideals, also groups and friendships. In the eleventh house people are linked in groups through friendship or a common purpose. They are able to share ideas and interests and their lives are enriched by what they share.

The sign and planets in the eleventh house can show the types of friends we are attracted to and the way we go about making them. For example Mars is impulsive and makes friends quickly, whereas Saturn would be reserved and shy but attracted to more serious types of people or those who are in an older age group.

It can show us the type of groups we are attracted to and how we fit in. For instance Mars or Aries may have difficulty fitting into a group that quashed the individuality. They would constantly strive to make their mark or take over leadership. Our role in the group can also be shown by the signs or planets. Gemini or Mercury would act as secretary and take the minutes, Moon or Cancer would make the tea, Jupiter or Sagittarius will run the newsletter, and Leo will most likely take the chair.

With many planets in the eleventh there is often a need to be involved with a group or a wide social circle which would be their support system through life. In the eleventh we yearn for a more ideal society so this area deals with our hopes and wishes. Here we discover how we relate, not on a   one-to-one but to the whole human race.

The Twelfth House

The twelfth house is the house of Pisces and is associated with hidden resources and motivations, clandestine activities, associates and enemies, hospitals, institutions of confinement and karma, and is sometimes called the house of secrets and sorrows. The twelfth house is sometimes called the house of the unconscious mind and consequently is connected with repression. The sign on the twelfth and the planets in it can show us what kind of emotions, needs and past events we are repressing. It is as though the individual cannot accept the energy as part of the self and so represses it into the unconscious mind. But these unacceptable energies must still manifest themselves. If the conscious mind is unwilling or unable to accept them they have only two places left to surface. They manifest, either in the body then the twelfth house becomes the house of deeper illness. Or they manifest in the environment which can be expressed as individuals working against you., which is the domain of the sixth house.

For instance Mars in the twelfth house in a woman's chart may mean she has trouble expressing her assertive energy, she may have trouble being positive. She may experience it through the relationships that she attracts, they could be strong, aggressive, domineering or arrogant people. For men with the Moon or Venus in the twelfth they may have difficulty expressing the feminine side, although with these placements they may often experience it through nursing or caring as a profession.

The twelfth house is also considered to be the house of the collective unconscious and in spiritual terms it is the mystical longing for union with our source, a desire to return to our creator and a direct experience of being part of something greater than ourselves.

For Pisces, the twelfth house, the sign of the two fishes, is always faced with a choice. Their individual separateness and the desire

76

to blend with the whole. There may be susceptibility to drugs or alcohol which is a way to break down boundaries or to escape from difficulties. Others will get in touch more directly through meditation and prayer or devotion to God. There is always difficulty with boundaries when you have a strong twelfth house emphases. It can reveal patterns, urges and compulsions which operate from below the level of conscious awareness, and yet do significantly influence our choices and our attitudes and our directions in life, as they are stored in the unconscious memory and filter through.

The twelfth house may show the overall psychological state of the parent which has filtered through to the unborn child which is developing in the womb. The twelfth house is also the house of karma so we may experience in this house difficulties and troubles that we have brought in from previous lives and that have to be dealt with at some time in this lifetime. Whether we believe in reincarnation or not placements in the twelfth describe influences which have come from sources which we cannot obviously see or remember.

House Systems

The question of which house system to use lies mainly with the Astrologer who through experience will find the system which best fits his or her methods. The equal house which is used throughout this book is probably one of the most commonly used amongst astrological students. It is easy to set up as the circle is divided equally into 30⁰ sections and therefore does not contain complicated mathematical formula. One of its best assets for students is that aspects can be drawn in to complete the chart pattern with no distortion, which makes it the easiest to learn and to interpret. However, there are several house systems which have been popular in their time so I will briefly describe some of the better known systems. It is considered by some astrologers that the house cusp is not the 'beginning' of a house, but the peak of the houses energy so that planet which lies 3⁰ or 4⁰ off say the fourth house cusp will have third and fourth house energies.

Placidus House System

This is one of the more difficult systems to mathematically calculate but became popular in the 19th Century when Raphael produced a placidean table of houses so the house cups could be found without any calculation. It was first developed by a Spanish monk Placidus de Titus, it is a time system and the house cusps are found by trisecting the time it takes for any degree of the ecliptic to travel from one angle to another that is from the ascendant to the midheaven, or midheaven to the descendent. The problem with this system is the distortion of the houses in latitudes greater than 66.5⁰ so that in very high latitudes some degrees of the ecliptic can never become the ascendant.

Koch System

This system is another time system and has currently become more commonly used with the advent of computers and its use by the Huber School. The mathematical calculation using trigonometry is complex and although tables were produced in 1971 by Dr Walter Koch, they did not supersede the placidus system. Its disadvantage like the placidus system is that it fails in the polar regions.

Topocentric System

Another time system which has been tested and results show that it is a good system to use for timing events. Again the calculation of the house cusps is complicated.

However, it differs from other systems in that it has been derived theoretically. It has the advantage that there are no house distortions in the polar region although below 50* latitude the house cusps fall within 1⁰ of placidus. Topocentric houses are generated by trisection of the cone radius. The cone of rotation is produced by the natural rotation of the horizon around the topocentric axis. The constant speed at which the cone rotates enables space and time to be divided equally.

Porphyry System

This system uses the ecliptic as its circle of reference although it takes the Ascendant to be the cusp of the first house, but unlike the equal house the Midheaven coincides with the cusp of the tenth house. the space between the angles is then trisected equally along the ecliptic. This system was criticised for the equal division of space as no logical reasoning could explain it.

Campanus System

Johannes Campanus was a well known mathematician of the 13th Century. He used the prime vertical as a frame of reference instead of the ecliptic. He then divided the prime vertical into equal 30* segments but accepted that the angles should correspond to the first and seventh and fourth and tenth house cusps. This system like other space systems fails in high latitudes.

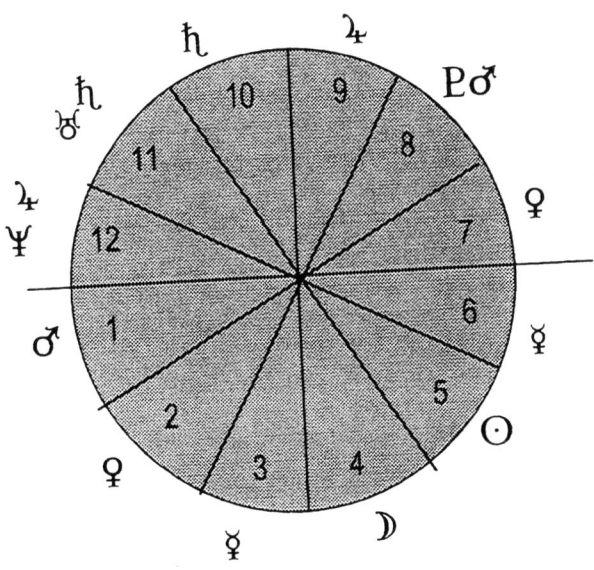

Planetary Rulerships of the Houses

Chapter 9

Sun Placements

Sun in houses
When reading the following chapters remember that any aspects can alter these interpretations considerably.

Sun in First House
There is a desire to be in control of their own lives and their surrounding environment, also of any situation they may find themselves in. Often bright and cheerful people who appear to exude confidence.

Sun in Second House
Security is important and the ability to be in control of their own finances. There are often many opportunities to accumulate wealth. They may have to watch a tendency to be possessive of either things or people.

Sun in Third House
These people need to shine in their local environment or amongst siblings, they develop good communication skills quite early on. They have a thirst for knowledge and enjoy learning, but they have the potential to be rather bossy or dominating.

Sun in Fourth House
Home life is very important to these people, they must have a base either to work from or retreat to as they dislike continuous exposure. They may be strongly influenced by their parents or the past and could get locked into this. There may be inner doubts or lack of confidence.

Sun in Fifth House

These people need to find their creativity to show their specialness, or it will always seem as if their sun shines behind the clouds. They are interested in sports and leisure activities and this can be more greatly emphasised than work. They work well with children on creative levels once they have found their own talents.

Sun in Sixth House

These people could be workaholics, they express all their energies and creativity in the area of work so that it creeps into their leisure time. They may also be overly concerned with health and if not actively working in connection with health they may have a tendency towards hypochondria or develop phobias. They are overly anxious and worry a great deal and may have a desire to create a perfect world.

Sun in Seventh House

Interaction with others is important for these people as they learn a great deal from all relationships and may often feel they are fated in some way. They may often work with relationships or in a partnership needing someone else to bounce their ideas off. It is a good position for diplomats and arbitrators as they are tactful and seek a balanced view.

Sun in Eighth House

There is a strong interest in the occult and reincarnation with this position and these people may do a lot of self analysis in an effort to rid themselves of any psychological problems connected to the past. They enjoy a mystery and love delving in hope they will uncover long forgotten secrets or unresolved problems. They are fairly emotionally stable even if not overly expressive.

Sun in Ninth House

These people have high ideals and expectations of life. They are the explorers in life and are driven by an inner restlessness to see and experience as much as they can.

Travel usually plays an important part at some time in their lives. They seek higher knowledge either through travel, or by further education. They have their own special philosophies which although learned early on can be changeable.

Sun in Tenth House

These people are career oriented and success and a high profile provides the status they desire. They are very ambitious and can be dictatorial and arrogant if these needs are thwarted. Well balanced they exude a lot of charisma and give others confidence by their efficiency. They are highly motivated and have what it takes to inspire others.

Sun in Eleventh House

These people also have high ideals but on more humanitarian levels than for self aggrandisement. They seek truth and wisdom and have respect for the views of others. They enjoy working within a group but would exude leadership qualities as their ability to organise would come out. Their own goals and desires could be pursued within a group situation.

Sun in Twelfth House

There is a desire to help others in need with this position but there is often a lack of confidence in their own abilities. They may be of a quiet nature seeking their own company or seclusion from the world. They may have clairvoyant abilities or at least an interest in the occult. Positively they use their talents to help others but negatively they may seek to escape from their responsibilities, not able to take the harsher elements of life.

Chapter 10

Moon Placements

Moon in Signs and Houses

Moon in Aries

These people have emotional and impulsive natures, they have an uncontrolled temper which flares up suddenly, but it is only temporary and soon forgotten. They are independent and they dislike convention and discipline. The mother plays an important or dominating part in the life, but it is not always a sympathetic relationship. Very high spirited and courageous, unless deliberately provoked, for when their feelings are aroused they act impulsively and carelessly and may often act before they think, so that they may regret their actions when they have calmed down. Insistent on having their own way, they very rarely obey those in authority over them.

Moon in the First House

These people find it difficult to view life objectively as they can be swamped in their own feelings and emotions. They desire to be loved and protected and will adapt to fit the needs of another. As they grow in confidence they want to nurture and protect everyone around.

Moon in Taurus

Quiet, persistent, determined, they are conservative by nature and resist change. They tend to have many friends and attract wealth and the good things in life, they often desire to acquire money houses or land. They spend their money conservatively, and like to hold onto it not because they are mean but because they like security, however, they can be materialistic and nurture their own needs. There is often a tendency to succeed into their father's or family businesses. It is a favourable placement for singing, music or painting, they are sensuous, sociable and good natured. They like the comfort and security of familiar surroundings, and as a loving and affectionate person, they need love and affection around them. Emotionally they are stubborn and it is hard for them to change their attitudes, they prefer the familiar attitude as well as familiar objects.

Moon in the Second House

Talents may lie in their ability to care for others and may earn their money in professions where caring is the prime factor such as nursing, child care or catering. These are sentimental people and may be attracted to the past and collect items linked to the past. They feel emotionally secure when they are financially solid.

Moon in Gemini

A lover of gathering information, books, scientific or literary pursuits, they tend towards occupations of a mental nature. They like to change residences frequently and travel about a good deal. They are skilful and dextrous and are likely to have more than one occupation or their minds like their jobs can change frequently. Their rapidly swinging emotions make them quite restless, they get bored quickly and their attention wanders if they spend too much time on one objective. If not well placed they may show a lack of straightforwardness and honesty. There is a tendency to talk incessantly and they can be the type of person who never gets off the telephone. They are nervous and fidgety and they are apt to spread themselves too thinly so that they cannot cope with all they've taken on.

Moon in the Third House

These people may have found themselves in the position of mothering other siblings either by choice or necessity. Everything they do is to help them feel secure whether it is the gathering of knowledge or caring for everyone in their immediate environment.

Moon in Cancer

There are strong ties to the mother, they are imaginative, emotional and changeable, with some ability for mimicking, acting or expressing the thoughts and emotions of others. There is a tendency towards mediumship, psychism, music, painting and poetry. Their sensitivity to others can make them imagine slights where none were intended. They are often moody, and can withdraw and sulk. If the Moon in this sign receives difficult aspects there may be a tendency to dominate and live out their dreams through the lives of their children. Feelings are more important to them than logical thinking which seems cold and boring, they get very attached to ideas, points of view, or certain objects for reasons they don't understand. They are easily hurt by criticism, because they are unusually sensitive to other people's feelings. They know how the other person feels before anything is said.

Moon in the Fourth House

The home is important to these people, it may be seen as a retreat or sanctuary which protects them from the outside world. There may be many moves as they continually search for a place that feels secure for they are sensitive to all family difficulties. Possible interest in genealogy in an attempt to discover their roles in life.

Moon in Leo

They are ambitious people and do not hesitate to come before the public as they like to be the centre of attention and will often act in a way that attracts attention, they also tend towards being in positions of authority and prominence. They are very susceptible to love affairs and are popular with the opposite sex and they make sincere lovers. A great deal of intuition, love of music, painting and poetry, plus a love of pleasures and luxuries such as perfumes, jewels, antiques and clothes. They have a need to love and be loved but they are inclined to dramatise everything including emotional scenes. They are emotionally very warm and if they like someone they let them know it. They need plenty of reassurance for the better they feel about themselves the less they need to show off.

Moon in the Fifth House

This position may be someone who yearns for children but it may also bring back memories of their own childhood which could affect these desires. There is a strong instinctive need to be creative, they may enjoy the theatre and they could find themselves involved with the public in some way.

Moon in Virgo

Excellent mental powers and capable of following intellectual pursuits. They have good memories and learn easily. They may be rather serious but usually cheerful, neat and like order around at all times and it bothers them to have anything out of place, (a place for everything and everything in its place) is their motto. They are often quiet and easy going, irresolute, unambiguous and unpretentious. They have many friends especially female friends. There is a regard for hygiene and personal cleanliness and they are particular about food and diet. They prefer to work behind the scenes, they are curious but do not ask personal questions. Sometimes they can be excessively occupied with detail blinding them to the more important issues.

Moon in the Sixth House

This position may find someone who is ritualistic, feeling secure and safe with the adoption of daily routine. They need to watch their diet as there is a tendency to eat for comfort. In a work situation they tend to care for the needs of others, ever ready with the aspirin or the tea and sympathy. Often put frustrated mothering instincts on to family pets.

Moon in Libra

Generally popular with a fondness for music and poetry. They are peace-loving and do not like to start fights with others. They like life to be beautiful and do not like to think about things that are not pleasant. They are affectionate, good natured, kind in manner and gain friends easily. They are fond of company, society and friends, in fact much of their fate will come through their associations with friends, they will be greatly swayed and influenced by people. They are easily upset by inharmonious relationships and there is always a special link to the parents especially the mother.

If weakly placed or aspected, they may be over-dependent on others for emotional security. They rely very much on their charm to get them out of things they don't want to do, people generally like them because they can exercise a very genuine charm.

Moon in the Seventh House

These people may look towards their partner for nurturing and mothering, seeking a partner who shows emotional and caring qualities. Security will be an important reason for this person to set up home with another. There could be difficulties if the partner turns out to be highly emotional and needs most of the caring.

Moon in Scorpio

They are firm, determined, self reliant and assured, well able to stand alone and fight their own battles. They can also be abrupt, plain-spoken, positive, energetic and capable of hard work. Conservative and averse to change especially if forced upon them from the outside, difficult to influence and may be very obstinate. Sometimes they are irritable, angry and revengeful.

If the Moon receives difficult aspects it may bring questions regarding overeating and overindulgence in alcohol is likely. They have very intense feelings but they may find them hard to understand because they are so complicated and deep. They need a great deal of reassurance from those close to them or they will have to cope not only with feelings of jealousy but they may also feel lonely and misunderstood. They are very fond of anything secret or mysterious and as they like to learn about the world around them they become good psychologists as they have a deep intuitive nature.

Moon in the Eighth House

This position is very sensitive to the moods and feelings of the mother and may have been deeply affected during childhood. Any strong feelings running through the family will be picked up when the Moon is in this position. They may care for others who are going through emotional traumas helping them by sharing their experience and knowledge.

87

Moon in Sagittarius

Their manner is restless and unsettled either in body or mind, they are fond of physical exercise and enjoy walking, they are also inclined to travel or change their residence frequently. Their nature is candid, honourable, kindly and good humoured, their intuition is active and they may have the gift of clairvoyance. They are idealists and they want the world to be a beautiful place and people to be good and are disappointed when they are not. In the lower type of chart there may be an interest in gambling and amusements only. Difficult aspects to the Moon could cause narrow mindedness, arrogance and an egotistical holier-than-thou attitude. They are also very curious and want to know the answer to every question, this curiosity often makes them want to travel and see places very different from the one they live in now. They are very independent and resent anyone trying to keep them from doing what they want. Being optimistic and cheerful they don't stay gloomy for very long and when others are around usually feel good about life. They will often be interested in any subject that teaches them about the universe and their place in it.

Moon in the Ninth House

This position gives an instinctive ability to see what is ahead, they feel their way intuitively. They have a strong philosophy of life that developed from childhood. They may feel a strong link with a special place overseas and may live overseas at some time.

Moon in Capricorn

These people can achieve either popularity or notoriety but they are generally in the public eye in some way. There is often a degree of administrative ability especially if the Sun is in a Cardinal sign or if there is a Cardinal sign rising. There is nearly always some drawback or difficulty attached to their occupation which may cause them to suffer in some way, even though they have not deserved it. They can be fond of shows, rather selfish, careful with money matters, cautious and calculating, they know how to influence others but often think too little of the feelings of others. The less desirable characteristics of this placing depends upon the rest of the nature of the chart. They do however take life seriously and are generally hard workers though they are often shy and insecure about their own worth, often rather uncomfortable with their feelings they can sometimes appear cold by nature. It is as though their feelings seem out of place inside them almost as a difficulty rather than a pleasure. They don't show their loving feelings very readily but they need love as much as anyone else. They need the sort of parents they can look up to and model themselves on. When their emotional needs conflict with their practical needs they often take care of the practical needs first but they must remember that they will never by happy if emotional needs are continually denied.

Moon in the Tenth House

The mother is an important figure to these people, and they may choose a career that will reflect their own mothering qualities. They are extremely conscious of their reputations as they often come before the public at some time in their lives. Their emotions and feelings are often vulnerable when they are confronted with the media in any way.

Moon in Aquarius

This position gives an inclination towards astrology, fortune telling, dreaming, visions, mediumship and the occult generally. They are usually attracted by original, eccentric, unusual or novel subjects. They tend to join secret societies or brotherhoods such as the freemasons. They usually have an interest in politics, education, scientific work and they may join a movement or public body relating to these. They are sociable and sympathetic and they like to have the good opinion of others, though they may be very independent, unorthodox and unconventional at times.

It is a slightly unfavourable position for the constitution for if there are difficult aspects to the Moon there could be afflictions to the eyesight. They seek freedom of emotional expression and demand freedom to come and go as they please within the domestic situation, thus they are likely to have unusual family relationships. They feel that they can control their own feelings and don't like to be around those who can't because great displays of emotion bothers them. They rely on their intellect to solve problems rather than on moods, feelings and impulses. They need to learn to be more tolerant of the emotional differences between themselves and others. They value their freedom very highly and can be very stubborn if someone tries to force them to follow a path they are reluctant to follow. They like to experiment with life but definitely on their own terms.

Moon in the Eleventh House

These people are attracted to friends who mother them in some way. Or these are the people who organise and care for others in group situations they always make the tea or get stuck with the washing up. These people feel secure in group situations which often become a second family to them.

Moon in Pisces

They are usually quiet, retiring, easy going, restless and fond of variety, They change their minds easily and are not always to be depended upon. This Moon position makes them easily discouraged when they meet with misfortune and opposition in life. There is a liking for reading, and for poetry and music that appeals to the emotions and feelings. With writing they are usually fluent, copious and imaginative, but diffuse. They are inclined to be spiritual but it is usually more emotional than intellectual, they are prone to feel rather than to reason out. There is a tendency towards mediumship, clear dreaming, and various psychic powers. It is not a favourable position for robust health. They are kind and sympathetic, and because of their sensitivity to the feelings of others are easily hurt and could develop a persecution complex. Sometimes they are excessively shy. They are also very sensitive with strong feelings, a lively imagination can make them very creative but it is also often easier for them to daydream than live in the real world. They need to learn to stand up for themselves and resist those who are more aggressive instead of avoiding conflicts.

Moon in the Twelfth House

A sensitive placement, they may absorb all the feelings going on around them. There may be a complicated relationship with the mother that may be hidden in the unconscious, and not easy to access except through dreams or meditation. These people are very protective of their own feelings and desires and keep them hidden from the outside world.

Chapter 11

Mercury Placements

Mercury in Signs and Houses

Mercury in Aries
They are quick witted, observant, sharp, sometimes given to exaggeration, and they can be sarcastic, enthusiastic or excitable. They are often clever at writing or speaking but their interest span favours only short pieces of writing rather than long complicated works. They have fertile minds and are quick and inventive, and can often be the cleverest in the family.

Mercury in the First House
This position will portray an active mental nature, someone who needs to communicate or who appears to be a great thinker. They are likely to be intensely curious about everything and avidly store information which they then impart onto their particular circle. Changes of environment may be common in early childhood.

Mercury in Taurus
They are usually slow to make up their minds, but are fixed and determined when they have done so. Patient and persevering in the acquisition of knowledge. They are fond of money and possessions and may make money by occupations that come under Gemini or Virgo. This placement conveys a sociable and friendly disposition with some inclination to religion, art, music or poetry. Anger and irritation is apparent when Mercury has difficult aspects.

Mercury in the Second House

There may be a natural talent for writing or speaking with Mercury in this position and it may be that money will be earned by making good use of these talents. The acquisition of information adds to their security, so lack of education could give feelings of inadequacy.

Mercury in Gemini

These people will be inclined to study though perhaps in a rambling and aimless fashion. They tend to study more that one subject at a time or quickly change from one to another without going into anything in sufficient depth. They can be fun and others are attracted by their agile mind and sense of humour, they may also have a gift of mimicry.

Mercury in the Third House

This is the natural house of Mercury so it is strongly placed here. This may indicate good early learning abilities and a flair for languages. Aspects to Mercury in this house may show relationship with other siblings. There could be a tendency to have strong opinions before it is backed up with knowledge.

Mercury in Cancer

They are quiet, good humoured, easy going and sociable. They are sometimes changeable, their minds grasp many subjects with a wide comprehensive view of things. Their memories are good and their minds sound and strong, if not always quick or alert. They often have a sense of rhythm and motion which shows in dancing or athletics or mentally in music or poetry. They are often dreamy and can be very intuitive especially where the family are concerned.

Mercury in the Fourth House

This position of Mercury may be someone who uses their home as a place of learning, these people often have large libraries and are interested in history. They may come from an intellectual background, one of their parents having chosen an academic career. Many changes of residences can also be common especially in early years.

Mercury in Leo

They are strong minded and positive, but can also be kind hearted, easy going, fond of pleasure and self indulgent. They are also able to talk a great deal about themselves and they are capable of directing, managing for, or controlling others. They are fond of children, of music, singing, poetry or the fine arts. They may give up much of their time to follow mental or pleasure pursuits and neglect other duties, that are less exciting.

Mercury in the Fifth House

A need to express themselves creatively is important for these people. They enjoy exchanging ideas and solving mind games. They have a natural affinity to young people and may make good teachers in this area. They love variety and their romantic nature is stimulated by different and interesting people.

Mercury in Virgo

They learn readily, are fond of science, especially computer science, and studying and reading generally, they have good memories. They make excellent secretaries and clerks, as they have very active and analytical minds and are able to think things out in great detail. Although they may achieve much in the areas of writing and study it does not always favour public success.

Mercury in the Sixth House

These people tend to take on too much work and find themselves with stress related problems. They need to learn to relax and to not get involved with what everyone else is doing. There is a tendency to live on their nerves and there may be a critical dimension that sets in when watching others work.

Mercury in Libra

They enjoy studying, writing, reading and educational pursuits generally, in conjunction with another person. There are harmonious relationships with brothers, sisters, cousins etc., but if Mercury receives difficult aspect then there could be problems with communication in their partnerships. It gives a love of society and comradeship, a fondness for intellectual pleasures and amusements.

Mercury in the Seventh House

These people above all need to choose partners with whom they can communicate. Physical attraction soon wears thin if there is nothing to say. Their partners need to be intellectually stimulating and it may be difficult to settle for just one as variety helps to keep them stimulated. A tendency to imitate or copy others during the relationship plus an attraction to younger people.

Mercury in Scorpio

They have strong opinions and can be obstinate and difficult to convince. They can pursue a train of though with great mental concentration. They are lively and active in mind, witty yet sarcastic, and will have a great flow of words and command of language (unless there is a difficult aspect from Saturn), they are dextrous and inventive. They are fond of looking into mysteries and solving problems, they make powerful hypnotists and healers of the mind.

Mercury in the Eighth House

This position gives Mercury's curiosity a deep and probing ability. They love a mystery and would move heaven and earth to solve it. They encourage others to talk about their personal life, but keep quiet about their own. There is a fascination with death and reincarnation as they explore the deeper secrets of life.

Mercury in Sagittarius

Their minds can be just, generous and sincere, and there is often an aptitude for medicine, science or literature. They are very active mentally and perhaps also physically, but they are also very changeable. There may be an ability to write but this will tend to be in subjects like religion, philosophy or science. Their mental abilities do not show to their best advantage during youth or early life, these people take time to settle down being interested in a great many fields during early years.

Mercury in the Ninth House

A busy position for Mercury with an inclination to travel, there is an attraction to more abstract concepts. There could be some confusion here as Mercury likes to dip into many different areas yet in this house he gets caught in the depth of his studies and may find it a struggle to finish what he has begun. May have many friends overseas.

Mercury in Capricorn

They are cautious, diplomatic, subtle and profound, their whole nature is seldom ever seen on the surface. They can influence other people through the mind. There is always a serious side to their character, and this may be a calculating one at times, with an inclination towards serious and profound studies. This position is favourable for winning prizes in education. They are often better educated than their brothers and sisters, they tend to hold government posts and can be fairly ambitious.

Mercury in the Tenth House

Attracted to a profession where Mercury skills are used in communication, sales, writing, lecturing, printing etc. Reflecting good mental abilities would be important to these people. Career needs to contain a lot of variety or there will be a tendency to keep changing direction. Good communication is likely between one of the parents if there are no difficult aspects.

Mercury in Aquarius

They have a strong intellect, a good memory and a comprehensive mind. They can be of fixed opinions, averse to change and not easily influenced in their ideas, but enjoy variety. They are capable of hard work mentally, they are original and deserving of a good education. They tend to travel for the sake of achieving an objective and not just for the mere sake of travelling. This is a strong position for Mercury for good clear objective thinking, it also strengthens the intuition, they tend to know where they are going.

Mercury in the Eleventh House

Often manages to get involved in group situations where they often play a significant role as spokesperson or group secretary. Interested in other people's thoughts and ideas as it is found to be stimulating but is equally interested in voicing own opinions. Is likely to be busy and active and accumulate many friends.

Mercury in Pisces

These people work quietly, subtly, and in the dark, they make good detectives and can have analytical skills, they are good at discovering mysteries. If Mercury receives good aspects they can have much ability as an imaginative writer. They may gain fame through singing, music, or writing. They can be scatty or vague tending to day dream with their heads in the clouds or they could put their imagination to some use and make good romantic novelists. They can be highly intuitive and telepathic and their minds are based on unconscious emotional patterns of past experiences.

Mercury in the Twelfth House

Tendency to be a dumping ground for other peoples thoughts which can interfere with their own thought processes. There is a lot of restless searching and probing into the unconscious and a general curiosity about the meaning of life. They can be very sensitive and insecure about their own talents and abilities and may in some way sacrifice themselves for others.

Chapter 12

Venus Placements

Venus in Signs and Houses

Venus in Aries
These people can be impulsive and unstable in their affections, they are very ardent and find it difficult to restrain their feelings. Their enthusiasm to 'clock' up as many emotional experiences as possible could make them inclined to marry early and perhaps hastily. They have a positive cheerful attitude and can be quite popular and creative, although they do tend to be self centred, as whatever makes them happy is okay. These people want action in their relationships and to keep them happy you would need to be physically active and imaginative.

Venus in the First House
With Venus in the first house it is important for these people to look attractive and it is often not that difficult for them. They put themselves out to be amicable and are very susceptible to flattery. They can be charming but lazy, friendly, but selfish. Their ability to form relationships is very important to them.

Venus in Taurus
These people give constant and lasting affection, they are loyal but can be possessive. Their homes are usually beautiful and artistic and personal beauty is often important to them as they seek to make themselves as attractive and youthful as possible. They are sensual and enjoy touching and physical closeness is important.

Venus in the Second House

Venus in this position, the house of natural talents, often bestows charm and good looks. They love beauty and surround themselves with beautiful possessions. A sordid environment would throw these people off balance. They can be possessive and put too much emphasis on possessions and greed. They may gain their money in the beauty field or other venusian pursuits.

Venus in Gemini

These people are usually sociable, good humoured and friendly and they like variety in their romantic and social lives. This is a favourable position for popularity and marriage and there is generally more than one love affair or marriage. There is a tendency to some flirting and inconstancy in love. They are excellent at moving around at parties and making everyone feel welcome. They can talk to anyone with equal ease.

Venus in the Third House

These people know exactly what to say and how to say it, and the author of "How to Win Friends and Influence People" probably had Venus in the third. They can be kind and gentle to younger ones and generally have a good relationship with other siblings. They are sensitive to the needs of others and attract confidences from their peers.

Venus in Cancer

These people are emotional, affectionate, kind hearted and imaginative, and their sensitivity makes them easily hurt. They value financial and domestic security and their moods can be fluctuating and unpredictable. Their homes are important to them and they often seek to stay in them than go out to public places of entertainment. Their relationship with their children is important and can be possessive at times. They need to be careful not to live emotionally through their children.

Venus in the Fourth House

This person needs peace and harmony in their home environment and would find it difficult to live with constant arguments or any unpleasantness. They would spend a lot of time in the home creating the right atmosphere. They are likely to have inherited a creative and artistic flair which would be put to good use in the family home.

Venus in Leo
They are lovers of life and rather theatrical in their behaviour. They are kind hearted and their sympathies are easily moved. They are usually popular and fond of society, company, friends, and pleasures of all sorts. They may have considerable creative talent and usually have a vivid colour sense. They are fond of children and are romantic but if Venus has difficult aspects in this sign it can produce someone who is snobbish, excessively proud and selfish.

Venus in the Fifth House
These people need to express themselves creatively, they are true romantics and will love to be "in love". This placement can also show that you may have creative and charming children and that you are likely to encourage them in their creativity. It is likely that your children will be a source of pleasure for you if other aspects in your chart do not make you push them beyond their capabilities.

Venus in Virgo
These people tend to over analyse their relationships and are very critical of those they love cutting the spontaneous flow of affection. They can be extremely fastidious about personal hygienic and their appearance. They do have an innate sense of order and cleanliness and often make good cooks and dieticians. The can often be very shy with feelings of social and sexual inadequacies, they can often use possessions and status as a substitute for personal affection.

Venus in the Sixth House
Venus in this position enjoys harmonious working conditions and has a dislike of dirty or heavy work. However, this can also be someone who enjoys their work and puts their own particular style into what they do., There is also a tendency to fall in love with co-workers so that many of their relationships come from a working environment.

Venus in Libra

Marriage and harmonious relationships are extremely important to these people, they can be bestowed with general physical beauty. They are often well liked because they have a genuine desire to please. They have high standards for social conduct and manners for they dislike coarseness and uncouth behaviour. They dislike disagreements and discord and if exposed to them too frequently they become nervous and upset.

Venus in the Seventh House

With Venus in the seventh there is a tendency to be a bit of a romantic with a need to be in a relationship. You may idealise your partner or may be continually searching for the right partner and no one seems to fit into your ideal. Attractiveness is more important to you for romance to blossom, you expect your partner to make an effort to look good and you are drawn to those who do.

Venus in Scorpio

With Venus in this sign the emotions and sexual desires are strong and passionate and they can be very jealous and possessive. They often lack reason and delicacy because of the intensity of the feelings. There is a certain magnetism and attraction to the opposite sex but if they are rejected they can become disillusioned, revengeful and bitter. If Venus is badly aspected then you may get the type of person who uses his/her sex appeal to manipulate people, this applies mainly in a woman's chart. Difficult aspects in a mans chart shows he would find it difficult to relate to women.

Venus in the Eighth House

This is a rather seductive position for Venus who is most capable of making others feel at ease and relaxed in a sensual situation. They love to delve into mysteries and often create intrigue if it does not happen naturally. They are often charismatic but may find it difficult to stay in a relationship. They often do well financially through their partners.

Venus in Sagittarius

These people are friendly, vivacious, sociable and outgoing. They are often outspoken and honest about their inner feelings. Their feelings tend to be rather fickle and they are often attracted to more than one person at a time. They are imaginative with a sense of the romantic and beautiful, they like music and poetry and they may show a love of nature and sports. Their frank nature is often construed as tactlessness.

Venus in the Ninth House

There is often a tendency for someone with Venus in the ninth to live abroad or marry a foreigner, failing this there is always an interest in foreign cultures and overseas. There is a philosophical air about them and they love to study on a deep level and if they are involved in teaching the love of their subject often comes across to students.

Venus in Capricorn

These people often repress their emotions and sexuality when they are in a group, but they can be capable of being very sensual in private. There tends to be a sense of aloneness about them which can make them mysterious and attractive to others. They are often popular with the older and more mature people, as they relate to them more easily. They often seek to improve their status through marriage, they are proud and reserved in public and dislike displays of emotion and affection, considering such conduct beneath them.

Venus in the Tenth House

A warm and sociable nature developed from a closeness with one of their parents. There is always a need to present themselves in the best possible way to the public. They would never allow their image to slip, they endeavour to remain cool and charming in every situation. They often choose to work in artistic and creative areas in an attempt to find beauty in what they do.

Venus in Aquarius

This indicates a detached but warm emotional outlook. They tend to be friendly with everyone but not necessarily on a personal basis. They are often popular and well liked as there is a sparkling, effervescent and unusual quality in their manner, they generally have many friends. Their social and sexual morality may be unorthodox departing from the acceptable normal. Their romantic encounters are often sudden and casual and not always very stable, to keep the relationship alive it is necessary to allow them as much freedom as they need.

Venus in the Eleventh House
These people often find a niche for themselves in the right group situation, this is where they make their friends. They may be the mediator in a group situation where they are able to soothe ruffled feathers. There may be a tendency to use the group situation to climb from one social group to another, judging themselves by their acceptance by others.

Venus in Pisces
These people are often deeply compassionate and sympathetic and usually very spiritual. They have a high capacity to understand the feelings of others, and can easily put themselves in anothers position. They are romantic and sensitive and need clear demonstrations of affection from others to prevent them from feeling lonely and disappointed. They hesitate to express their feelings as they are afraid of being hurt through rejection. They tend either to become emotionally dependent on others or have others emotionally dependent on them. There is also a tendency towards martyrdom, with strong leanings towards blaming their partners for their own weaknesses.

Venus in the Twelfth House
Like Venus in Pisces this is a sensitive placement tending to find all the lame ducks when they are searching for a relationship. There is sometimes a strong need to escape from the harsh realities of life, as they tend to become very emotional and sentimental. If life becomes too difficult they can resort to alcohol or drugs to help obliterate painful memories. There is a need to care for others and they may often work in a caring profession or for some large institution.

Chapter 13

Mars Placements

Mars in Signs and Houses

Mars in Aries

This position gives energy, activity, forcefulness, combativeness, positiveness, enterprise, originality, self-assurance, and the desire to be at the head of things. Though it increases the vitality it also increases danger by accidents, fire, wounds and surgical operations. These people are often impulsive, imprudent, they act in haste, and they dislike secrecy or restrictions, some of the most important events in their lives will be due to their own acts. They use up their energy and their force rapidly so they are more inclined to 'wear out' than grown old gracefully.

Mars in the First House

This position of Mars gives tremendous energy and if not properly used can lead to irritation and aggressive behaviour. There is a strong urge to shape their own lives. They would benefit from regular exercise which would help them stay in control. They have stamina and strength and need to live an active life, they are the people who make things happen as they are too independent or reluctant to depend on anyone else.

Mars in Taurus

These people are firm and obstinate and they feel that any obstacle that they encounter can be overcome without difficulty. They work carefully and slowly but their thoroughness makes up for lack of speed. Their possessions will be important to them and they are likely to work hard for what they want in life, but they must remember not to be too possessive about their friends. They may have difficulty in expressing their anger unlike those with Mars in Aries, but they will rise to any challenge with great tenacity.

Mars in the Second House

These people are very determined in their pursuit of possessions, they have a strong desire nature and are so impatient that they make most of their purchases on impulse. They can be very resourceful and hardworking, they respond to any challenge and will stand up and defend the things they value.

Mars in Gemini

These people work quickly but they have trouble directing their energy at a single task for any length of time. They rarely finish tasks because it is more exciting to move on to something else so it is possible that they do not master skills completely. They have quick minds and like to argue and discuss topics, they are rather impulsive and may make their decisions too rapidly, which they may regret later. Fortunately they have the tendency to shrug off mistakes or brush them under the carpet where they do not have to face them.

Mars in the Third House

This can indicate a very busy environment and someone with this placement can move around it very quickly. There may be arguments with other siblings as here is the person who could be verbally aggressive when their activities are blocked or frustrated. They may be very restless or highly strung and may need to make a conscious effort to relax.

Mars in Cancer

This position gives a fluctuation of mood with a tendency to act according to the mood. They are sensitive to harsh words from others and they can become quite angry though they may have trouble releasing their anger. There may be difficulties or disagreements with their families but there will also be much loyalty. They expend a lot of energy within the home and if there are difficult aspects, they could come from a background of constant arguments and bickering.

Mars in the Fourth House

A strong desire to have a home of their own and a lot of energy may go into achieving this. There may have been some conflict with one of the parents which could have involved some angry confrontations. There may be many arguments in the home if they do not make a conscious effort to relax.

Mars in Leo

These people are very proud and work on their own initiative, and they do their best to be reliable if they know someone is depending upon them. They have considerable self confidence and courage with a good understanding of themselves. They are quite stubborn and the more they are pushed the more they resist, and they can sometimes appear arrogant and domineering.

Mars in the Fifth House

This is a competitive placement, they love sport especially the energetic kind which involved plenty of action and an element of risk. They put a lot of effort into all they do whether it is winning a game or creating a work of art. They may have rebellious and energetic children who will keep them on their toes.

Mars in Virgo

These people work carefully and systematically and with great attention to detail. They often work with tools to make useful objects and are willing to take time to master difficult techniques so they have the ability to become master craftsmen. They will have a strong sense of responsibility but they must try to be more tolerant of other people's ways and not be too critical. They apply their critical abilities to themselves when learning something new, the keyword here is perfection.

Mars in the Sixth House

This may be someone who shows their leadership qualities in the area of work. They work at top speed and find it difficult to have patience with the slower mortals. They may be too quick for their own good but they are happiest in a place which generates activity and is constantly busy. There is a tendency to push themselves too hard which could lead to overstrain and exhaustion. However, this is the person who will tackle the complaints board for you and come out winning.

Mars in Libra

These people have a strong sense of co-operation and are willing to make compromises to get along. There seems to be a fluctuation of energy with this position sometimes feeling very energetic and sometimes feeling very lazy. They can also be extremely competitive. Their natural charm makes them a popular champion and a graceful loser. Too much time may be spent on making choices.

Mars in the Seventh House

This could be the person who "marries in haste and repents in leisure" although there is unlikely to be any repenting as this Mars will get themselves out of something just as quickly as they got into it. They need to be assertive in their relationships and consequently may be attracted to assertive or aggressive partners until they find that quality within themselves.

Mars in Scorpio

These people have a strong will and they know what they want and they apply steady pressure until they get what they want. When they are upset they do not always explode immediately they tend to make biting and sarcastic remarks and can hold a grudge for quite a long time. They can be quick tempered and fight with the sharpest weapons, as their most deepest emotions are often involved. They have very strong likes and dislikes it is hard for them to be neutral about anything.

Mars in the Eighth House

This person can be very passionate and sexually oriented, however they have to take care that they do not use their sexuality as a vehicle for aggression. They have very strong feelings and tackle everything with a degree of passion, with difficult aspects here there could be problems involved with inheritances or financial battles over possessions after divorce proceedings.

Mars in Sagittarius

These people have much physical energy and they find a good release for it being out-of-doors and in the fresh air, they are often restless and being outdoors gives them a sense of freedom. They rebel against any form of restriction and they often have athletic ability and play a lot of sport. These people also have an inclination to travel far afield at some time in their lives as they are natural explorers. They dislike day to day routine matters, and take a long time to settle down.

Mars in the Ninth House

There are very strong views on education here and much energy is put into achievement. There may also be a strong desire to travel and keep on the move. They will believe passionately in their own particular philosophy and have their own image of God, they are likely to get involved in many arguments defending their beliefs.

Mars in Capricorn

These people are quite ambitious and have a phenomenal energy to work hard for what is important to them. They are practical, idealistic and work for tangible results. They must learn to avoid measuring people's worth according to their income or social prestige, there are many important values that cannot be measured this way, but they may be in danger of learning this too late. They are quite courageous but their natural caution makes them not willing to fight unless the point is quite clear.

Mars in the Tenth House

Their aim in life is to be respected for their courage and drive to succeed in their own particular field, in which they endeavour to be leaders. There may have been a fiery relationship with a parent who may also exhibit the same drives and who has been instrumental in the climb to the top. A tendency to be too pushy and ruthless in achieving their goals.

Mars in Aquarius

These people are quite inventive and original, but they often do things because they are different not necessarily because they are better. They do not follow orders very well and when they were young they probably had trouble with people in authority over them. They are often political or have a special aptitude towards anything technical especially computers. You frequently find Mars in this position as well as Mars in Virgo, in the charts of those who repair electronic equipment, or are involved in new technology.

Mars in the Eleventh House

This position of Mars may be attracted to group interaction but there may be some difficulty here as Mars needs to express not only individuality but assertiveness. The needs of the individual could conflict with the needs of the group unless leadership qualities are taken up. There is a tendency to be fairly assertive when making friends and to be attracted to those who are active and energetic.

Mars in Pisces

These people are very sensitive and their energy often depends on their moods. It is quite difficult for them to be self assertive as excessive emotions stand in the way and people take advantage of them because they are unsure of themselves. These people grow more sure of themselves as they get older and they can be a tremendous help to those around them, they have as much potential for success as everyone else, except they do not have as much push or ruthlessness. They dislike direct confrontations with people and they can become highly emotional and are prone to tears. It is a favourable position for psychology and for working hospitals, as well as psychic matters.

Mars in the Twelfth House

With Mars in the twelfth house there is an innate dislike of confrontation as with Mars in Pisces, so there is a tendency to keep all the anger inside which could be hazardous to the health. Here we have someone who likes to work behind the scenes they can be fairly directive in a subtle way. Not always saying what they mean it can take some time to figure them out. Energy may be used or wasted by not distinguishing boundaries, by going the long way round to tackle a problem.

Chapter 14

Jupiter Placements

Jupiter in Signs and Houses

Jupiter in Aries
These people often have enormous self confidence and feel entitled to display pride with sometimes a touch of arrogance. They have an ability to stand alone against all odds if necessary unless there was any adverse pressure from their parents, then they may have been made to feel that it is them against the world. There may be an attitude of self importance as they believe strongly in their own ability, however this could appear as arrogance and could arouse resentment in others. There is much enthusiasm and they have the ability to inspire confidence in others, as nothing seems impossible to them. Over confidence could lead to carelessness and impatience.

Jupiter in the First House
A philosophical personality with a tendency to do things is a big way. They are often larger than life and are not easy to dismiss or overlook. These personalities are generous and open, love to exaggerate but can be a bit tactless. They always have far reaching goals but often find the journey more rewarding than the goal. They have a sixth sense and a zany sense of humour.

Jupiter in Taurus
These people have a strong desire nature and are likely to accumulate material possessions and use them as a protection against the unpredictable and challenging outside world. They will always prefer comfort to deprivation and pleasure to work. There is a tendency for them to attract wealth and they may find it a challenge

by learning to develop a healthy attitude towards possessions rather than how to acquire them. They have a fondness for luxury and good food and have a rather self indulgent attitude. Jupiter here is steady and patient but tends to stick to old methods rather than try out new ones, though status is very important to them.

Jupiter in the Second House

A person with Jupiter in the second may feel secure by having a well tested philosophy for life, perhaps handed down by parental influence, yet with Jupiter there is always the need to expand their views further. They may need to always aspire to gain more than they already have on a material level and are often quite fortunate in their achievements. With Jupiter in this position they may find the need to apply for further education, as they may need knowledge to feel secure, hoping that it will provide a doorway towards more skilled employment.

Jupiter in Gemini

These people often neglect their emotional and spiritual needs and use their minds solely as a tool to gain advancement in the world. They may exclude everything from their lives that does not have an intellectual principle but they find it difficult to stick to a subject long enough to acquire any useful knowledge or firm foundation. They are likely to enjoy travelling to a variety of different places and find it stimulating. However, they are able to see life with a kind of logical detachment, and if they understand the larger, more important issues of life they are able to communicate that understanding to others.

Jupiter in the Third House

There is likely to be a good relationship with brothers and sisters and to be well thought of in the neighbourhood. There is generally a thirst for knowledge, they may gather information which will bring them pleasure, and which they can impart amongst their various acquaintances and be heralded as a 'mine of information'. There may be many changes of residence or extensive travel during their childhood. There is always an inner restlessness with these people as they set their goals much higher than average.

Jupiter in Cancer

This is a good placement for Jupiter as these people are often able to take care of and protect others for they feel emotionally secure and protected themselves. They like tradition and prefer anything old rather than the new and untried. They either receive financial help from their parents or tend to become wealthy in later life, as their happy outlook attracts good fortune and comfortable situations. They like to feel they belong and put down roots. They are able to find something positive in even the most difficult situations.

Jupiter in the Fourth House

This may be someone who was born with an innate understanding of the good things in life. There is often a desire to own property or land and to them big is beautiful. They do things in style, enjoy the open air life and often settle down somewhere overseas. Exploring is in their nature and they would grow restless if confined. There is a possibility they will settle overseas at some point in their lives even though they are likely to eventually return to their roots.

Jupiter in Leo

These people have strong constitutions and plenty of vitality, they are generous and benevolent but expect admiration and appreciation in return. There are usually leadership qualities and their greatest talent is the ability to inspire confidence and enthusiasm. They have a special love of children and often make excellent teachers. They are very sociable and enjoy getting together with friends, however although they enjoy company they have a strong need to be appreciated and well thought of, and can be extremely hurt if someone challenges their integrity.

Jupiter in the Fifth House

With Jupiter in this house the creative vision knows no limits, they believe everything is possible, the word "cannot" would not be in their vocabulary. They are life's gamblers and risk takers on many levels. If they are interested in sport it would be because there is a touch of danger such as fast cars or parachuting as they are the adventurous types. There may be a philosophical attitude and sometimes there may be many children, or children with Jupitarian traits.

Jupiter in Virgo

There is often a conflict with Jupiter in this sign as Jupiter inclines towards large scale projects, growth and expansion and Virgo tends to pay precise attention to detail and it is not possible to be too detailed about large projects and these people like everything done exactly right. It will either lead to overwork or they must learn to delegate work to others however hard this is for them. These people often enjoy pleasant working conditions and are well paid and respected for what they do, they are tidy people and cannot tolerate chaos. There is usually a good relationship with co-workers and they have integrity and are usually honest. If there are difficult aspects there may be a tendency to drift from job to job, if working conditions are not conducive to their personalities.

Jupiter in the Sixth House

Jupiter in the sixth may take dietary concerns to extremes. This means there is a tendency to overeat and gain weight at a phenomenal rate, or else they are able to be overly health conscious and eat virtually nothing. Their health is usually good if they control their weight. This may also be someone who takes on too much at work, but whatever they do, they do to the best of their ability. They often make good employers as they make an effort to teach their employees how to do the work to their best ability.

Jupiter in Libra

These people usually have strong principles regarding marriage and relationships, so there is a likelihood of a lasting marriage and a fulfilling home life. They are often popular and well liked and are generous in their consideration of the wishes and needs of others. If there are difficult aspects to Jupiter there may be a tendency to make moral decisions for others, or there may be lawsuits arising from financial or marital problems. However they have considerable diplomatic skills and an ability to influence others.

Jupiter in the Seventh House

If Jupiter's placement is where we are vulnerable to excesses then in the seventh this is likely to result in many relationships. Jupiter in this position finds it difficult to find all they need in one partner. They also need freedom in their relationship but may find it difficult to grant their partner the same. They may struggle with jealousy but ultimately need the independence to do their own thing. There is usually a tendency towards more than one marriage.

Jupiter in Scorpio

Scorpio is the natural ruler of the 8th house which will give these people an interest in the occult, reincarnation and other related subjects. The combination of Scorpio's intensity and Jupiter's enthusiasm in everything they enter into is done wholeheartedly and they give it all they have got. However, they do have a strong sense of privacy revealing little about themselves.

Jupiter in the Eighth House

Jupiter in this position benefits through other peoples money, through legacies, business deals, tax rebates or even fortunate marriages. They understand the meaning of sharing and are usually more fortunate than most. They may also be involved in legal matters to do with finances as a career choice. They enjoy sharing different philosophies and spend time searching for new meanings to their life. Sexual experiences are to be shared but can lead to an excessive sexual appetite.

Jupiter in Sagittarius

These people have a strong desire to be free and experience life in their own way. They are often attracted to foreign travel and study foreign cultures, religions, races and social systems. They have a far sighted outlook on life and can often have prophetic insights into the future. They are deep thinkers, interested in philosophy and religion and the nature of mans purpose for being. There is a desire to expand their knowledge or any area of their life without others imposing any restrictions or limitations on them. They may attract money later in life.

Jupiter in the Ninth House

There is a continual search for knowledge and the basic truth of life, they can have great vision and insight but benefit most when teaching others what they have discovered along their journey of life. Philosophy, religion and further education are their ways of gaining wisdom and enlightenment. This position could also be someone who chooses publishing or printing as a career and perhaps they are the ones most likely to get a book published themselves, or who harbour it as a lifelong desire.

Jupiter in Capricorn

This position can give great integrity and moral conduct in business ethics and positions of trust. They enjoy taking positions of responsibility and are usually conservative with interests in education, politics and moral conduct. There is often a strong drive for power prompted either by personal ambition or by a sense of duty to society, they often allow this duty to interfere with their home life. They often manage to obtain wealth usually through hard work and therefore detest extravagance and waste.

Jupiter in the Tenth House

With Jupiter in the tenth the mother or father could be a source of inspiration and wisdom and depended upon for guidance throughout their life. There may be some claim to fame with this position, but there is also leadership and authority which takes them into the public eye at some time. Career may involve travel or have some connection with overseas. Professional status may be important to them or they may be involved in law or education.

Jupiter in Aquarius

These people are democratic because they hold no prejudices and they desire to spiritually share and experience with people from different areas of life. They realise that tolerance, respect and co-operation are essential for a successful social order. There is often a strong interest in astrology, philosophy, karmic law and reincarnation. They have an easy acceptance of others which makes them popular and easy to be with. Many social reformers have Jupiter in Aquarius.

114

Jupiter in the Eleventh House

Jupiter in the eleventh is likely to aspire to high ideals and expectations from life. They are likely to enjoy group situations where they can expand their personal philosophies. Friendships are likely to be varied from all walks of life and to be plentiful. The invitations may be so abundant they are spoiled for choice. They have many goals and the faith to believe they will achieve them.

Jupiter in Pisces

These people have great emotional depth especially in understanding and compassion. They often are champions of the underdog and the less fortunate. With aspects to Uranus, Neptune or Pluto there is often psychic ability. Their spiritual understanding can be more universal than the Jupiter in Sagittarius person. They may seek seclusion and are often associated with spiritual retreats, ashrams, churches and monasteries where they seek spiritual renewal through meditation. They are so sensitive to others needs and feelings that they need solitude and a chance to rest and renew themselves without the intrusion or interference of others.

Jupiter in the Twelfth House

Jupiter in this position may have a strong psychic ability that often develops later in life. They are sometimes considered lucky but this could be attributed to their deep faith that everything will turn out well, but there does seem to be a protective quality with this position. Here is the ability to expand the unconscious mind through meditation or prayer. There is an ability to be drawn deeply into spiritual life, there is a healing quality which is given freely to all they come in contact with.

Chapter 15

Saturn Placements

Saturn in Signs and Houses

Saturn in Aries
There is often lack of self assertion of a positive kind, and a need to enforce one's will and to control the immediate environment. However any confidence they appear to have is more often a defensive manoeuvre which sometimes attempts to attack first, because it is fearful of attack. Any difficulties are generally due to their own actions, directly or indirectly. Their fate in life is largely of their own choosing, especially their career. There is a touch of selfishness with this position and they have few close friends but many acquaintances and they may be rather gloomy and fond of seclusion. It is often difficult for people with this Saturn position to see themselves as others see them.

Saturn in the First House
These people may spend the first half of their life feeling self conscious or inadequate in some way. They may appear quiet and withdrawn through lack of confidence It is natural for them to approach everything in life with caution. However, confidence develops alongside achievements and they do have the perseverance to keep on trying. Because they believe everything to be so difficult it can sometimes result in a pleasant surprise when they find that it is not.

Saturn in Taurus
These people are strong willed, very firm and persistent in pursuing their purpose. It is not always a good position for money matters, finances tend to grow slowly or they may lose money through

investments. There is strong materialism here and a tendency towards being very careful with their spending.

Saturn in the Second house
Saturn placed in the second house often means that these people will experience difficulties in the financial side of life. Money just does not seem to come their way and they struggle with understanding their own self worth and value. It is when they begin to discover their inner resources and value themselves that their financial difficulties begin to improve. There is a tendency to stick to traditional ways of making money and although this position is not prohibitive towards achieving wealth it does mean that you need to work very hard in order to make any headway.

Saturn in Gemini
There may be troubles and difficulties in their early years especially with education. They may have some learning difficulties although there may be considerable intellectual ability. There is often strength of character, ability for scientific work or for invention and discovery. They usually have an excellent sense of timing which aids their successes.

Saturn in the Third House
With Saturn in the third there may be difficulties of self expression, somehow they never seem able to say exactly what they mean. A difficult childhood as an only child or one who has too many responsibilities when young can make these people feel they have missed out on a great deal, and are uncomfortable relating to others especially an emotional level. There may also have been some childhood problems that made early learning difficult, such as illness, or changes of school through moving away, that made it difficult to settle down.

Saturn in Cancer
This position may make emotional expression difficult which may cause estrangement from the family. It may be that the early life was cold or austere or beset by problems leaving them with emotional scars and inhibitions, but they do nevertheless take family responsibilities very seriously. They often incur financial struggles

117

and domestic strain. They hide their inner feelings from public view and build a shell around themselves which can inhibit the expression of true warmth of their personalities. It can also produce a sluggish metabolism which causes overweight and water retention, or it leads to under nourishment and bony appearance.

Saturn in the Fourth House

Those with Saturn placed in the fourth may go through life with an insecurity coming from the lack of parental support they had in earlier life. Their expectations of life are not high in that they would not expect their needs to be met. These are the people that ultimately have to parent themselves, pay attention to their inner child and discover their own strengths so that they learn to support themselves. A difficult relationship with one of the parents may have played a part in an inner lack of confidence, although some of the difficulties here may not necessary be the fault of the parent as it may have been circumstances beyond their control.

Saturn in Leo

These people have a need for importance and recognition and they seek to gain positions of power and leadership. Physical ailments with Saturn in this sign take the form of stiffness of the back and heart trouble. Their need to defend their ego can result in stubbornness and rigidity plus there is a danger of developing dictatorial and dogmatic attitudes. Difficult aspects to Saturn can bring disappointments in love or problems through children, as well as losses through financial speculation.

Saturn in the Fifth House

These people may find a lack of spontaneity in their lives, all creative endeavours including children seem to include a lot of responsibility that can sometimes prove to be too great for them to make the effort. They take love affairs seriously and they have to learn to have fun and relax a little and release some to their creative energy. In fact they take everything to do with leisure or pleasure seriously enough to take the fun out of it. They need to learn to live a little.

Saturn in Virgo

These people are practical, exacting, and hardworking. They are concerned with detail, accuracy, precision and are meticulous, especially in work. They have a strong and capable intellect and are able to deal with profound subjects. There is often a disappointment in the career and their ambitions may be thwarted by ill health or setbacks from parents. Overwork and worry can lead them into ill health and they may have nervous problems or digestive trouble.

Saturn in the Sixth House

With Saturn placed in the sixth there may be issues surrounding health, this does not necessarily mean poor health but can often include a rigid routine that indicates exceptional concern for health. Other difficulties may come through their attitude to work, they may feel tied down by daily routine yet at the same time lost without it. There are often problems in the work area that must be sorted out before any advancements can be made in their career.

Saturn in Libra

This is a strong position for Saturn and these people often have much social awareness and social responsibility. This position is favourable for partnerships, especially with older or more serious persons, position, power and dignity is often gained through the partner, or there is some financial gain and improved status. People with this position often become lawyers, judges and mediators, and are inclined to achieve their goals through the co-operation of others.

Saturn in the Seventh House

Saturn placed here can indicate someone who works with relationships and sometimes it can seem like pure hard work. They may expect grief from relationships, perhaps even rejection and there is a tendency for life to fulfil their expectations. They may look for someone with strength to look after them or they can be the strong ones and attract those who are weak in some way so that they can 'parent' them. Most of the difficulties in their lives come through their interaction with others, so they may end up alone to avoid continuous strife.

Saturn in Scorpio

This position produces very forceful, strong and turbulent characters. There is a tendency for them to be rather critical and they are usually perfectionists in their work. They accept responsibilities with a serious emotional intensity and they learn to deal calmly with them as they arise. Thoroughness, persistence, determination and a fanatical drive for success that is equalled by only a few other positions. They are likely to harbour deep resentment if they feel they have been dealt with unjustly.

Saturn in the Eighth House

Saturn here may produce a fear of letting go and giving themselves to another. Sexual problems may be experienced as they hold themselves under such firm control that something gives. It can give rise to anger and frustration and conflicts when it comes to shared resources. There is an attraction to banking, insurance and generally other peoples resources with this position.

Saturn in Sagittarius

This position gives intense intellectual pride, they fear disapproval or censure and feel resentful if they have been spoken about unjustly. It tends to give some degree of power, prominence, authority or responsibility in religious matters. In some cases there is an inclination towards philosophy of some kind or towards politics. If their religious views are orthodox they will be serious and devout, but if unorthodox, it will bring philosophical or original thinking and an enquiring mind which will embrace new views, yet with equal seriousness. If it is badly aspected they may become unpopular and notorious.

Saturn in the Ninth House

Saturn in the ninth is often involved with tradition, and is conservative and often judgmental. Travel is often experienced as fraught with difficulties such as lost luggage, delays and misunderstandings. If travel is to further their education or for the purpose of pursuing a career then difficulties are often much less.

Saturn in Capricorn
People with this position know that everything has its price and that everyone must contribute to the work of the world. It does indicate strong ambitions for worldly power, status and authority which is manifested through business or politics. They often have a strong sense of family pride and honour though those born to wealthy and prominent families run the risk of being extremely cold about human values because they lack the experience of personal struggles without resources. This position can reach the heights of spirituality or the depths of materialism and selfishness, but it does give the necessary drive to overcome difficulties.

Saturn in the Tenth House
This is a placement where Saturn is comfortable, status and achievements are very important to these people, they work hard for their rewards. Working in a structured environment is important and they often make good teachers, they are patient and disciplined and make excellent organisers.

Saturn in Aquarius
People with this position are mentally ambitious, and they have the capacity for well organised mental concentration. The mind is impersonal and scientific, the concern for impartial truth is paramount. It gives a sense of justice and responsibility in relationships, they are generally level headed and offer good advice based on universal laws. If badly aspected they may be selfish and domineering and expect others to play the game by their rules and serve their personal interests.

Saturn in the Eleventh House
This is the house of friendships and with Saturn placed here friendships are taken seriously. They are often attracted to either serious minded people or those who are older in years. They tend to be more selective when it comes to choosing friends and they are not interested in those who do not come within the criteria for selection. They do not fit easily in a group situation and may suffer from isolation or loneliness. However, when friends are made they are often for life. There may be some fear attached to setting their sights too high as life seems to be such a struggle.

Saturn in Pisces

In this position these people tend to be trapped in their memories of the past, they can have an over active or fearful imagination, that generates all types of anxieties and neuroses. On the positive side these people can have emotional understanding and humility and the willingness to work for those less fortunate. If it is well aspected they are capable of deep meditation with profound spiritual understanding. If it is badly aspected it can result in paranoia, excessive worry, and regret over past mistakes. These people need a certain amount of quiet and solitude in order to tap their inner resources. In some cases it can be a sign of poor health.

Saturn in the Twelfth House

This can be a difficult position to interpret for there is often a fear of what is in the unconscious or what would happen if it was released, so here there are feelings of fear over lack of control. This position may involve repressing some part of themselves which involves feelings of guilt or inadequacy. There may be a fear of exposure to another person, which could manifest as a fear of intimacy. Anxiety is common depending upon the sign yet they often contain a deep inner wisdom that sees them through their most difficult crises.

Chapter 16

Uranus Placements

Uranus in Signs and Houses

Uranus in Aries
These people need freedom to act in their own independent way, they have courage, daring, initiative and resourcefulness. They can also be blunt and outspoken, they demand change and their spirit of adventure is strong, they need constant new experiences to keep them happy. They like their own way and to be independent.

Uranus in the First House
There is an electric energy about these people which is usually obvious within minutes of meeting. There is often something unusual about their life, they are independent, original and need a great deal of freedom to find themselves. They can generate energy that makes them exciting to be around. At least life will never be boring when in their company, however their inconsistency may be too much for some people to handle.

Uranus in Taurus
Attachment to home and possessions can dampen their individual expression and their need to be practical in an original way. There may be many ups and downs in their financial affairs, sudden losses or gains. It can give unusual artistic and musical talent. They may find it difficult to express their originalities through such a practical and earthy sign.

Uranus in the Second House

There is a tendency towards financial ups and downs with Uranus in this position. There is a dislike of being bound by possessions or burdens of life. There is a need to feel free from any type of material restrictions. Money is likely to be earned in unusual ways and personal talents could include originality, intuition and inventiveness with a clear insight into what you attempt. These people are just not attracted to any situation that is conventional and routine.

Uranus in Gemini

This position increases the mental power and activity, it gives originality and ingenuity, and possibly some eccentricity. They are restless and often have a fondness for travel, and may be very inventive and intuitive.

Uranus in the Third House

This is the original and inspired thinker, they can be rational and logical as they are able to see things from a detached viewpoint. Often a difficult placement for early school life as these children find structure and routine difficult as it stifles their originality. Here you may find the child labelled as restless or disruptive as they struggle to fit into classroom routine. They may have a rather detached attitude to the rest of their family, perhaps breaking contact with other siblings in later life.

Uranus in Cancer

These people have very sensitive feelings and emotions, they are easily touched and quickly moved. There may be trouble or estrangement in the domestic affairs. There may be some mediumship and dreaming or occult experiences.

Uranus in the Fourth House

There may be an unusual or disruptive early home life so that these people have difficult settling down and may always need a place to run to or escape to if they do decide to put down roots. There is generally something unconventional about the home life. It may be a meeting place for groups concerned with humanitarian principles, or it may be used as a base rather than a home.

Uranus in Leo

There may be some difficulty with the father or obstacles in their family lives. They disregard convention and have a love of freedom and independence, they may have a rebellious disposition. They are often fickle and changeable in their love affairs. It is a good position for a public or professional career.

Uranus in the Fifth House

This is the person with the unusual hobby or creative outlet but whatever they do will be touched with originality and often a touch of genius. As this is also the house of children you may expect to have fairly independent and detached children who will want to make their own way in life as soon as possible. They will experiment and you may have to watch them meeting life with their unusual potential which may or may not be acceptable. There may also be a tendency towards short-lived and exciting love affairs that keep the adrenaline going.

Uranus in Virgo

There may be difficulties in your working life with thwarted ambitions. The intellectual ability is often increased, the mind is often subtle and penetrating, independent and original. May need to be careful with diet as allergies to food may be a concern.

Uranus in the Sixth House

These people bring their unusual qualities into the area of work. They are experimental and find new and different ways to do things which is rarely the same as anyone else. They always approach any task or work in their own unique way. The difficult side of Uranus in this position is the tendency towards allergies, this may be because they are often anxious and highly strung and may have some difficulty repressing this. These people need some mind body exercise such as yoga to help them to relax.

Uranus in Libra

There is often hasty engagements and marriages with this position which often lead to separation or divorce. The imagination, taste, and aesthetic faculties are increased and there may sometimes be remarkable intuition.

Uranus in the Seventh House

With Uranus in the seventh there is a need for freedom within a relationship. Any form of restriction through jealousy and possessiveness will send them running in the opposite direction. They are attracted to partners who are open and honest and who are in some ways different from their usual crowd. A problem may occur if other aspects of the chart shows a need for security, security for with Uranus in the seventh this will be difficult to come to terms with over longer periods. There is a need for frequent interaction with others and exchange of ideas and experiences will be stimulating.

Uranus in Scorpio

This position gives strength of mind, acuteness, incisiveness, wit, mental grasp and comprehensiveness, if the rest of the chart shows intellect. They do possess determination and powers of concentration. though you may occasionally find that it shows an aggressive, rebellious nature and one who enjoys being at war with the world.

Uranus in the Eighth House

These people can be curiously detached and experimental with the sexual side of their nature yet can also be capable of expressing great passion. However, again there is this conflict which in spite of their strong sexual feelings there is the need to be free and retain their individuality, the blending of two into one does not come easily and they have difficulty letting go. There is an intense interest in the occult especially astrology. There can be intuitive flashes of insight that leads them into new realms of understanding.

Uranus in Sagittarius

This position increases the imagination and inventiveness, as well as religious sentiments and the higher emotions. There may be a tendency to dreams or visions and there will be a strong inclination to travel.

Uranus in the Ninth House

An unusual philosophy of life may prevail here, there may be a tendency to follow their own instinctive truths, and find their own path rather than follow anyone else's although they may be motivated to join groups where they discuss and exchange ideas. There may be unusual experiences through travel or the desire to visit places that are different and this may awaken them to change worn out ideas. They need constant stimulation with new dreams and visions for the future.

Uranus in Capricorn
These people are thoughtful, serious and reserved, but they usually have strong ambitions, are steadfast and persevering. There may be danger of family discord, especially in their early life, such as separation from their father in some way. It is a good position for public occupations connected with governing bodies.

Uranus in the Tenth House
With Uranus in this position the vocation is likely to be unusual, a good position for astrologers. Whatever work these people take on has to be fulfilling or in some way serve humanity. There is a strong independent streak and this person is likely to express their own ideas and beliefs regardless of how controversial they may be. They may have seen one of their parents as being overly independent or not always there in spirit perhaps wishing themselves elsewhere. They learned independence at an early age and are more than capable of looking after themselves when the need arises.

Uranus in Aquarius
This position increases the mental power and gives originality and independent minds that are inventive and resourceful. They work well in association with others and it is favourable for benefits from partners or marriage.

Uranus in the Eleventh House
There is a strong affinity towards others with a united sense of purpose, they may be drawn to shared experiences of a group situation and make good facilitators. They enjoy the sharing involved in groups but yet may fear the loss of their own individuality, so they seek to express their ideas strongly and attempt to take leadership. They are attracted to people who are different and their friends may be slightly offbeat or eccentric in some way. Their

goals and objectives in life may be constantly changing as their vision of the future takes on different dimensions.

Uranus in Pisces

This position tends towards inner religious feelings, occult experiences, dreams and a keen interest in all psychic matters. There may be unexpected misfortunes with this position, possibly caused through such a diverse spiritual outlook. These people find it difficult to realise what fulfils them.

Uranus in the Twelfth House

A difficult position for Uranus as exploring the unconscious can take them to new and discovered depths that could be difficult to handle. There may be a yearning for freedom and a fear of being contained which may take them beyond safe boundaries. They may seek to retreat from life temporarily and emerge as a completely changed person. Settling down and establishing roots may be too difficult causing them to become drifters or remote from reality. There can be a touch of genius here which can be taken too far. Being out of touch with reality could make these people struggle to stay grounded.

Chapter 17

Neptune Placements

Neptune in Signs and Houses

Neptune in Aries
This position may give a love of travel for its own sake, much sympathy, and considerable intuition in regard to spiritual matters. They may find it difficult to express their true identity.

Neptune in the First House
Neptune in the first absorbs what is around it and finds it hard to establish the separate identity that the first house requires. Here there may always be a sacrifice to make, the sacrifice of individuality to become united with others. They may take on everyone else's troubles and they resent being taken advantage of. They may become the rescuer of the weak or find themselves continually rescued. There is always the possibility that they become drifters having no real purpose other than to escape the harsher reality of life. They have their dreams but they may always be dreams as they can lack the determination to make them work. A birth with Neptune conjunct the Ascendant may be surrounded with mystery or they may actively not to have wanted to be born at all.

Neptune in Taurus
This position is often good for money and business, though they may never be wealthy they will never be without. It is favourable for friendship and marriage.

Neptune in the Second House

Their biggest talent is their compassion for others and they may find work in a field where they care for those less fortunate. The problem here is that their generosity could leave them broke and a soft touch for a sob story. They are not realistic with finances and may be an easy target for fraud, or in some instances commit fraud. In some cases they may worship money above all else, and not until later in life do they discover the emptiness behind the materialism. There is often a tendency to always be provided for with Neptune in this house even if they never become materially rich.

Neptune in Gemini

This position gives strength to the intuitions and imagination and often gives prophetic or symbolical dreams. They may have musical taste and mental sensitivity.

Neptune in the Third House

There is a strong psychic ability here as Neptune picks up the impressions and moods of those around. The mind may switch from a clear insight to being vague and woolly. There is an artistic quality here which could be expressed in poetry or creative writing. As children they may have imaginary friends if they are lonely and there may be difficulty adapting or identifying with their environment. There may be some learning difficulties here perhaps coping with dyslexia, they often grow up to be excellent teachers of children with special needs, as they intuitively tune in to ways of communicating that they understand.

Neptune in Cancer

This position often gives mediumship or some psychic ability. There is often close association with the mother and some benefit through her. There may be many changes of residence and if badly aspected there may be psychic experiences connected with their residence. (Haunting etc. accentuated perhaps in the fourth house.)

Neptune in the Fourth House

With Neptune in the fourth house there may be a very close or intangible bond with one of the parents, so much so that it becomes hard to separate. After a secure childhood they may find it hard to cope with the responsibilities and difficulties of adult life. They may find it difficult to develop their individuality away from the family structure. There can often be some mysterious misfortune in the early years in that a sacrifice has to be made. Sometimes Neptune is in this position in the charts of those who are adopted or brought up in a different environment from their family such as an orphanage. There may also be over idealisation of one parent and a longing to find their spiritual home.

Neptune in Leo

These people have warm affections and their feelings are active and powerful. they are usually very generous they love company and pleasure and may follow some dramatic pursuit.

Neptune in the Fifth House

A creative placement with a vivid imagination, these people can write reams of fantasy given good aspects to Neptune. However, it sometimes happens that these people are called to make sacrifices in the area of their creativity, something more important calls upon their time. It may seem that every time they try to do something for themselves another person needs their time and they are quickly able to feel guilty if they succumb to their own needs. There may be some sacrifice made connected to children, they may never find the time to settle down and be a mother or they may have to give up something to be with their children.

Neptune in Virgo

This is not a strong position for Neptune but there may be considerable success in employment's such as nursing, medicine or clerical work.

Neptune in the Sixth House

This position of Neptune may show delicate health with a tendency towards allergies, but more of an allergic reaction to substances that are ingested. There can also be a sensitivity to drugs or alcohol; inasmuch less would be needed to take effect. Often illnesses can be difficult to diagnose or come from an unknown origin and they can often disappear as quickly as they came which could indicate they are emotional in origin. Neptune here is more inclined to try alternative therapies than to stick to conventional medicine. There may be healing qualities with this position or a tendency to work in areas connected to health or caring for the well being of others.

Neptune in Libra

These people are generally popular, there is a great attraction to the opposite sex, friendships and partnerships in general. There may be a love of beauty and a taste for painting and music.

Neptune in the Seventh House

There is a tendency to be unrealistic about relationships, to have high expectations that are romantically inclined and to feel let down when reality takes over. There may be a sacrifice of your own needs for the sake of another or a tendency to pick up lame ducks and look after them until they recover and then discover either that they no longer need you or you feel you have no purpose without someone to care for. The positive side of this placement is the search for a soul mate - a spiritual partner who fulfils every need. The negative side is being deceived by those with whom you place your love and affection and which may result in scandal and an unpleasant divorce or separation, that somehow hits the media.

Neptune in Scorpio

The feelings are intensified in this position, it is often good for money by marriage or partnership, there may also be a love of luxury.

Neptune in the Eighth House

Neptune is quite at home in this house of sharing and sexual union, they are able to blend with one another with comparative ease. There is a tendency to go beyond boundaries and lose touch with reality which may result in an effort to ground themselves. They are very romantic and sometimes life can spoil that romantic illusion so they feel let down. There may be a magnetism that is picked up by the media so these people could find fame. It is not a good placement for business so special care should be taken with financial transactions or signing contracts, it is a good idea to seek professional advise before signing anything.

Neptune in Sagittarius
There may be an inclination to travel either for pleasure or necessity. There may be considerable religious, spiritual or poetical feeling. Dreams and other psychic experiences may be a prominent feature in their lives.

Neptune in the Ninth House
Here there is the person who seeks a spiritual life but their religious pursuits may not be strictly conventional. Their need to belong may see them involved with a guru or a religious cult, a complete fascination for anything that promises enlightenment. There is the possibility of disillusionment within their own particular philosophy in that it does not fulfil all the high ideals. Higher education appeals but sometimes as a means of escape or postponing the time when they have to take on responsibility and live in the real world. Travel may also be used as a form of escape from day to day living but there is the ability to find real pleasure and enjoyment from a much needed holiday.

Neptune in Capricorn
There may be trouble in the family in their early life especially through the father. It is generally good for financial affairs and making money generally.

Neptune in the Tenth House
Neptune in the tenth may represent some ideal image to the media which is worshipped in some way. Generally there is lack of direction with this position, sometimes there is a clear direction that gets foggy from time to time, causing these Neptunian people to give up something that has been working well because it is no longer fulfilling. There is always a yearning to follow a spiritual path which does not always lead to worldly success. If Neptune on the tenth represents one of your parents then the parent may have made a sacrifice for the child, or the child may have picked up feel-

ings of resentment and feel guilty if there was any sign of unhappiness. On a positive level the parent may have taught compassion and concern for all humanity.

Neptune in Aquarius

This is a good position for friendship, love and marriage. There is much sympathy and humanity and frequently there is much intuition. No doubt we will learn more about this position when Neptune enters Aquarius in 1998.

Neptune in the Eleventh House

An attraction to groups that have a humanitarian or spiritual vision. They see group activity as giving something to all humanity, there is a tendency to blend their individuality with that of the group. They will seek out friends who are supportive and caring, if there are difficult aspects to Neptune then there could be some deception that is likely to lead to disillusionment. Friends may be of an artistic nature, artists, healers or poets or people who drift through life with no ambitions. Their aspirations and goals may be unrealistic but generally of a spiritual nature.

Neptune in Pisces

These people are broadminded, charitable, and sympathetic. They often benefit through the help of others or they may be involved in charitable institutions and helping others.

Neptune in the Twelfth House

This is a strong placement for Neptune in its own house. The unconscious mind can be a source of inspiration and can be tuned into by meditation. These people may spend much time alone to recover and re-centre themselves and prevent outside chaos from entering their serene lives. There are strong escapist tendencies where they escape into a world of fantasy. They may suffer sorrow because life does not always live up to their expectations.

Chapter 18

Pluto Placements

Pluto in Houses

Pluto is only useful as a tool for interpretation by its house position and aspects. Therefore we have excluded any mention of Pluto in signs in this book.

Pluto takes approximately 248 years to go through all the zodiac signs so its journey through each sign takes several years, spending a disproportionate amount of time in each sign, and can be interpreted on a generation level only. It may be important by house position if it is strongly placed e.g. conjunct the angles or in the eighth house. The Pluto energy can also be directed into healing channels especially those who heal by touch will have Pluto in a prominent positions.

Pluto in the First House

With Pluto in the first, life appears to go through rather dramatic changes. In early years life may be a struggle and the birth itself could have involved a near death experience or a struggle to survive. There is the feeling of power and control around the first house Pluto and there may be a tendency to manipulate situations to suit them. They tend to be suspicious always anticipating disaster, but they do have real power for self transformation.

Pluto in the Second House

With Pluto in the second possessions may be seen as giving some kind of power or control and there may be an obsessive desire to gain possessions. Pluto fears destruction and chaos and may subsequently set up events so that life fulfils their fears. They may experience both wealth and poverty so they have to find an inner sense of security. Pluto may need some control over the environment to feel secure so these people may establish themselves as important figures in the local community.

Pluto in the Third House

Pluto in the third may give a penetrating mind that immediately sees through any subterfuge but this also makes them suspicious and looking for sinister motives where there are none. There may be a tendency to have power over other siblings if there are any, and they may need to be watched in early years for bullying. However these children may take on trauma if anything does happen to other siblings because of guilt feelings. Many may have felt their early environment to have been threatening in some way in that they may have been suddenly taken away from it through schooling or hospitalisation, so therefore expect many upheavals and changes which threaten their security.

Pluto in the Fourth House

There may be major issues from early childhood that are cut off from conscious awareness. They may seek therapy or self awareness groups to discover the true person beneath the surface, yet there is always the fear of what they will find underneath. There is the ability to rebuild life after major crises such as divorce or death of a loved one with Pluto in this position. One of the parents could have been seen as suffocating or manipulative so that it was difficult to break free but once that freedom is found it will take a lot to relinquish it. The fourth house often shows endings and with Pluto here it could be complete transformation when finishing with something is total.

Pluto in the Fifth House

With Pluto in the fifth there is a deep desire to be somebody special and they will exert the full force of their personality to make this happen. Their creative urge must somehow express the depth of their feelings which could result in some fairly dramatic works of art. However some may experience creative blocks that may need to be worked through if their creativity was blocked as a child. The fifth also being the house of children would indicate that the birth of a child would be a life changing or transforming experience. This may be because problems may be experienced during the pregnancy in a woman's chart. There may be a tendency to come face to face with part of themselves through their children.

Pluto in the Sixth House

Pluto in to the sixth could indicate that illnesses may have a psychological origin and it may be that difficulties encountered elsewhere in life may lead to disease. They are able to work in a single minded fashion and their desire is to do a job to the best of their ability. There may be difficulties with co-workers as there would be a dislike of taking orders and there may be jealous under-currents and a certain amount of intrigue. There is often a need to transform the working environment and in some cases there may be complete changes of profession.

Pluto in the Seventh House

Pluto in the seventh will often need to have control in partnerships although they will often attract someone plutonian in nature where there may be conflict as each strives to take control. In these instances it is better to keep all communication open as subtle manoeuvres can ultimately destroy. Pluto in this position often provokes the other person to end the relationship when they want it to finish as there is fear of making the decision. There is also the possibility of going through the death of a partner but this is more likely to manifest as the death of a relationship but they also have the capacity to completely transform their relationships.. This can often leave the seventh house Pluto filled with guilt, like the fourth it takes on the guilt. The seventh house of balance in relationships is a difficult one for Pluto planet of extremes, as they need to feel the pain of interaction with another and find it difficult to let go.

Pluto in the Eighth House

With this position they need to learn to direct their energies into more constructive channels. They need to learn to share on a deeper level, particularly of themselves. There can be a lot of repressed anger with Pluto in this position and counselling therapy of some sort may be needed to understand where or with whom the anger lies. A well aspected Pluto may help to channel the drives in fairly significant achievements, but there may be attempts to avoid close contact perhaps hoping it will avoid possible tragedy or trauma through relationships. Pluto here is also closely tuned into what is in the atmosphere and is very quick to pick up on any undercurrents.

Pluto in the Ninth House

Pluto here searches for a deeper awareness of the meaning of life and a tendency to ponder on the question of survival. There is a leaning towards fanaticism or obsession with spiritual or religious issues so that they feel they have a firm structure for their beliefs. A breakdown of the belief system can be totally devastating and they may go through periods of deep depression until they undergo a rebirth into a new system of beliefs that transforms their existence. They could have quite dogmatic viewpoints through fear of someone being able to break down their belief system. It is sometimes said these people may be suppressing frustration, because that they cannot find the reason behind existence. On a different level Pluto here may also experience control or manipulation from in-laws which could interfere with their relationship.

Pluto in the Tenth House

Here Pluto may see one of the parents as dark and overpowering, the presence of which may be felt as suffocating or restricting and difficult to break free from. There may be a tendency to withdraw from the mother completely and because the tenth house is also the outside world, they may also withdraw from the world and live in the seclusion of the family, and then they will deny they have any ambition. The pent up energy must come out at some point and it may be through controlling the family in more subtle or underhand ways. To pursue a career with Pluto in the tenth it must be meaningful and exciting and give them control over what they do, given this they will put everything they have in a single minded way to be successful even to the point of ruthlessly cutting out anything that gets in the way.

Pluto in the Eleventh House

Pluto here will be drawn to groups that are concerned with reform and transformation, to break down the structure of society to be born again into something more meaningful. However, aware of the destructive element that lies within Pluto may have trouble sitting comfortably in a group situation. Wherever Pluto is there is a psychological issue, on a group level it may be humanistic psychology, group awareness that transforms them into more enlightened souls. There can be an obsessive desire to move towards their goals to the exclusion of all else and their goals may be more powerful and strive towards greater heights than most other placements. The eleventh house is also to do with friendships so Pluto here may seek out relationships with people in powerful positions or those who will transform their lives on more profound levels and will endure and give support through many of life's crises.

Pluto in the Twelfth House

There is an inner anxiety with Pluto in the twelfth that comes with change, they are afraid of letting go of one life style or set of beliefs to make room for another. They are afraid of the unknown and what is beneath the surface in the unconscious mind, so they endeavour to keep a balance because what they really fear is death. They see danger around every corner yet at the same time appear to have some kind of divine protection. Much of what Pluto fears may come out in dreams or meditation so they may be good subjects for dream therapy. They have a strong investigating nature and would make good detectives, using psychological knowledge of the criminal mind, which also makes a master criminal. Pluto here is sensitive also to what is in the atmosphere and may pick up on the stresses of everyone around, and be the one who falls ill. It is often during a crisis that Pluto in the twelfth discovers how much strength he has to survive and succeed.

Name:	MARY
House System:	EQUAL

	Triplicities	-	Elements	
21	Fire	S	MC	
22	Earth	1		
23	Air	3	ASC	
24	Water	1		
25	Positive	8	MC	
26	Negative	2	ASC	

	Quadruplicities	
27	Cardinal	3
28	Fixed	5
29	Mutable	2

30	Dignity	
31	Detriment	
32	Exalted	☉
33	Fall	

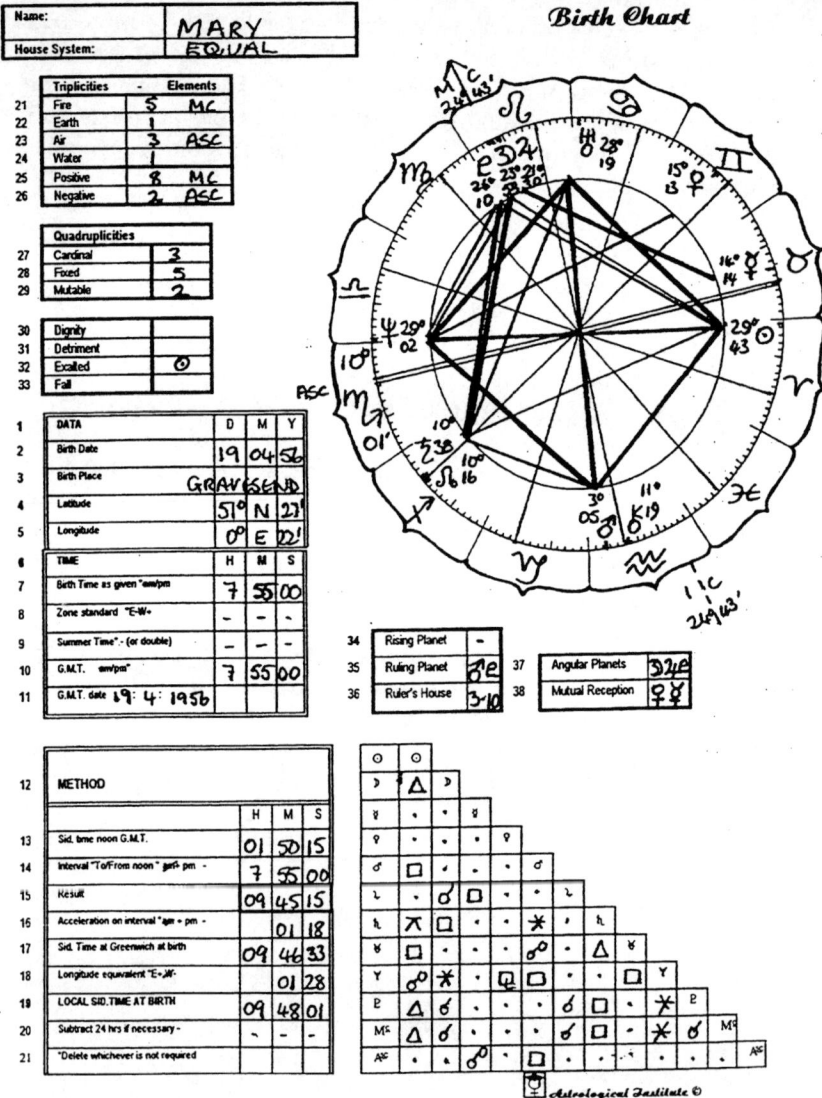

	DATA	D	M	Y
1	DATA	D	M	Y
2	Birth Date	19	04	56
3	Birth Place	GRAVESEND		
4	Latitude	51° N	27'	
5	Longitude	0° E	02'	
6	TIME	H	M	S
7	Birth Time as given "am/pm"	7	55	00
8	Zone standard "E-W"	-	-	-
9	Summer Time" - (or double)	-	-	-
10	G.M.T. am/pm	7	55	00
11	G.M.T. date	19: 4: 1956		

34	Rising Planet	
35	Ruling Planet	
36	Ruler's House	3-10
37	Angular Planets	
38	Mutual Reception	

12	METHOD	H	M	S
13	Sid. time noon G.M.T.	01	50	15
14	Interval "To/From noon" am-pm -	7	55	00
15	Result	09	45	15
16	Acceleration on interval "am + pm -		01	18
17	Sid. Time at Greenwich at birth	09	46	33
18	Longitude equivalent "E+W-		01	28
19	LOCAL SID. TIME AT BIRTH	09	48	01
20	Subtract 24 hrs if necessary -	-	-	-
21	"Delete whichever is not required			

Astrological Institute ©

140

Chapter 19

Calculation Data

To begin to calculate a birth chart you must have with you the ephemeris for the year in question, a table of houses, blue, black, green and red pens, 1 pencil, 1 small ruler and access to an atlas which contains the latitudes and longitudes listed in the back. In addition you will need blank birth charts and calculation forms such as the examples shown in this book.

We are now going to calculate a birthchart for Mary born on the 19th April, 1956 in Gravesend, Kent at 7.55 p.m.

If you look at the Chart Form on page 140 you will see that each section is numbered. These correspond to the numbered information following.

1. This section is headed Data. This is where we put the infor mation that we are going to use to calculate our birthchart.

2. Birth Date. In this section write in the birth date for Mary in the boxes provided headed D M Y (Day, Month, Year). So here you put 19 04 56.

3. Here we fill in where Mary was born. She was born in Gravesend so write this in the space provided.

4. This section is the latitude of birth, you will find this by look ing at the back of an atlas which should give you the latitude and longitude of cities and large towns of the world. While you are looking up the latitude jot down the longitude for the next section. Mary's birth latitude was 51⁰ N 27'. Write 51⁰ under column D: N under column M: and 27' under Y.

5. This is where you put the longitude which you have already found from the back of your atlas. Mary's longitude is 0º E22'. Place this in the space provided in the same format as the latitude.

6. This section is marked 'Time'.

7. Here we write under H M S (Hours, Minutes, Seconds, the exact birth time as given by your client. Mary's birth time is 7h 55m. Enter this in the space provided.

8. The Zone Standard does not apply in this country but it does apply to births abroad in places like United States of America. New York for example is 5 hours slow on Greenwich Meantime. It is in this section we would write the 5 hours to be added on to a birth time to bring it up to Greenwich Meantime. An example of this is shown later in the book.

9. Where you see Summer (or Double) Time you need to refer to the Tables for British Summer Time which you will find on page 168/169. Remember during the war years and 1947 Summer Time was kept on all the year, plus an extra hour was added during the summer months. In 1956 summer began on April 22nd so as Mary was born on April 19th we **do not** need to take any time off, so we leave this section blank.

10. Under GMT (Greenwich Meantime) we enter the final time when all calculations have been made, and in our example there is nothing to be subtracted so we enter 7h 55m pm. Remembering to delete am or pm whichever is applicable.

11. GMT Date is where the correct date of birth is entered after adjustments have been made. The date can be different if one or two hours is taken off when adjusting for British Summer Time. For example a person born at 12.30 a.m would go back to 11.30 pm the day before. This would then be treated as a pm birth for the day before. This can also occur for overseas births when we take into account the different Time Zones.

12. This is the section headed 'Method'.

13. This is where we enter the Sidereal Time for the birth at noon GMT. To do this we need to open the ephemeris at the year in question (1956) and turn to the section headed April. Look across the headings and the first column is headed **DAY**, run your finger down that column until you come to the day 19 under the month of April, underline the whole row in pencil if it helps you. The second column is headed Sid.Time. This is the column we need to find the Sidereal Time at noon, so under 19 April you will find the amount of 1.50.15. Enter these figures in the column provided on your birth chart

    H M S

14. Now we move to the **Interval TO/FROM Noon**. This is the part where most people make mistakes. If you understand that the figures in the ephemeris are taken at Noon then for an a.m. birth we must work back from noon. In the case of a p.m. birth such as Mary's the interval equals the Birth Time minus noon. So in this example if the birth was 7h 55m pm the interval would be simply 7h 55m. So 07.55.00 is entered in this column.

Example

To find the interval for a) pm birth and b) am birth

The birth time here is to be taken after zone standard and Summer time have been calculated. On form 1B on page 158 you would take the calculated time as at point 10.

a)   pm birth   b)   am birth

   19.55 birth time   12.00 Noon
   12.00 Noon   07.55 am birth time
   -------   -------
   07.55 interval   04.05 interval

15. The next line is easy addition as long as you remember there are 60 seconds in a minute, and 60 minutes in an hour. So add

143

07.55.00 to the Sidereal Time at Noon and where it says Result enter the answer 09.45.15.

16. The acceleration is calculated because Sidereal Time is short of Mean Time by nearly 10 seconds for each hour. Refer to Table B on page 161 The acceleration is found by running your finger across the top row until you come to 7h (which is highlighted), and then running your finger down the column until you come to the nearest minute to 55 which is 56 and in that column you will see 1.18.2. This is 1 minute 18 seconds, (also highlighted). Write this in under the minutes and sec onds column alongside Acceleration on Interval.

17. As all PM births are added, you add 1 minute 18 seconds to your previous result of 09.45.15 which gives a total of 09.46.33. This is written alongside Sidereal Time at Greenwich at Birth. Note: remember pm births all data is added but if it is an am birth all data is subtracted.

18. The Longitude Equivalent is found by multiplying the longi tude by 4 or referring to Tables A1 or A2 on pages 162/163. If the longitude has degrees then we use Table A2 which gives the answer in hours and minutes. In Mary's chart the longi tude is in minutes only so we use Table A1 which gives us our answer in minutes and seconds. So if you run your finger down the first column until you come to 22', the answer is on your immediate right (highlighted) which is minutes and sec onds and that is 1 minute 28 seconds. Write this in where is says **Longitude Equivalent** * E+ W-.

19. If the longitude is East we ADD and if it is West we SUB TRACT. Gravesend is east so we add 1 minute 28 seconds to 09.46.33, so that the local Sidereal Time at Birth is 09.48.01. We write this in the space provided.

20. If during your addition or subtraction you accumulate more than 24 hours then 24 hours must be subtracted here.

The Exact Ascendant

Now we come to a slightly more difficult part where we calculate the exact ascendant. We open the table of Houses at the page which is closest to the Latitude on your birth chart; in some cases this will be exact but in this example it is 51°27. We have to look at the tables either side of this figure which will be Tables for Taunton at 51°01 and London which is 51°32. We begin Phase one of our calculation with the Table for the Lesser Latitude (If your latitude is exact then you miss out Phase 2 of the calculation).

If you look in the Table of Houses you will discover each page is divided into six sections, the left hand column for each section is headed 'Sidereal Time'. We look in this column to find the birth sidereal time that we have calculated. We may not find the exact sidereal time we are looking for so again we take the figures either side, one being later and one earlier. To find Mary's birth sidereal time we need to look at the fifth section on this page, which begins with a sidereal time of 08.08.44. For Mary whose birth sidereal time is 09.48.01 the later sidereal time is 9.49.08 and the earlier sidereal time is 9.45.16. Put these in the table as follows:-

Phase 1 To find the ascendant at the Lesser Latitude

If there is not a table for the birth latitude (51° 27') then we must use the table either side beginning with the lesser latitude (51* 01').

Later Sidereal time	09.49.08
Earlier Sidereal time	09.45.16

	3.52 (A)

We then find the Log of (A) = 0.7929

To find the log of A turn to log table on page 164/165. We take the 3.52 which is 3' and 52 seconds and run our finger across the top to 3 and down to 52 which should come to the highlighted figures of 0.7929

Birth Sidereal time	09.48.01
Earlier Sidereal time	09.45.16

	2.45 (B)

We then find the Log of (B) = 0.9409

To find the log of B repeat as for A.
We then take the ascendant at the earlier sidereal time and subtract it from the ascendant at the later sidereal time as follows:
Move across in Table of Houses to column marked Ascendant, to
find these figures.

Ascendant at L.S.T.	$10^0 26$ Scorpio
Ascendant at E.S.T.	$09^0.45$ Scorpio

	.41 (C)

We then find the Log of (C) = 1.5456

Formula for calculating the exact ascendant is: (C) - (A) + (B) = D

$$1.5456$$
$$.7929$$

$$0.7527+$$
$$0.9409$$

$$1.6936 \quad = (D)$$

Look up 1.6936 in your logarithm table and you will find it equals
29'. You then add the 29' to the ascendant at the earlier sidereal
time.

Ascendant at E.S.T.	$09^0.45$ Scorpio
	00 .29

	$10^0.14$ Scorpio (E) 1

146

Phase 2 To find the Ascendant at the Greater Latitude

Now we move to the next table which is for London at 51⁰32' and repeat the same procedure.

Later Sidereal time	09.49.09
Earlier Sidereal time	09.45.16

	3.53 (A)

We then find the Log of (A) = 0.7910

Birth Sidereal time	09.48.01
Earlier Sidereal time	09.45.16

	2.45 (B)

We then find the Log of (B) = 0.9409

We then take the ascendant at the earlier sidereal time and subtract it from the ascendant at the later sidereal time as follows:

Ascendant at L.S.T.	10⁰.11 Scorpio
Ascendant at E.S.T.	09⁰.31 Scorpio

	.40 (C)

We then find the Log of (C) = 1.5563

Formula for calculating the exact ascendant is: (C) - (A) + (B) = D

$$
\begin{array}{l}
1.5563 \\
.7910 \\
\hline
0.7653+ \\
0.9409 \\
\hline
1.7062 \quad = (D)
\end{array}
$$

Look up 1.7062 in your logarithm table and you will find it equals 28'. You then add the 28' to the ascendant at the earlier sidereal time.

Ascendant at E.S.T. $09^0.31$ Scorpio
                       .28

                       $09^0.59$ Scorpio (E) 2

We must then take the Greater Latitude from the Lesser Latitude to enable us to find the birthplace latitude.

Greater Latitude $51^0.32$
Lesser Latitude $51^0.01$

                      .31   = (F)

We find the log of (F)   1.6670

Birthplace Latitude $51^0.27$
Lesser Latitude $51^0.01$

                         .26   = (G)

We find the log of (G)   1.7434

PHASE 3

Find the difference between E in phase 1 and E in phase 2

From (E) Phase 1 $10^0.14$
Take (E) Phase 2 $9^0.59$

                      .15   = (H)

Log of (H)   1.9823

Now we use the formula G + H - F = K

(G)	1.7434
(H)	1.9823 +

	3.7257
(F)	1.6670 -

	2.0587 = (K)

Now look up in your logarithm tables 2.0587 to find the Anti-Log. The nearest is 2.0444 which equals 13 minutes. Therefore, the Anti-Log of K = 13'.

IMPORTANT: If the sidereal time at birth falls between 06.00.01 and 17.59.59 (Approx. 6am and 6pm) then K is subtracted from E in phase 1.

If the sidereal time at birth falls between 18.00.01 and 5.59.59 (approx. 6pm and 6 am) then K is added to E in phase 1.

Remember this is Birth Sidereal Time not Birth time. In this example Mary's Birth Sidereal Time is 09.48.01 which falls between 06.00.01 and 17.59.59 so therefore we subtract K (13') from E in phase 1.
10º14 - 13' = 10º01' Scorpio which is the exact ascendant.

Phase 4

The calculation for the Midheaven is now simple. There is always a one degree difference each day for the midheaven. The log of 1⁰ is 1.3802 (J).

We take A from Phase 1 and subtract it from J and add the result to B from Phase 1. We use this formula (J - A + B =).

We then look the result up in the log table and convert to degrees and minutes.

```
          (J)  1.3802
          (A)   .7929 -
               --------
               0.5873
          (B)  0.9409 +
               --------
               1.5282
```

Look up 1.5282 in your logarithm-tables on page 166/67 and you will find it equals 43', you then add the 43' to the degree at the earlier sidereal time which is listed under column '10' (meaning the 10th house). In this example the sign at the top of the column is Leo and the degree is 24^0 so the exact Midheaven is 24^0 43'.

Calculation Form for the Exact Position of Planets

FORM A (see details on page 152)

	D	M	Y
	19	04	56
Birth date			
	H	M	S
Birth time as given am/pm..	07	55	0
Zone Standard E- W+	-	-	-
*Summer- (double-)time	-	-	-
G.M.T.	07	55	0
am/pm*			
G.M.T. date .....:.........:......			
(a) Interval TO or FROM Noon	07	55	0
(b) Log. of Interval		.4817	

PLANETS	☉	☽	☿	♀	♂
(c) Daily motion of planets *	00°23 29°24 ------ 59'	3'19 19'21 ----- 13'58	15'29 13'37 ----- 01'52	15'50 14'55 ----- 00.55	03'31 02'53 ----- 00.38
(d) Log. of the motion	1.3875	.2351	1.1091	1.4180	1.5786
(e) Find Log. of Interval	.4817	.4817	.4817	.4817	.4817
(f) Addition of (d)+(e)	1.8692	.7168	1.5908	1.8997	1.0603

*If am birth, take planets on birth date from day before.
If pm birth, take planets on birth date from day after.
(see note over page for explanation)

151

Sign containing the Planet	☉ ♈	☽ ♌	☿ ♉	♀ ♊	♂ ♒
(g) Noon position of the Planet on date of birth	29.24	19.21	13.37	14.55	02.53
(h) Anti-log of (f) If am (g) - (h) *(Reverse if Retrograde)* If pm (g) ₊ (h)	.19	4.36	.37	.18	.13
(i) Position of Planets at Birth time	29.43	23.57	14.14	15.13	03.06

* Delete where applicable

TABULATE PLANETS IN NUMERICAL ORDER

Sign containing Planet		Planets in Numerical Sign Order	Sign containing Planet		Planets in Numerical Order
♈	☉	29°43	♐	♄	1°39
♉	☿	14°14	♒	♂	3°06
♊	♀	15°13	♏	A^sc	10°01
♋	♅	28°18	♐	♌	10°17
♌	♃	21°30	♉	☿	14°14
♌	☽	23°57	♊	♀	15°13
♌	M^c	24°43	♌	♃	21°30
♌	♇	26°11	♌	☽	23°57
♎	♆	29°03	♌	M^c	24°43
♏	A^sc	10°01	♌	♇	26°11
♐	♄	01°39	♋	♅	28°18
♐	♌	10°17	♎	♆	29°03
♒	♂	03°06	♈	☉	29°43

How To Use Calculation Form A

To begin with fill in the data on the top right hand column which you can copy off your birth chart. When you come to interval (a) write in the interval TO or FROM noon as shown in our example 7 hrs. 55 mins and then convert to logs (b). In this example it is 4817.

An important note to remember when finding the motion of the planets for the day of Birth is that if a birth is a.m. then planets of the day before are taken from the birth day. If the birth is p.m. then planets from the birth date are taken from the day after birth to find the planetary motion for the birth day.

In the first column marked (c) write in the daily motion of the planet from the Sun to Mars, using the formula as written above in bold type. In your logarithm table find the log of the daily motion and write this in column marked (d). We have already worked out the log of the interval which is .4817' we now write this figure all the way along in the column marked (e). We then add rows (d) + (e) and write the answer in (f).

We now look in the ephemeris and find which signs contain the planets and write these into row headed Sign Containing the Planet. The noon positions on the day of birth straight from the ephemeris are then written into row (g).

We then look up all the anti log for each column in row (f) in our logarithm tables on page 164/165 and convert them back to degrees and minutes or just minutes, and enter them into row (h). If it is an a.m. birth you subtract (h) from (g) and if it is a p.m. birth you add (h) to (g) and write the answer in row (i).

At the bottom of the form under Tabulation of Planets in Sign and Numerical Order, put in all the planets already calculated together with all the planets taken from the ephemeris from Jupiter onwards.

Now we come to complete the rest of the chart form as seen on page 140. We have already completed numbers 1-20 but before we complete 21-38 we must write in on the Chart Wheel the information we have already calculated. Take your red pen and write the glyph and degrees and minutes of the Ascendant (10^0 01' Scorpio). Now enter all the other signs of the zodiac anti-clockwise around the Chart Wheel beginning from the Ascendant. All signs except the Ascendant are written in the outer ring in blue or black ink.

The ascending degree of 10^0 01' Scorpio is the degree that begins the first astrological house. Make a small pencil mark at 10^0 of each astrological sign then join up the pencil points from one sign to the opposite until you get 12 equal segments. These are the astrological houses and you will notice each house contains 30^0. This is called the Equal House System and is the system used throughout the book. It may be helpful to number the houses beginning with the First House (1) just below the ascending line and written anticlockwise around the chart in the same sequence as the signs. The best placement for these is as close to the centre of chart as possible.

Copy the planets from the section **Tabulate the Planets in Sign and Numerical Order** from page 151 on to the chart. Write the glyphs for the planets around the wheel in the second ring with their degrees and minutes. **All the planets must be facing you and not upside down.**

Before we go any further you can check that you have calculated your chart correctly. If a person was born at 6 a.m. the Sun will be conjunct the ascendant, if they were born at Noon the Sun will be conjunct the Midheaven, if they were born at 6 p.m. the Sun will be conjunct the descendant, if they were born at Midnight the Sun will be conjunct the I.C. This is just an approximate way of checking that you haven't made a glaring error at this point.

Now it is time to begin filling in numbers 21 to 38 on your birthchart.

21. This is where we enter the Elements known as the Triplicities. We need to count how many planets are in Fire signs. Write the amounts in the small column next to the element and in the wider column fill in the glyphs of the planets in that element. This includes the MC and the Ascendant.

22. This is the Earth element repeat the same procedure as above.

23. Repeat the same procedure as 21.

24. Repeat the same procedure as 21.

25. This is how many planets you have in positive signs. Add together Fire and Air and this will give you the amount of planets in Positive Signs. Write the number in the space pro vided. You can if you wish write in the planets, but this is not necessary.

26. This is how many planets you have in negative signs. Add together Earth and Water and this will give you the amount of planets in Negative Signs. Write the number in the space provided.

27. In this section we write in the Qualities known as the Quadruplicities. The first one is Cardinal, if you do not know which are the Cardinal Signs refer to diagram on page 10. Then count the planets and write in the amounts in the space provided.

28. This space is for Fixed Signs, the same procedure as for 27.

29. This space is for Mutable Signs, the same procedure as for 27.

Here we have a section 30 to 33 where we place planets that are in Dignity or Detriment, Exalted or Fall. To be able to do this refer to diagram on page 42.

30. This section is for planets in Dignity.

31. This section is for planets in Detriment (those opposite the sign they rule).

32. This section is for planets in Exaltation.

33. This section is for planets in Fall (those opposite the sign of their Exaltation).

34. This is the Rising Planet. If you have a planet that lies with in 8^0 either side of the Ascendant, that is in the First or Twelfth House then it is rising. Enter that planet in the space provided.

35. The Ruling Planet is the planet that rules the sign on the Ascendant, it is often called the Lord of the Chart and is significant.

36. This is where we place the number of the house that contains the Ruling Planet.

37. Angular planets are planets that are within 8^0 either side of the Angles, that is Ascendant/Descendant axis and MC/IC axis. Write the glyph of any such planets in the space provided.

38. This is the section where we enter planets that are in Mutual Reception. This means that two planets are in each others signs, such as the Sun in Scorpio and Pluto in Leo. So every Scorpio born in the Pluto/Leo era will have the Sun and Pluto in Mutual Reception.

Calculation Form to Find the Sidereal Time at Birth in Northern and Southern Hemispheres.

Form 1B

This Calculation form can be used for Northern and Southern Hemisphere Births follow the numbered points on page 136. Details for Overseas births and Southern Hemisphere are detailed overleaf.

1	**DATA**	D	M	Y
2	Birth Date			
3	Birth Place			
4	Latitude			
5	Longitude			
6	**TIME**	H	M	S
7	Birth Time as given *am/pm			
8	Zone standard *E-W+			
9	Summer Time* - (or double)			
10	G.M.T. am/pm*			
11	G.M.T. date : :			
12	**METHOD**	H	M	S
13	Sid. time noon G.M.T.			
14	Interval *To/From noon * am/pm			
15	Result			
16	Acceleration on interval *am/pm			
17	Sid. Time at Greenwich at birth			
18	Longitude equivalent *E+ W-			
19	**LOCAL SID.TIME AT BIRTH**			
20	Subtract 24 hrs if necessary -			
20a	**SOUTHERN HEMISPHERE BIRTH ADD 12 HRS**			
	Subtract 24 hours if necessary			

Asc .... MC.............................. *** Remember for Southern Latitudes you must Reverse the Signs.**

Overseas Births

When a person is born overseas in the Northern or Southern Hemisphere their birth time must be converted to Greenwich Mean Time. To find the different time zones refer to the table on page 158.

For example if a person is born in New York you will see from the table that New York is five hours slow (West) of Greenwich (that is five hours behind Greenwich) So to bring it up to Greenwich Mean Time you write 5 hours in the section marked (8.) and ADD it on to the birth time. Another example is a person born in Western Australia which is 8 hours ahead (East) of Greenwich. In this example we write the 8 hours next to Zone Standard and subtract it from the birth time.

When you need to work out the interval from or to Noon, use the final calculation of the birth time as at Greenwich (10) which may not be the same as the birth time you were first given.

When you have a birth from the Southern Latitude, fill in the form in exactly the same way as for the Northern Hemisphere the only difference to the form occurs when you reach No. 20a at this point you add 12 hours to your calculation so far, and subtract 24 hours from final result if necessary. Then you take this final result and look it up in your table of houses for Northern Latitudes use the same procedure as for Northern Latitudes to find the exact ascendant. When you get your final result you then reverse the signs. This means that if the ascendant is 10^0 15' Taurus you reverse it to become 10^0 15' Scorpio. If the MC is 5^000 Aquarius then reverse it to become 5^000 Leo. So all you must remember for Southern Hemisphere births is to **ADD** 12 hours and reverse the Ascendant and Midheaven.

The reason for this reversal is because you are using a table of houses for Northern Hemisphere. A table of houses for the Southern Hemisphere would be almost identical as for the Northern Hemisphere by degrees and minutes but the signs would be reversed.

Zone Standards

Longitude	Hour	COUNTRY
+ 0	+ 0	Greenwich Mean Time
+ 15 E	+ 1	Belgium, Austria, Czechoslovakia
+ 30 E	+ 2	Egypt, Bulgaria, Cyprus
+ 45 E	+ 3	Iraq, Kenya
+ 60 E	+ 4	Seychelles, Mauritius
+ 75 E	+ 5	Chagos Islands (Indian Ocean)
+ 90 E	+ 6	Pakistan East
+ 105 E	+ 7	Thailand, Southern Sumatra
+ 120 E	+ 8	Western Australia, Hong Kong
+ 135 E	+ 9	Japan, Korea
+ 150 E	+ 10	British New Guinea, Queensland
+ 165 E	+ 11	New Caledonia, Solomon Islands
- 180 W	+ 12	New Zealand, Fiji
- 165 W	- 11	Samoa
- 150 W	- 10	Hawaiian Islands
- 135 W	- 9	Yokon
- 120 W	- 8	Nevada, California, Los Angeles
- 105 W	- 7	Montana, Utah Wyoming, USA
- 90 W	- 6	Nicaragua, Manitoba, Texas USA
- 75 W	- 5	Peru, Jamaica, Michigan USA
- 60 W	- 4	Bermuda, Chile, Guadeloupe
- 45 W	- 3	Argentina, Brazil Eastern
- 30 W	- 2	Greenland
- 15 W	- 1	Madeira, Iceland
- 0	- 0	Greenwich Mean Time

Greenwich is used as the Prime Meridian or the Zero degree point, and the world is then divided into 15⁰ portions which makes 24 equal divisions.

All countries should be checked in a 'Time Changes for the World' handbook for the exact time difference, as many countries operate daylight saving time and this can vary from pre-war years to present time.

All areas West of Greenwich are slow on Greenwich and all areas to the East of Greenwich are fast or ahead. Therefore births that are West of Greenwich must have time added on to their birth times and those born East of Greenwich must have time subtracted from their birth times.

World Map Showing the Greenwich Meridian

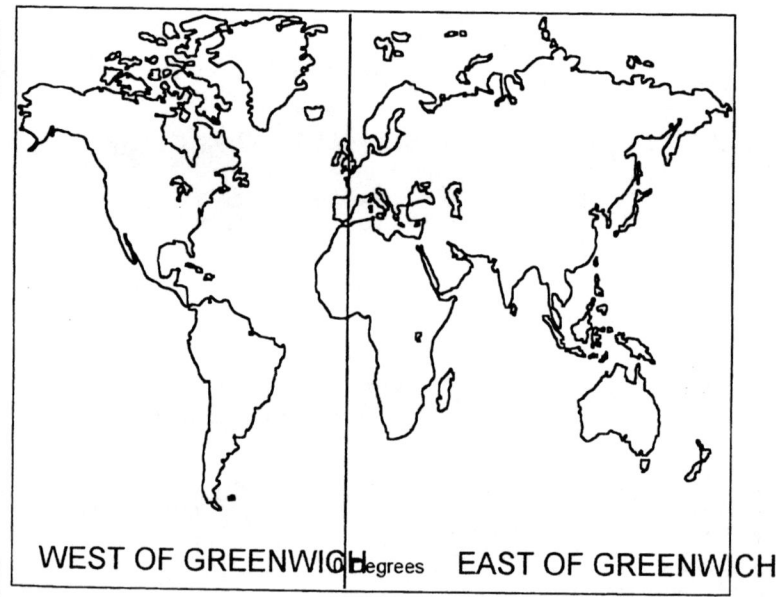

WEST OF GREENWICH 0 Degrees   EAST OF GREENWICH

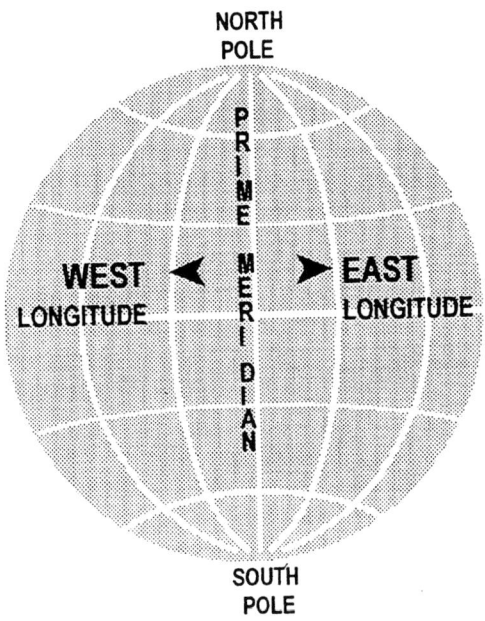

NORTH
POLE

WEST
LONGITUDE

EAST
LONGITUDE

PRIME MERIDIAN

SOUTH
POLE

The Prime Meridian is a fixed point for zero longitude throughout the world and is a place of reference for locating any place in the world. The Meridian at Greenwich was designated to be zero longitude and areas that are east of Greenwich are minus zones which means that they are ahead in time and areas that are west of Greenwich are plus zones and are behind Greenwich in time.

This means that if you are born west of Greenwich then you must add the difference in time to your birth time and if you are born east of Greenwich then you must subtract the difference in time to your birth time in order to bring your birth time to Greenwich Mean Time.

TABLE B   TO FIND THE ACCELERATION ON THE INTERVAL

m	0h	1h	2h	3h	4h	5h	6h	7h
	m s	m s	m s	m s	m s	m s	m s	m s
00	0 0.00	0 10.0	0 20.0	0 30.0	0 39.4	0 49.3	0 59.1	1 10.0
04	0 0.70	0 11.0	0 20.4	0 30.2	0 40.1	0 50.0	1. 0.0	1 10.0
08	0 1.30	0 11.2	0 21.0	0 31.0	0 41.0	0 51.0	1 0.5	1 10.3
12	0 2.00	0 12.0	0 22.0	0.32.0	0 41.4	0 51.3	1 1.1	1 11.0
16	0 2.60	0 13.0	0 22.3	0 32.2	0 42.1	0 52.0	1 2.0	1 12.0
20	0 3.30	0 13.1	0 23.0	0 33.0	0 43.0	0 53.0	1 2.4	1 12.3
24	0 4.00	0 14.0	0 24.0	0 34.0	0 43.4	0 53.2	1 3.1	1 13.0
28	0 4.60	0 15.0	0 24.3	0 34.2	0 44.0	0 54.0	1 4.0	1 14.0
32	0 5.30	0 15.1	0 25.0	0 35.0	0 45.0	0 55.0	1 4.4	1 14.3
36	0 6.00	0 16.0	0 26.0	0 36.0	0 45.3	0 55.2	1 5.1	1 15.0
40	0 6.60	0 16.4	0 26.3	0 36.1	0 46.0	0 56.0	1 6.0	1 16.0
44	0 7.20	0 17.1	0 27.0	0 37.0	0 47.0	0 57.0	1 6.4	1 16.2
48	0 8.00	0 18.0	0 28.0	0 38.0	0 47.3	0 57.2	1 7.0	1 17.0
52	0 8.50	0 18.4	0 28.3	0 38.1	0 48.0	0 58.0	1 8.0	1 17.0
56	0 9.20	0 19.1	0·29.0	0 39.0	0 49.0	0 59.0	1 8.3	1 18.2

m	8h	9h	10h	11h	12h	13h	14h	15h
	m s	m s	m s	m s	m s	m s	m s	m s
00	1 17.0	1 29.0	1 39.0	1 48.4	1 58.3	2 08.1	2 18.0	2 28.0
04	1 20.0	1 30.0	1 39.2	1 49.1	1 59.0	2 09.0	2 19.0	2 29.0
08	1 20.2	1 30.0	1 40.0	1 50.0	2 00.0	2 09.4	2 19.3	2 29.2
12	1 21.0	1 31.0	1 41.0	1 50.4	2 00.2	2 10.1	2 20.0	2 30.0
16	1 22.0	1 31.3	1 41.2	1 51.0	2 01.0	2 11.0	2 21.0	2 31.0
20	1 22.1	1 32.0	1 42.0	1 52.0	2 02.0	2 11.4	2 21.3	2 31.1
24	1 23.0	1 33.0	1 43.0	1 52.4	2 02.2	2 12.1	2 22.0	2 32.0
28	1 24.0	1 33.3	1 43.2	1 53.0	2 03.0	2 13.0	2 23.0	2 32.4
32	1 24.1	1 34.0	1 44.0	1 54.0	2 04.0	2 13.4	2 23.2	2 33.1
36	1 25.0	1 35.0	1 45.0	1 54.3	2 04.2	2 14.0	2 24.0	2 34.0
40	1 25.4	1 35.3	1 45.1	1 55.0	2 05.0	2 15.0	2 25.0	2 34.4
44	1 26.1	1 36.0	1 46.0	1 56.0	2 06.0	2 15.4	2 25.2	2 35.1
48	1 27.0	1 37.0	1 46.4	1 56.3	2 06.2	2 16.0	2 26.0	2 36.0
52	1 27.4	1 37.3	1 47.1	1 57.0	2 07.0	2 17.0	2 27.0	2 36.4
56	1 28.1	1 38.0	1 48.0	1 58.0	2 08.0	2 17.2	2 27.2	2 37.0

m	16h	17h	18h	19h	20h	21h	22h	23h
	m s	m s	m s	m s	m s	m s	m s	m s
00	2 38.0	2 48.0	2 57.4	3 07.3	3 17.1	3 27.0	3 37.0	3 47.0
04	2 38.4	2 48.2	2 58.1	3 08.0	3 18.0	3 28.0	3 38.0	3 47.4
08	2 39.0	2 49.0	2 59.0	3 09.0	3 18.4	3 28.3	3 38.2	3 48.0
12	2 40.0	2 50.0	2 59.4	3 09.2	3 19.1	3 29.0	3 39.0	3 49.0
16	2 40.3	2 50.2	3 00.0	3 10.0	3 20.0	3 30.0	3 40.0	3 49.3
20	2 41.0	2 51.0	3 01.0	3 11.0	3 20.4	3 30.3	3 40.1	3 50.0
24	2 42.0	2 52.0	3 01.4	3 11.2	3 21.1	3 31.0	3 41.0	3 51.0
28	2 42.3	2 52.2	3 02.0	3 12.0	3 22.0	3 32.0	3 41.4	3 51.3
32	2 43.0	2 53.0	3 03.0	3 13.0	3 22.4	3 32.2	3 42.1	3 52.0
36	2 44.0	2 54.0	3 03.3	3 13.2	3 23.0	3 33.0	3 43.0	3 53.0
40	2 44.3	2 54.1	3 04.0	3 14.0	3 24.0	3 34.0	3 43.4	3 53.3
44	2 45.0	2 55.0	3 05.0	3 15.0	3 24.4	3 34.2	3 44.1	3 54.0
48	2 46.0	2 55.4	3 05.3	3 15.2	3 25.0	3 35.0	3 45.0	3 55.0
52	2 46.2	2 56.1	3 06.0	3 16.0	3 26.0	3 36.0	3 45.4	3 55.2
56	2 47.0	2 57.0	3 07.0	3 17.0	3 26.3	3 36.2	3 46.0	3 56.0

TABLE A₁   TO CONVERT MINUTES INTO LONGITUDE EQUIVALENT OF TIME

'	M	S	'	M	S	'	M	S	'	M	S	'	M	S	'	M	S
01	00	04	31	02	04	61	04	04	91	06	04	121	08	04	151	10	04
02	00	08	32	02	08	62	04	08	92	06	08	122	08	08	152	10	08
03	00	12	33	02	12	63	04	12	93	06	12	123	08	12	153	10	12
04	00	16	34	02	16	64	04	16	94	06	16	124	08	16	154	10	16
05	00	20	35	02	20	65	04	20	95	06	20	125	08	20	155	10	20
06	00	24	36	02	24	66	04	24	96	06	24	126	08	24	156	10	24
07	00	28	37	02	28	67	04	28	97	06	28	127	08	28	157	10	28
08	00	32	38	02	32	68	04	32	98	06	32	128	08	32	158	10	32
09	00	36	39	02	36	69	04	36	99	06	36	129	08	36	159	10	36
10	00	40	40	02	40	70	04	40	100	06	40	130	08	40	160	10	40
11	00	44	41	02	44	71	04	44	101	06	44	131	08	44	161	10	44
12	00	48	42	02	48	72	04	48	102	06	48	132	08	48	162	10	48
13	00	52	43	02	52	73	04	52	103	06	52	133	08	52	163	10	52
14	00	56	44	02	56	74	04	56	104	06	56	134	08	56	164	10	56
15	01	00	45	03	00	75	05	00	105	07	00	135	09	00	165	11	00
16	01	04	46	03	04	76	05	04	106	07	04	136	09	04	166	11	04
17	01	08	47	03	08	77	05	08	107	07	08	137	09	08	167	11	08
18	01	12	48	03	12	78	05	12	108	07	12	138	09	12	168	11	12
19	01	16	49	03	16	79	05	16	109	07	16	139	09	16	169	11	16
20	01	20	50	03	20	80	05	20	110	07	20	140	09	20	170	11	20
21	01	24	51	03	24	81	05	24	111	07	24	141	09	24	171	11	24
22	01	28	52	03	28	82	05	28	112	07	28	142	09	28	172	11	28
23	01	32	53	03	32	83	05	32	113	07	32	143	09	32	173	11	32
24	01	36	54	03	36	84	05	36	114	07	36	144	09	36	174	11	36
25	01	40	55	03	40	85	05	40	115	07	40	145	09	40	175	11	40
26	01	44	56	03	44	86	05	44	116	07	44	146	09	44	176	11	44
27	01	48	57	03	48	87	05	48	117	07	48	147	09	48	177	11	48
28	01	52	58	03	52	88	05	52	118	07	52	148	09	52	178	11	52
29	01	56	59	03	56	89	05	56	119	07	56	149	09	56	179	11	56
30	02	00	60	04	00	90	06	00	120	08	00	150	10	00	180	12	00

163

TABLE A$_2$ **TO CONVERT DEGREES INTO LONGITUDE EQUIVALENT OF TIME**

°	H	M	°	H	M	°	H	M	°	H	M	°	H	M	°	H	M
01	00	04	31	02	04	61	04	04	91	06	04	121	08	04	151	10	04
02	00	08	32	02	08	62	04	08	92	06	08	122	08	08	152	10	08
03	00	12	33	02	12	63	04	12	93	06	12	123	08	12	153	10	12
04	00	16	34	02	16	64	04	16	94	06	16	124	08	16	154	10	16
05	00	20	35	02	20	65	04	20	95	06	20	125	08	20	155	10	20
06	00	24	36	02	24	66	04	24	96	06	24	126	08	24	156	10	24
07	00	28	37	02	28	67	04	28	97	06	28	127	08	28	157	10	28
08	00	32	38	02	32	68	04	32	98	06	32	128	08	32	158	10	32
09	00	36	39	02	36	69	04	36	99	06	36	129	08	36	159	10	36
10	00	40	40	02	40	70	04	40	100	06	40	130	08	40	160	10	40
11	00	44	41	02	44	71	04	44	101	06	44	131	08	44	161	10	44
12	00	48	42	02	48	72	04	48	102	06	48	132	08	48	162	10	48
13	00	52	43	02	52	73	04	52	103	06	52	133	08	52	163	10	52
14	00	56	44	02	56	74	04	56	104	06	56	134	08	56	164	10	56
15	01	00	45	03	00	75	05	00	105	07	00	135	09	00	165	11	00
16	01	04	46	03	04	76	05	04	106	07	04	136	09	04	166	11	04
17	01	08	47	03	08	77	05	08	107	07	08	137	09	08	167	11	08
18	01	12	48	03	12	78	05	12	108	07	12	138	09	12	168	11	12
19	01	16	49	03	16	79	05	16	109	07	16	139	09	16	169	11	16
20	01	20	50	03	20	80	05	20	110	07	20	140	09	20	170	11	20
21	01	24	51	03	24	81	05	24	111	07	24	141	09	24	171	11	24
22	01	28	52	03	28	82	05	28	112	07	28	142	09	28	172	11	28
23	01	32	53	03	32	83	05	32	113	07	32	143	09	32	173	11	32
24	01	36	54	03	36	84	05	36	114	07	36	144	09	36	174	11	36
25	01	40	55	03	40	85	05	40	115	07	40	145	09	40	175	11	40
26	01	44	56	03	44	86	05	44	116	07	44	146	09	44	176	11	44
27	01	48	57	03	48	87	05	48	117	07	48	147	09	48	177	11	48
28	01	52	58	03	52	88	05	52	118	07	52	148	09	52	178	11	52
29	01	56	59	03	56	89	05	56	119	07	56	149	09	56	179	11	56
30	02	00	60	04	00	90	06	00	120	08	00	150	10	00	180	12	00

164

	PROPORTIONAL LOGARITHMS FOR FINDING THE POSITIONS OF PLANETS							
	DEGREES OR HOURS*							
Min	0	1	2	3	4	5	6	7
00	3.1584	1.3802	1.0792	9031	7781	6812	6021	5351
01	3.1584	1.3730	1.0756	9007	7763	6798	6009	5341
02	2.8573	1.3660	1.0720	8983	7745	6784	5997	5330
03	2.6812	1.3590	1.0685	8959	7728	6769	5985	5320
04	2.5563	1.3522	1.0649	8935	7710	6765	5973	5310
05	2.4594	1.3454	1.0614	8912	7692	6741	5961	5300
06	2.3802	1.3388	1.0580	8888	7674	6726	5949	5289
07	2.3133	1.3323	1.0546	8865	7657	6712	5937	5279
08	2.2553	1.3258	1.0511	8842	7639	6698	5925	5269
09	2.2041	1.3195	1.0478	8819	7622	6684	5913	5259
10	2.1584	1.3133	1.0444	8796	7604	6670	5962	5249
11	2.1170	1.3071	1.0411	8773	7587	6656	5890	5239
12	2.0792	1.3010	1.0378	8751	7570	6642	5878	5229
13	2.0444	1.2950	1.0345	8728	7552	6628	5866	5219
14	2.0122	1.2891	1.0313	8706	7535	6614	5855	5209
15	1.9823	1.2833	1.0280	8683	7518	6600	5843	5199
16	1.9542	1.2775	1.0248	8661	7501	6587	5832	5189
17	1.9279	1.2719	1.0216	8639	7484	6573	5820	5179
18	1.9031	1.2663	1.0185	8617	7467	6559	5809	5169
19	1.8796	1.2607	1.0153	8595	7451	6546	5797	5169
20	1.8573	1.2553	1.0122	8573	7434	6532	5786	5149
21	1.8361	1.2499	1.0091	8552	7417	6519	5774	5139
22	1.8159	1.2445	1.0061	8530	7401	6505	5763	5129
23	1.7966	1.2393	1.0030	8509	7384	6492	5752	5120
24	1.7781	1.2341	1.0000	8487	7368	6478	5740	5110
25	1.7604	1.2289	0.9970	8466	7351	6465	5729	5100
26	1.7434	1.2239	0.9940	8445	7335	6451	5718	5090
27	1.7270	1.2188	0.9910	8424	7318	6438	5706	5081
28	1.7112	1.2139	0.9881	8403	7302	6425	5695	5071
29	1.6960	1.2090	0.9852	8382	7286	6412	5684	5061
30	1.6812	1.2041	0.9823	8361	7270	6398	5673	5051
31	1.6670	1.1993	0.9794	8341	7254	6385	5662	5042
32	1.6532	1.1946	0.9765	8320	7238	6372	5651	5032
33	1.6398	1.1899	0.9737	8300	7222	6359	5640	5023
34	1.6269	1.1852	0.9708	8279	7206	6346	5629	5013
35	1.6143	1.1806	0.9680	8259	7190	6333	5618	5003
36	1.6021	1.1761	0.9652	8239	7174	6320	5607	4994
37	1.5902	1.1716	0.9625	8219	7159	6307	5596	4984
38	1.5786	1.1671	0.9597	8199	7143	6294	5585	4975
39	1.5673	1.1627	0.9570	8179	7128	6282	5574	4965
40	1.5563	1.1584	0.9542	8159	7112	6269	5563	4956
41	1.5456	1.1540	0.9515	8140	7097	6256	5552	4947
42	1.5351	1.1498	0.9488	8120	7081	6243	5541	4937
43	1.5249	1.1540	0.9462	8101	7066	6231	5531	4928
44	1.5149	1.1498	0.9435	8081	7050	6218	5520	4918
45	1.5051	1.1455	0.9409	8062	7035	6205	5509	4909
46	1.4956	1.1413	0.9383	8043	7020	6193	5498	4900
47	1.4863	1.1372	0.9356	8023	7005	6180	5488	4890
48	1.4771	1.1331	0.9330	8004	6990	6168	5477	4881
49	1.4682	1.1209	0.9305	7985	6975	6155	5466	4872
50	1.4594	1.1170	0.9279	7966	6960	6143	5456	4863
51	1.4508	1.1130	0.9254	7947	6945	6131	5445	4853
52	1.4424	1.1091	0.9228	7929	6930	6118	5435	4844
53	1.4341	1.1053	0.9203	7910	6915	6106	5424	4835
54	1.4260	1.1015	0.9178	7891	6900	6094	5414	4826
55	1.4180	1.0977	0.9153	7873	6885	6081	5403	4817
56	1.4102	1.0939	0.9128	7854	6871	6069	5393	4808
57	1.4025	1.0902	0.9104	7836	6856	6057	5382	4798
58	1.3949	1.0865	0.9079	7818	6841	6045	5372	4789
59	1.3875	1.0828	0.9055	7800	6827	6033	5361	4780
	0	1	2	3	4	5	6	7

* The same tables can be used for converting minutes and seconds.

165

	PROPORTIONAL LOGARITHMS FOR FINDING THE POSITIONS OF PLANETS							
	DEGREES OR HOURS*							
Min	8	9	10	11	12	13	14	15
00	4771	4260	3802	3388	3010	2663	2341	2041
01	4762	4252	3795	3382	3004	2657	2336	2036
02	4753	4244	3788	3375	2998	2652	2330	2032
03	4744	4236	3780	3368	2992	2646	2325	2027
04	4735	4228	3773	3362	2986	2640	2320	2022
05	4726	4220	3766	3355	2980	2635	2315	2017
06	4717	4212	3759	3349	2974	2629	2310	2012
07	4708	4204	3752	3342	2968	2624	2305	2008
08	4699	4196	3745	3336	2962	2618	2300	2003
09	4690	4188	3737	3329	2965	2613	2295	1998
10	4682	4180	3730	3323	2950	2607	2289	1993
11	4673	4172	3723	3316	2944	2602	2284	1988
12	4664	4164	3716	3310	2938	2596	2279	1984
13	4655	4156	3709	3303	2933	2591	2274	1979
14	4646	4148	3702	3297	2927	2585	2269	1974
15	4638	4141	3695	3291	2921	2580	2264	1969
16	4629	4133	3688	3284	2915	2574	2259	1965
17	4620	4125	3681	3278	2909	2569	2254	1960
18	4611	4117	3674	3271	2903	2564	2249	1955
19	4603	4109	3667	3265	2897	2558	2244	1950
20	4594	4102	3660	3258	2819	2553	2239	1946
21	4585	4094	3653	3252	2885	2547	2234	1941
22	4577	4086	3646	3246	2880	2542	2229	1936
23	4568	4079	3639	3239	2874	2536	2223	1932
24	4559	4071	3632	3233	2868	2531	2218	1927
25	4551	4063	3625	3227	2862	2526	2213	1922
26	4542	4055	3618	3220	2856	2520	2208	1917
27	4534	4048	3611	3214	2850	2515	2203	1913
28	4525	4040	3604	3208	2845	2509	2198	1908
29	4516	4032	3597	3201	2839	2504	2193	1903
30	4508	4025	3590	3195	2833	2499	2188	1890
31	4499	4017	3583	3189	2827	2493	2183	1894
32	4491	4010	3576	3183	2821	2488	2178	1889
33	4482	4002	3570	3176	2816	2483	2173	1885
34	4474	3994	3563	3170	2810	2477	2168	1880
35	4466	3987	3556	3164	2904	2472	2164	1875
36	4457	3979	3549	3157	2798	2467	2159	1871
37	4449	3972	3542	3151	2793	2461	2154	1866
38	4440	3964	3535	3145	2787	2456	2149	1862
39	4432	3957	3529	3139	2781	2451	2144	1857
40	4424	3949	3522	3133	2775	2445	2139	1852
41	4415	3942	3515	3126	2770	2440	2134	1848
42	4407	3934	3508	3120	2764	2435	2129	1843
43	4399	3927	3501	3114	2758	2430	2124	1838
44	4390	3919	3495	3108	2753	2424	2119	1834
45	4382	3912	3488	3102	2747	2419	2114	1829
46	4374	3905	3481	3096	2741	2414	2109	1825
47	4365	3897	3475	3089	2736	2409	2104	1820
48	4357	3890	3468	3083	2730	2403	2099	1816
49	4349	3882	3461	3077	2724	2398	2095	1811
50	4341	3875	3454	3071	2719	2393	2090	1806
51	4333	3868	3448	3065	2713	2388	2085	1802
52	4324	3860	3441	3059	2707	2382	2080	1797
53	4316	3853	3434	3053	2702	2377	2075	1793
54	4308	3846	3428	3047	2696	2372	2070	1788
55	4300	3838	3421	3041	2691	2367	2065	1784
56	4292	3831	3415	3034	2685	2362	2061	1779
57	4284	3824	3408	3028	2679	2356	2056	1774
58	4276	3817	3401	3022	2674	2351	2051	1770
59	4268	3809	3395	3016	2668	2346	2046	1765
	8	9	10	11	12	13	14	15

* The same tables can be used for converting minutes and seconds.

166

Time changes in Great Britain

During the periods shown below the time has been advanced by one hour. Before 1981 the time was advanced at 2.00 am GMT on the day shown. From 1981 onwards and during the war years the time was advanced at 1.00 am GMT. From 18th February 1968 to 31st October 1971 Time was advanced by one hour to bring us in line with Mid European Time, this was an experimental period and was not continued after October 1971.

Daylight Saving hours 1940 - 1947 including War Years

Remember that the clock was put forward by one hour from 1 January 1941 through to 7 October 1945 plus an extra hour was added during the period entered in italics. If your time of birth was during the period entered in italics then you must subtract 2 hours from your birth time. 1946 and 1947 are included in this table as the time was not entirely back to normal until after 1947.

1940	25 February to 31 December +1	1943	15 August to 31 December +1
1944	1 January to 2 April +1	1944	4 April to 15 August +2
1941	1 January to 4 May +1	1944	15 August to 31 December +1
1941	4 May to 10 August +2	1945	1 January to 2 April +1
1941	10 August to 31 December +1	1945	2 April to 15 July +2
1942	1 January to 5 April +1	1945	15 July to 7 October +1
1942	5 April to 9 August +2	1946	14 April to 6 October +1
1942	9 August to 31 December +1	1947	16 March to 13 April +1
1943	1 January to 4 April +1	1947	13 April to 10 August +2
1943	4 April to 15 August +2	1947	10 August to 2 November +1

1916 21 May to 1 October	1958 20 April to 5 October
1917 8 April to 17 September	1959 19 April to 4 October
1918 24 March to 30 September	1960 10 April to 2 October
1919 30 March to 29 September	1961 26 March to 29 October
1920 28 March to 25 October	1962 25 March to 28 October
1921 3 April to 3 October	1963 31 March to 27 October
1922 26 March to 8 October	1964 22 March to 25 October
1923 22 April to 16 September	1965 21 March 24 October
1924 13 April to 21 September	1966 20 March to 23 October
1925 19 April to 4 October	1967 19 March to 29 October
1926 18 April to 3 October	**1968-71 18 Feb 68 - 31 Oct 71**
1927 10 April to 2 October	1972 19 March to 29 October
1928 22 April to 7 October	1973 18 March to 28 October
1929 21 April to 6 October	1974 17 March to 27 October
1930 13 April to 5 October	1975 16 March to 26 October
1931 19 April to 4 October	1976 21 March to 24 October
1932 17 April to 2 October	1977 20 March to 23 October
1933 9 April to 8 October	1978 19 March to 22 October
1934 22 April to 7 October	1979 18 March to 28 October
1935 14 April to 6 October	1980 16 March to 26 October
1936 19 April to 4 October	1981 29 March to 25 October
1937 18 April to 3 October	1982 28 March to 24 October
1938 10 April to 2 October	1983 27 March to 23 October
1939 16 April to 19 November	1984 25 March to 28 October
1940 - 1947 see following table	1985 31 March to 27 October
1948 14 March to 31 October	1986 30 March to 26 October
1949 3 April to 30 October	1987 29 March to 25 October
1950 16 April to 22 October	1988 27 March to 23 October
1951 15 April to 21 October	1989 26 March to 29 October
1952 20 April to 26 October	1990 25 March to 28 October
1953 19 April to 4 October	1991 31 March to 27 October
1954 11 April to 3 October	1992 29 March to 25 October
1955 17 April to 2 October	1993 28 March to 24 October
1956 22 April to 7 October	1994 27 March to 23 October
1957 14 April to 6 October	1995 29 March to 22 October

Chapter 20

Aspects

An aspect is the angular relationship between two planets, if two planets were in a square aspect then that means they are 90⁰apart. For a square aspect an orb of 8⁰is allowed, which means that 8⁰ either side of the aspect is within orb. If you had Venus in Libra at 20⁰and Mars in Aries at 13⁰ there is 7⁰difference, but as long as it is within the specified orb then it is in aspect.

SYMBOL	NAME	°	ORB	MEANING
☌	Conjunction	0	8	Blended power
⋎	Semi-sextile	30	2	Lack of ease
∠	Semi-square	45	2	Tension
✳	Sextile	60	6	Opportunity
q	Quintile	72	2	Artistry
□	Square	90	8	Difficulty
△	Trine	120	8	Ease
⚼	Sesquiquadrate	135	2	Strain
⚻	Quincunx/Inconjunct	150	2	Stress
☍	Opposition	180	8	Tense Awareness

The Conjunction   (Red)

This is a powerful aspect and indicates two planets together in the same degree in the same sign. However an 8* orb is allowed which means they can as far apart as 8*. It produces a more concentrated energy and force so that the planets involved are more easily expressed. The person uses the combined qualities of the two planetary energies often with little realisation of the effect this has on others. The ease with which the conjunction is expressed depends upon the compatibility of the two planets involved. For example if Saturn and the Moon are together it is more difficult to express the qualities of the Moon than when Venus and the Moon are conjunct.

The Sextile (red line)

This aspect shows how a person thinks and what opportunities are available to pursue subjects which are of interest. The mentality is sharpened and there is considerable skill in gathering information. It provides an avenue to express your creativity and often indicates more flexibility.

The Square (Black line)

This is a powerful aspect, and surpasses the conjunction in stimulating human reaction. It creates tension and demands action for the planets involved are almost always in signs which are naturally hostile to each other. Therefore positive action is necessary for it to be used constructively. The initial action of a square is to cause frustration and difficulties when the psychological factors of both planets are involved, so adjustment must be made for energies to be used positively. The square indicates a conflict of interests but unlike the opposition, it will be expressed subjectively and internally and become a definite problem area in life if not properly resolved. It is an area of inner tension brought about through an inability to restructure and transmute the energies indicated by the planets.

The attempt on the part of the individual to transcend his or her squares provides the necessary energy for personal growth. Thus we term squares dynamic aspects, since without them there is little desire to succeed. The square aspect does not let one rest until the problem indicated is either accepted or solved. A person with none or few squares may be easily lead by others and harbour no really driving ambition. These aspects show that there are lessons to be learned about how to use the energies constructively, otherwise negative effects are certain. The greatest tests in life come through the square aspects. They show the major crises that must be dealt with for the soul to evolve and grow toward greater conscious awareness of the self. Squares enable people to face difficulties and obstacles in their lives which builds character and strength to cope with whatever the future may bring.

The Trine (Red Line)

This is a positive aspect though it lacks the power to counteract the intense pressure of the negative aspects, but it is available to soften their effects when used with understanding and deliberation. In general the trine is a beneficial aspect and tends to blend the natures of the planets involved with ease. A person with many trines and few squares will either sail through life with comparative ease or are devastated during a crises.

The Quincunx or Inconjunct (Green line)

This aspect links planetary influences between signs that have no sympathy for each other by element or quality and are therefore functioning under great strain, so supreme effort must be made to express the qualities harmoniously. Usually it feels more like an irritating itch that it is difficult to find relief from.

The Opposition (Black line)

The conflict and uneasiness of the opposition aspect is projected on to other people. It is an easier aspect than the square, and easier to resolve the conflicts, it sometimes feels you are being pulled in two opposite directions and the task is to find a balance between the two planetary energies and the two houses involved. Any planets which are trine or sextile to either end of the opposition will be instrumental in solving the difficulty. The opposition is an aspect of challenge but the situation is usually accompanied by less tension than is indicated by the square.

The Sesquiquadrate (Green line)

This aspect represents a square, 90^0, and a semisquare, 45^0, linked together. They represent a challenge similar to a square but perhaps less intense.

How to Fill in an Aspect Grid

If you are unable to see patterns then there is no easy way but to calculate the differences mathematically between two planets. If you are able to see patterns fairly easily then the way I find aspects may be helpful to you.

Begin with conjunctions because it is easy enough to see whether two or more planets are situated in the same sign if they are with 8^0 of each other then they are in conjunction. The next step is to look for oppositions, these are planets that are in opposite signs to each other so if you have a planet for instance in Aries at 10^0 then look to Libra the opposite sign and see if you have any Planets in this sign between 2^0 and 18^0 (allowing for the 8^0orb) if you do then it would be in opposition. Once you have the oppositions then it is fairly easy to discover the squares. Another tip here is that if you have a planet in a fixed sign (Leo) then a square aspect would be a planet in another fixed sign that is Taurus or Scorpio, of course, Aquarius would be opposite. The same applies to planets in cardinal or mutable signs they are all square to the same quality either side of it.

To find the inconjunct or quincunx then again look to the opposite sign and then look at the signs either side of it if there is a planet in the same degree then it is inconjunct. For example a planet at 10^0 Aries - you would find Libra the opposite sign and look at the signs either side of it which are Virgo and Scorpio, if a planet is at 10^0 in either of these signs then it is inconjunct.

To find Trines is now straightforward they are planets that blend together easily because they are in the same element. If you have Mars at 10^0 Aries then you would look to see if there is anything from 2^0 - 18^0 Leo or Sagittarius (the other two fire signs) to see if they were in trine aspect. A sextile would be half of that degree. So planets in sextile would also be compatible which is Fire to Air or Earth to Water. This may sound very complicated to begin with but you will soon get used to the patterns.

Aspect Grïd

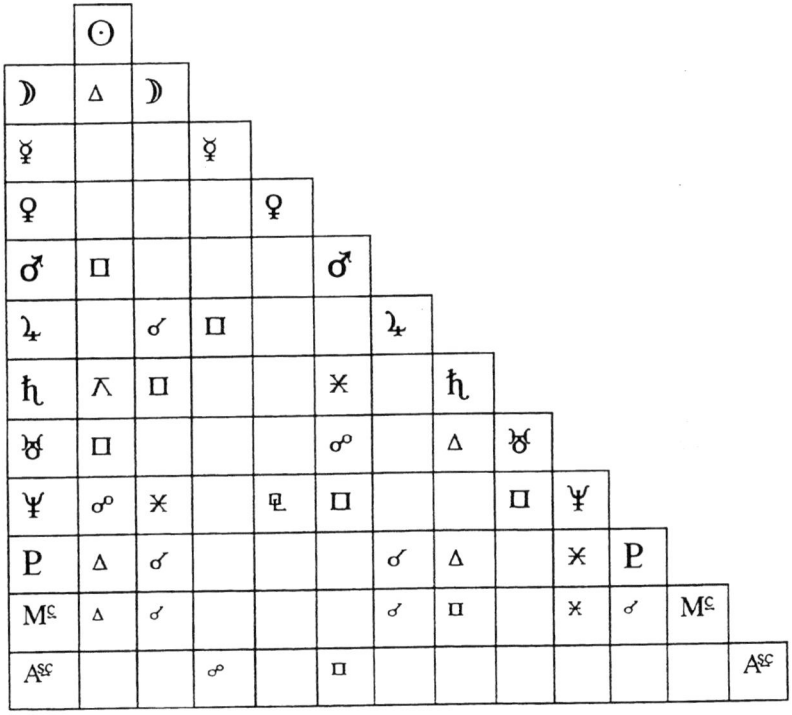

This aspect grid has been filled in for Mary's Chart which is shown on page 140.

Other Planetary Configurations

The **Stellium** is a group of planets (no less than three) that are conjunct within the same sign or within the sign either side. In other words a multiple conjunction in the same sign or adjacent signs. The house that the stellium is found will be an important area of life.

The **Easy Opposition** occurs when a regular opposition exists between two planets while a third planet is sextile to one end and trine the other. The challenge of the opposition can then be resolved through the affairs of the planet, sign and house position of the third planet forming the sextile and trine.

The **Finger of Fate** or sometimes referred to as YOD is formed when one planet is quincunx two others which are sextile to each other. It points the way to some special task in life which can be beneficial to the persons growth if the situation is handled wisely.

The **T-Square** is formed when two planets are in opposition and both are square to a third. the third planet becomes the focal point of the tension and challenge of the configuration. In the T-square, constant pressure has to be applied by the person to keep the energies of the three planets from unbalancing the life. It can however, indicate the particular struggle which forces the individual to grow. It is frequently found in the chart of prominent individuals for it often adds strength to the character. The focal planet in a T-square is the planet which squares both ends of the opposition. Another important point is the degree opposite the focal planet regardless of whether there is another planet in this position. The position by sign and house opposite to the focal indicates the area of life where such resolution and consequent growth may be found. This is called the karmic degree.

The **Grand Cross** or **Karmic Cross** is a difficult pattern to master, although it leads to great strength and growth if used wisely by the person in question. It is the same as the T-square but the position opposite the third planet square to the opposition is filled by another planet: and four squares are formed. The karmic cross calls for a very self contained individual, possessing a great supply of inner strength and stamina. The square is a symbol for Saturn, and it asks the individual to learn lessons of timing, limitations, and endurance. Depending on the planets involved some Astrologers believe it is easier to handle than the T-square because the fourth planet is filled and this gives you the answer to the problem, or at least something to work on, whereas in the T-square you have freedom of choice in searching for the answer.

The **Grand Trine** is formed by the connection of three planets at three 120⁰ angles, thus forming an equilateral triangle. If the energies contained within the Grand Trine are not wisely directed it causes the individual to go round in circles. Too many trines can indicate laziness and an inability to focus on life's challenges. The Grand Trine may sometimes produce apathy and indifference to responsibility and is often found in the charts of criminals. The grand Trine can be very helpful if it is connected with squares in the chart, as it eases the tension or the squares give the drive that the trines lack. In certain cases it can be a bestower of benefits if the abundant flow of harmonious energy is carefully channelled. In any case, there is an intensification of the significance of the element in which the planets are placed.

The **Kite Formation** is an extension of the Grand Trine in that a fourth planet is in opposition to one corner of the triangle and therefore sextile the other two corners. This is much more stable and powerful configuration than the Grand Trine and the opposition gives a definite focal point for the direction of the abundant energy contained within this planetary picture.

The **Mystical Rectangle** involves two oppositions in an X configuration where the two shorter distances are sextile and the two longer distances are trine. It is said to represent practical mysticism. It effectively involves four easy oppositions so gives the power to blend the energies involved to a practical and positive use. It shows potential for awareness in bringing creative instincts to a satisfactory fruition.

Aspect Configurations

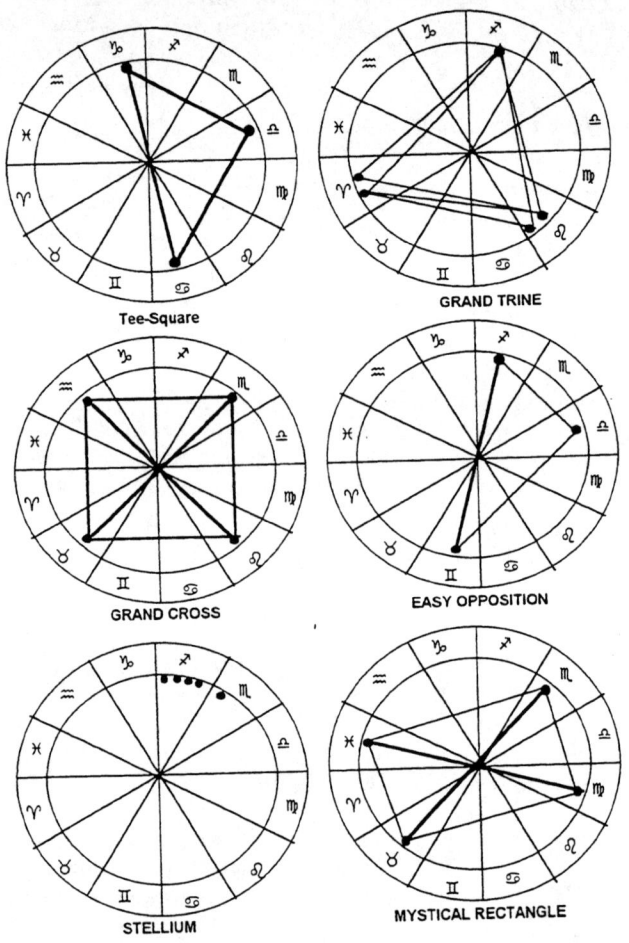

Tee-Square

GRAND TRINE

GRAND CROSS

EASY OPPOSITION

STELLIUM

MYSTICAL RECTANGLE

Diagram No. 12

176

Unaspected Planets

Unaspected planets sometimes represent certain energies which have not been integrated into the totality of the being. The task for the individual is to incorporate the forces embodied by the unaspected planet into their lives. If the unaspected planet is the Sun, the individual would usually find it extremely difficult to create a cohesive life pattern, then an Astrologer would be advised to study the aspects and placing of the Moon. Another way an unaspected planet may manifest itself is to use the pure energy of the unaspected planet only within the house and sign that it is "trapped" in.

Individual Unaspected Planets

Unaspected Sun

An unaspected Sun can sometimes indicate a lack of direction or of ambition, possibly brought on by not connecting with one of the parents. They may feel particularly insignificant, unable to make an impact resulting in a feeling that they are unable to express their personality, so they can be easily overlooked. There can sometimes be a lack of morality but not necessarily. A strong Moon helps in this instance.

Unaspected Moon

These people can appear to be very cold and are sometimes extremely sensitive. They find it hard to bring their emotions in their day to day life and they can have highly emotional periods which can become very unstable. Two personal examples of an unaspected Moon have been one young lady who was unable to bring the mothering aspect into her life, in other words she was unable to have a child of her own. Another one who although she had children was not inclined to look after them and eventually on a marriage break-up left her child with her husband. So these people can be overcome with emotional urges and they have a particularly strong desire for freedom.

Unaspected Mercury

There may be some difficulty here in expressing how they feel, or sharing personal knowledge with others. Sometimes they can act in a very unreasonable way, perhaps it could be said that they act in a way that does not include any reasoning. Intellect can be important to these people and they often appear to be strongly motivated to get themselves educated, but they can also be silent and untalkative. They can have a restless mind filled with new ideas.

Unaspected Venus

The Venus quality in their life seems to be rather erratic, finding it hard to be consistent in relationships, it's all or nothing. A lot of the things connected to Venus seem to be out of their control so there is an inability maybe to gain possessions or material things, or else they receive it without any desire. They may also find they have too many relationships at one time, or none at all. Very difficult to balance. Sometimes they may find it difficult to communicate on a relaxed level with associates.

Unaspected Mars

With an unaspected Mars there seems to be inconsistent energy; they always seem to be busy but the energy seems to be scattered leaving them unable to finish what they began. There can be flashes of violent temper but this only seems to be in effect if someone else's planets are aspecting the unaspected Mars. These people seem to generate work and do more than they actually need. One example of inconsistent energy came from someone who had an unaspected Mars in the twelfth and suffered from bouts of anaemia which was undiscovered for a while, so energy levels fluctuated with an inability to cope.

Unaspected Jupiter

This is not so easy to interpret but it has been known that people spend long periods of time in solitude, although this may not necessarily be chosen or self imposed. These people seem to find it difficult to incorporate travel into their life, but when and if they do then they have difficulty even calling it to a close and may spend the rest of their life travelling, and travel seems to come late in life.

Unaspected Saturn

An unaspected Saturn can be quite difficult in that it may be hard to incorporate discipline and responsibility into their life style. These people may be over cautious or have no caution at all. In other words they have no boundaries and may be totally irresponsible.

Unaspected Uranus

These people may feel restless and rebellious without any particular reason. There may be a continuous search for excitement or they may find their life is dull with no excitement at all. The energies of the planet always seem to fluctuate where there are no aspects to them.

Unaspected Neptune

An unaspected Neptune can sometimes be an overdose of Neptune on the psychic level. They may be very strongly directed towards a spiritual life at the very best, and at the worst may be a drifter with no particular morals.

Unaspected Pluto

There is an underlying need for control that seems to be missing in their life, they find that others can easily push them about. They may find blocks and find it difficult to get their anger out into the open, the difficulties of confrontation as with perhaps an unaspected Mars.

Applying and Separating Aspects

An applying aspect is when the angular relationship is less than exact. In other words if Venus is 7⁰ Aries and Mars is 10⁰ Cancer then Venus is applying to the Mars as it had not reached an exact aspect at the time of birth. This tends to indicate a situation that is gathering energy and momentum and preparing to release that energy so there is an increased intensity around an applying aspect.

A separating aspect has an angular value greater than the exact angular value, in other words it is moving out of aspect, so to use the same planets if Venus was 10⁰Cancer and Mars 7⁰Aries then Venus would be separating from an exact aspect to Mars.

To discover whether an aspect is in an applying or a separating phase check whether the faster moving planet at your time of birth is moving towards an exact angular relationship or out of aspect (separating).

Retrograde Planets

When a planet is retrograde it is symbolised in the ephemeris with the letter R with a cross through. What this means is that from an observers viewpoint on earth a planet appears to be travelling backwards in the zodiac. This retrograde motion of the planets occurs because the speed of each planet in its orbit around the Sun differs from the earth. Mercury and Venus are inside the earth's orbit, that is their orbit lies between earth and the Sun and therefore orbit the Sun at a greater speed than the earth, so when either of these planets catch up with or pass the earth then the planet appears to move backwards against the zodiac. See diagram 13 on following page.

From Mars to Pluto the planets lie outside the earth's orbit, when the earth appears to catch up with the outer planet it appears to stop in its orbit. This is noted in the ephemeris with an S (stationery), and as the earth moves forward in orbit the outer planet then appears to move backwards against the zodiac.

There is not any general agreement amongst Astrologers as to the meaning of a retrograde planet in the birthchart. Some believe that as it is only an apparent motion as seen from a viewpoint on earth then it cannot have any relevance. However, others say that during its retrograde cycle it is at its nearest point to earth so this must add strength. There are a few complete books on interpreting retrograde planets if you would like to pursue this further.

Diagram No. 13

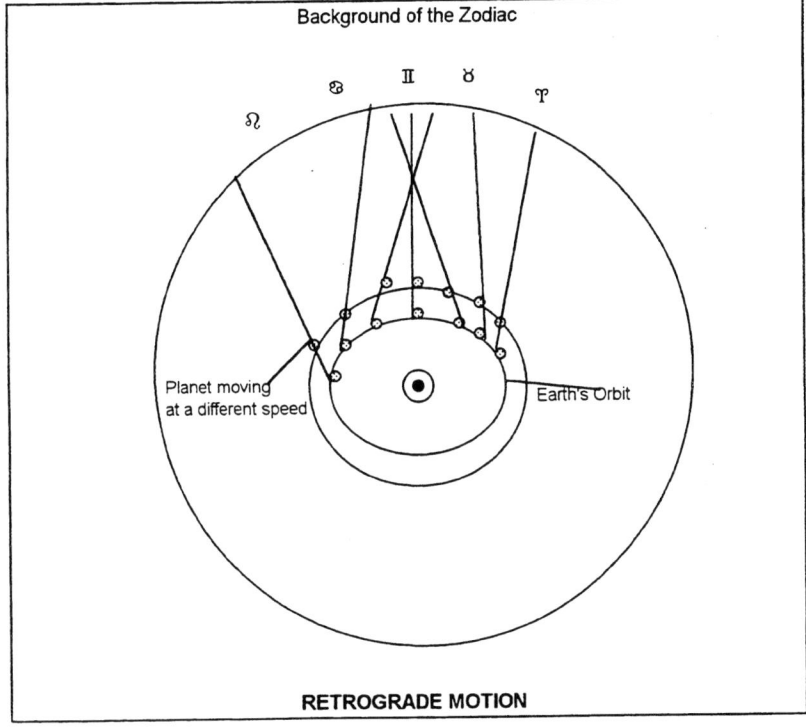

Chart Shapings

The shaping or pattern of a chart is fairly difficult for a student to recognise.

The Bowl

This is perhaps one of the easiest to recognise as all planets fall within six consecutive signs. This often indicates that a person is very self contained with a tendency to catalogue experience for use in humanitarian interests. They can be hard to approach except to their friends and they are very idealistic. The leading planet can be significant in this chart.

The Bucket

This is very similar to the bowl except one planet forms a handle and it is called the Singleton. These people have a single purpose which is indicated by the singleton planet. They are driven by achievement and they do have the ability to influence others. They are particularly adaptable and not over concerned with self preservation.

The Bundle

The Bundle often contains a Stellium, as the planets are grouped very closely together within about four signs. This may show someone who specialises in one particular area. They can be very narrow minded or have at the best very narrow interests which they concentrate on most of their life. Although this may be someone who can be very knowledgeable about ones subject it can also make a person very self centred, unable to see the other persons point of view as they always seem to be coming from one standpoint.

The Locomotive

The Locomotive is recognised by filling up eight of the twelve signs and leaving a space of four signs free. The leading planet, which is the planet leading clockwise, is the most important and is the driving force. Depending upon the leading planet these people usually have a great amount of energy and are often driven to complete a special task. They have strong inner compulsions and can be very practical.

Chart Shapings

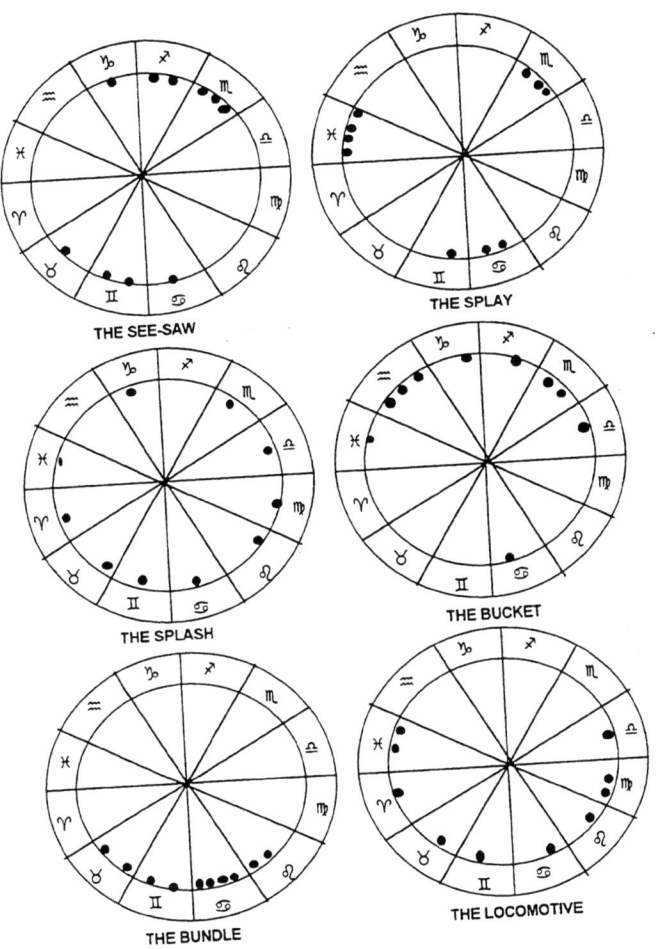

Diagram No 14.

The See-saw
In this type of chart you generally see many oppositions, so here you may have someone who sees two points of view and in fact may have difficulty coming down on either side. So these people can either be mediators or someone in a constant struggle as they try to balance the never ending contrasts in their lives.

The Splay
This is not an easy pattern to recognise but there may sometimes be a Grand Trine present. It tends to be the individualist, someone who dislikes being categorised, dislikes restriction or limitations, has many interests and is fairly intense. There is likely to be at least one Stellium present.

The Splash
This pattern is fairly easy to recognise as the planets are scattered throughout the chart, but this often indicates someone who has many interests but may have difficulty containing their energy. So they may appear to be very scattered, having trouble in achieving much in any one area.

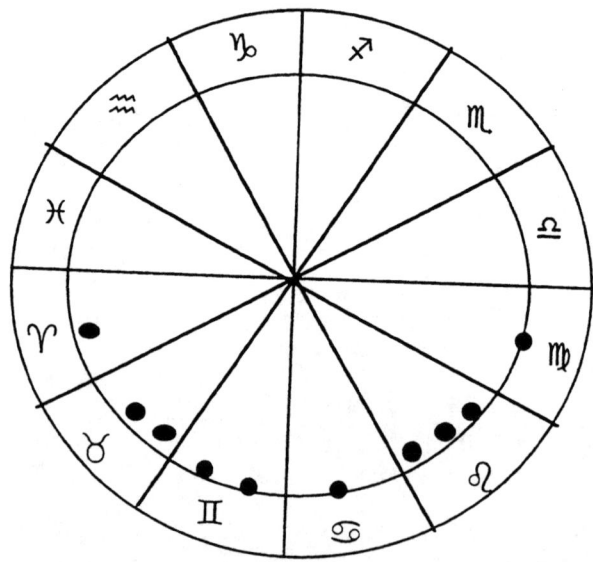

The bowl

184

Chapter 21
Understanding the Angles

Originally ancient astrologers plotted the planets against the background of fixed stars. Different characteristics were observed when people were born at different times of the year, when the sun appeared to be in a particular constellation.

Ancient astrologers saw the earth as the centre of the solar system rather than the sun, it is important to understand that astrology is based on the position of the planets in the heavens as seen from earth (Geocentric).

The ecliptic is the apparent path of the sun on its journey around the earth which takes a year to complete. The zodiac is an imaginary belt which follows the line of the ecliptic and spans about eight degrees each side.

When Hipparchus discovered that the zodiac belt was slipping slowly out of alignment with the fixed constellations (see precession of the equinoxes), then all calculating and observations in the heavens, had the zodiac belt not the constellations as a fixed reference.

The first point of Aries is taken when the Suns' path along the ecliptic crosses the equator from south to north. This occurs around the 21st March and is the first day of spring or the vernal equinox.

As the earth continuously rotates on its axis a different degree of the ecliptic will rise above the eastern horizon approximately every four minutes, and in your astrological chart it is the horizon's eastern point of the intersection with the ecliptic which determines the rising degree of ascendant for any given time and place.

Yet another significant point is when at midday the ecliptic intersects the great circle of the meridian and this point is known as the MC or (Latin medium coeli). The position of the planets given in the ephemeris from which we can calculate planetary movements are the geocentric measurements, that is as they are seen from earth. If the sun was the central point of reference it would be heliocentric.

The horizon and the meridian are always at 90* angles to each other. The individual birth chart is a 'frozen' map of the heavens for the time an individual is born, this can also be the case for countries, businesses, situations or indeed anything that is born in a moment of time.

Important points to remember

1.   The angles divide the chart into four parts with the
     Ascendant/Descendant, the vertical axis and the MC,
     Medium Coeli (more often known as the midheaven) and its
     polar opposite the Imum Coeli axis running horizontally.

2.   The twelve houses divide the circle into twelve portions,
     equal house system will divide the circle equally whereas
     other house systems show unequal portions.

3.   The four elements, the emphasis is shown with the spread of
     the planets.

The relevance of the angles astronomically are that any time in relation to the location of the observer a certain degree of the zodiac is rising over the eastern horizon whilst another degree is culminating at the medium coeli.

The Four Hemispheres

The Upper Hemisphere

This deals with the aspects of life that are less personal and more social. It represents the outer self, other people and the social world, where you can be more objective. There may be more inclination to stand up and be counted or to need recognition for your achievements when most of your planets fall in the upper hemisphere.

The Celestial Sphere

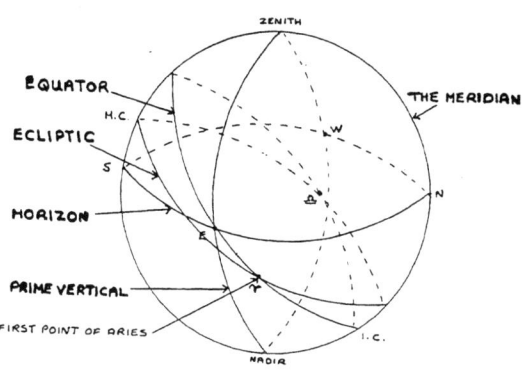

Diagram No. 15.

The Celestial Sphere shows the Great Circles of the Ecliptic, the Equator, the Prime Vertical, the Horizon and the Meridian. Any circle the plane of which cuts through the centre of the earth is a great circle. The Ascendant is the point where the Ecliptic intersects the horizon in the eastern sector. The Midheaven (MC) is the point where the Ecliptic intersects the great circle of the Meridian. The Ascendant and Midheaven form the angles of the birth chart and are the most important points in the Chart. The Vertex is where the Ecliptic meets the Prime Vertical in the West. All these points have opposite energies such as Ascendant/Descendent, Midheaven (MC/IC), Vertex/Anti vertex, the First Point of Aries/The first point of Libra. The Equator is tilted to the Ecliptic at an angle of approximately 23⁰ but is always changing. The Celestial Equator is the terrestrial equator extended out into the heavens.

The Lower Hemisphere
This is more personal and less social. It symbolises the inner self, ones closest family and associates and the less conscious mind. So therefore planets here are more subjective.

The Eastern Hemisphere
Energies situated in this half have more to do with the worlds perception of the self. They are considered to be more active and under personal control. There are people who control their destinies and rarely suffer with self doubt. They take the initiative and never wait for others, always to act and never to re-act.

The Western Hemisphere
This half symbolises one's experience and perception of the world. It is the part of the self that is acted upon, but is passive and not under one's personal control. Emphasis on the western side tends to lead to the subject being passive and out of control or a victim. There is a strong awareness of others.

The Four Hemispheres

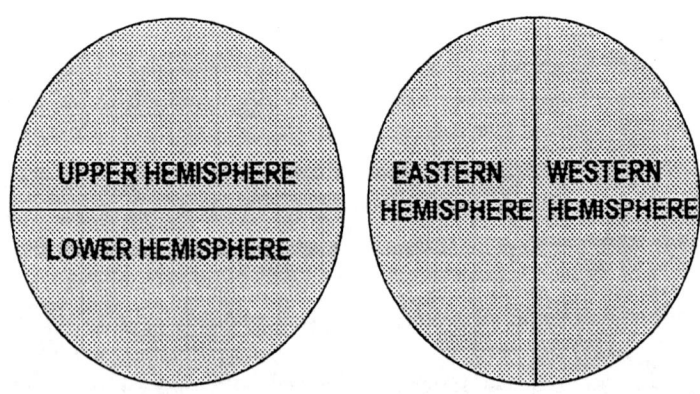

Diagram No. 16

Quick Table of Rising Signs

Your Ascendant is the following if your time of birth was:

If your Sun Sign is:	6 to 8 am	8 to 10 am	10 am to Noon	Noon to 2 pm	2 to 4 pm	4 to 6 pm
Aries	Taurus	Gemini	Cancer	Leo	Virgo	Libra
Taurus	Gemini	Cancer	Leo	Virgo	Libra	Scorpio
Gemini	Cancer	Leo	Virgo	Libra	Scorpio	Sagittarius
Cancer	Leo	Virgo	Libra	Scorpio	Sagittarius	Capricorn
Leo	Virgo	Libra	Scorpio	Sagittarius	Capricorn	Aquarius
Virgo	Libra	Scorpio	Sagittarius	Capricorn	Aquarius	Pisces
Libra	Scorpio	Sagittarius	Capricorn	Aquarius	Pisces	Aries
Scorpio	Sagittarius	Capricorn	Aquarius	Pisces	Aries	Taurus
Sagittarius	Capricorn	Aquarius	Pisces	Aries	Taurus	Gemini
Capricorn	Aquarius	Pisces	Aries	Taurus	Gemini	Cancer
Aquarius	Pisces	Aries	Taurus	Gemini	Cancer	Leo
Pisces	Aries	Taurus	Gemini	Cancer	Leo	Virgo

If your Sun Sign is:	6 to 8 pm	8 to 10 pm	10 am to Midnight	Midnight to 2 am	2 to 4 am	4 to 6 am
Aries	Scorpio	Sagittarius	Capricorn	Aquarius	Pisces	Aries
Taurus	Sagittarius	Capricorn	Aquarius	Pisces	Aries	Taurus
Gemini	Capricorn	Aquarius	Pisces	Aries	Taurus	Gemini
Cancer	Aquarius	Pisces	Aries	Taurus	Gemini	Cancer
Leo	Pisces	Aries	Taurus	Gemini	Cancer	Leo
Virgo	Aries	Taurus	Gemini	Cancer	Leo	Virgo
Libra	Taurus	Gemini	Cancer	Leo	Virgo	Libra
Scorpio	Gemini	Cancer	Leo	Virgo	Libra	Scorpio
Sagittarius	Cancer	Leo	Virgo	Libra	Scorpio	Sagittarius
Capricorn	Leo	Virgo	Libra	Scorpio	Sagittarius	Capricorn
Aquarius	Virgo	Libra	Scorpio	Sagittarius	Capricorn	Aquarius
Pisces	Libra	Scorpio	Sagittarius	Carpricorn	Aquarius	Pisces

This is only an approximate guide. To be absolutely certain of your ascendant it needs to be calculated as you are shown on Page 141.

189

The Ascendant

The ascendant is an energy point and there is some belief that it is the point where the spirit enters the body at the moment of a child's first breath. It is in fact the point between the womb and life in the outside world. So if the birth time is correct the qualities of the rising sign become the child's persona and shows the journey through life as well as through the birth channel.

There are many interpretations of the ascendant. First of all, it is the image of the personality as seen by others, so it is the first impression others have of you. It shows how you express yourself to the outside world, that is why when guessing the Sun sign of someone you hardly know it is more likely you will guess their ascendant.

The ascendant often reveals the quality of energy flow, vitalising the physical body i.e. Fire, Earth, Air or Water. The ascendant is more personal to the individual than their Sun sign because only by knowing the time of birth can one know the ascendant.

It is a way of expressing one's individuality, one's ego. Whereas the Sun reveals the way we understand and assimilate experience, the ascendant reveals the way we feel ourselves to be individual, our point of spontaneous action. In other words, the Sun is where you are going and the ascendant shows how you get there.

The ruler of your natal chart is the planet that rules the ascending sign. It is the lord of the chart. It appears to preside not only over your birth but over your whole life. The house position of the ruler is very important and seems to represent the area of life where you express your ascendant to the full. For further interpretation read the 'First House' on page 60.

190

♈	With *Aries* on the ascendant you will project yourself with a very energetic manner. You are positively able to act upon any ideas the minute they come into your mind which can be looked upon as impulsive. You can be very competitive and are likely to want to prove yourself all the time through your actions. The way others see you is very important to you and you like to be liked.
♉	With *Taurus* on the ascendant you are likely to express yourself through any of your material or financial dealings. Important expression in your gaining of any material resources. You like the good things in life and generally strive to create beauty in some form. You could appear very capable, steady and steadfast to others.
♊	With *Gemini* on the ascendant you are likely to express yourself thorough your search for knowledge. You are an original and creative thinker. You have a talent for helping others to clearly see and visualise your own ideas. Although you may appear to be scattered without a clear direction.
♋	With *Cancer* on the ascendant you expend a great deal of energy through your feelings. You identify strongly through your family or through any family concerns and like to be in a controlling position. Others will see you as someone to confide in, or someone who will look after them.
♌	With *Leo* on the ascendant you project yourself with dignity, energy and warmth although at times you may seem arrogant and overbearing. You are likely to express yourself where ever you see an opportunity and allow no one to stand in your way, and can often dominate a situation without being invited. Others are in no doubt of your ascendant as your aura projects your dynamic energy.
♍	With *Virgo* on the ascendant you are likely to be systematic, well organised and able to develop ideas and execute them. No detail is too small for you to notice or explain and perfection is your goal and there are no flaws in what you do. Others can only criticise your desire and need for perfection.

♎	With *Libra* on the ascendant you are likely to express your personality through co-operation with other people. Your personality tends to be focused and mirrored on those with whom you co-operate. Your actions express beauty and grace along with discipline, and a strong sense of justice. You are able to see a situation from several different viewpoints which gains you the reputation of being indecisive. You dislike being alone and tend to feel rather lost when you have to rely only upon yourself.
♏	With *Scorpio* on your ascendant you project yourself with energy and will power and are willing to stake your life to accomplish your aims. You cannot be convinced that something cannot be done, and you will do it or die in trying. You have a tremendous fixed emotionally intensity.
♐	With *Sagittarius* on the ascendant you manage to project yourself with friendly optimism. Your ambitions are geared to large scale goals and you tend to take many things for granted. You have the ability to influence others to your way of thinking and your optimism can be a source of inspiration to those with whom you come into contact with.
♑	With *Capricorn* on the ascendant discipline, systematic endeavour, hard work and patience are your characteristics. Everything you do has a purpose designed to achieve a practical end. You are serious, austere and reserved and tend to regard life with caution and trepidation.
♒	With *Aquarius* on the ascendant you are original, creative, independent and wishing to make your own unique contribution to the common good. You can be fun loving and friendly in a non-personal way. You find your source of power in a group activity with a close circle of friends.
♓	With *Pisces* on the ascendant you are sympathetic, adaptable and visionary. Your achievements are the result of your sensitivities to the subtle undercurrents of your surroundings. Your mystical insight enables you to penetrate the subtleties of human nature. You are probably musical and artistic.

With Aries on the ascendant you will project yourself with a very energetic manner. You are positively able to act upon any ideas the minute they come into your mind which can be looked upon as impulsive. You can be very competitive and are likely to want to prove yourself all the time through your actions. The way others see you is very important to you and you like to be liked.

With Taurus on the ascendant you are likely to express yourself through any of your material or financial dealings. Important expression in your gaining of any material resources. You like the good things in life and generally strive to create beauty in some form. You could appear very capable, steady and steadfast to others.

With Gemini on the ascendant you are likely to express yourself thorough your search for knowledge. You are an original and creative thinker. You have a talent for helping others to clearly see and visualise your own ideas. Although you may appear to be scattered without a clear direction.

With Cancer on the ascendant you expend a great deal of energy through your feelings. You identify strongly through your family or through family concerns and like to be in a controlling position. Others will see you as someone to confide in, or someone who will look after them.

With Leo on the ascendant you project yourself with dignity, energy and warmth although at times you may seem arrogant and overbearing. You are likely to express yourself wherever you see an opportunity and allow no one to stand in your way, and can often dominate a situation without being invited. Others are in no doubt of your ascendant as your aura projects your dynamic energy.

With Virgo on the ascendant you are likely to be systematic, well organised and able to develop ideas and execute them. No detail is too small for you to notice or explain and perfection is your goal and there are no flaws in what you do. Others can only criticise your desire and need for perfection.

With Libra on the ascendant you are likely to express your personality through co-operation with other people. Your personality tends to be focused and mirrored on those with whom you co-operate. Your actions express beauty and grace along with discipline, and a strong sense of justice. You are able to see a situation from several different viewpoints which gains you the reputation of being indecisive. You dislike being alone and tend to feel rather lost when you have to rely only upon yourself.

With Scorpio on your ascendant you project yourself with energy and will power and are willing to stake your life to accomplish your aims. You cannot be convinced that something cannot be done, and you will do it or die in trying. You have a tremendous fixed emotionally intensity.

With Sagittarius on the ascendant you manage to project yourself with friendly optimism. Your ambitions are geared to large scale goals and you tend to take many things for granted. You have the ability to influence others to your way of thinking and your optimism can be a source of inspiration to those with whom you come into contact with.

With Capricorn on the ascendant discipline, systematic endeavour, hard work and patience are your characteristics. Everything you do has a purpose designed to achieve a practical end. You are serious, austere and reserved and tend to regard life with caution and trepidation.

With Aquarius on the ascendant you are original, creative, independent and wishing to make your own unique contribution to the common good. You can be fun loving and friendly in a non-personal way. You find your source of power in a group activity with a close circle of friends.

With Pisces on the ascendant you are sympathetic, adaptable and visionary. Your achievements are the result of your sensitivities to the subtle undercurrents of your surroundings. Your mystical insight enables you to penetrate the subtleties of human nature. You are probably musical and artistic.

The Midheaven

The midheaven or MC signifies the point we are working towards as we grow older. Something that we are searching or striving for, it symbolises a point we spontaneously flow towards and grow towards as we move through life. Although we may express some of the qualities whilst we are young it does require effort to obtain the optimum expression of these qualities.

For example, Aries on the midheaven may indicate that a person admires strength and courage and therefore feels empowered to work and develop his or her assertive qualities.

With Scorpio on the midheaven a person may respect charismatic and powerful qualities in others and therefore seek to use his or her own abilities to the utmost.

The ruler of the midheaven is important due to the fact that it's house position so often shows where your real vocation comes into clearest focus.

Planets in the tenth house or conjunct midheaven represent ways of being, qualities or types of activities that are extremely important to the individual, and which he or she respects. A person will often exhibit those qualities or express these energies publicly in order that others might think well of them. Hence, the connection of the tenth house with one's reputation.

The planets appear to be important, perhaps more so than the sign. For example, if Uranus is in the tenth you will strive towards being independent and original. If Aquarius is your midheaven look for Uranus its ruler in your chart, and it will show you the area of your life where your true vocation lies.

Aries on the Midheaven

Aries on the Midheaven or Mars conjunct, it may show that you admire people who show courage and assertiveness in their chosen task. You will at some point try to integrate the qualities of this

195

sign in your life, you will want to take leadership roles and are prepared to put all your energy into what you choose to do. Chosen careers may include, Surgeon, Engineer, Dentist or a Military career.

Taurus on the Midheaven

Taurus on the Midheaven or Venus conjunct would be concerned with security and comfort. They may be threatened by anything too adventurous but instinctively know when something is a sound proposition. They are practical and loyal but not leaders. Their chosen career may be to do with the earth such as farming or gardening, or they may choose investment such as stockbroker, or accounting or they may choose the Venusian side and follow the world of beauty or they may follow a singing career.

Gemini on the Midheaven

With Gemini on the Midheaven or Mercury conjunct it, you might admire versatility but you would also admire a talent for communication. Eternally curious the Gemini MC would be seeking information about everything and then passing it on to all and sundry. So the Geminian career is likely to be any area where communication is the key such as information bureaus, telecommunication, public relations, journalism or on another level they may be the village gossip.

Cancer on the Midheaven

Cancerians like to be the key figure in a family situation so they are often attracted to careers that involve a fraternity of some sort. They are the carers and that often involves being in control as the mother controls her family. So the career a Cancerian is attracted to could be police force, catering (Chef), nursery nurse, childminding, housekeeper, alternative medicine, They may do something connected to herbs, medicinally or grow and sell them, and any profession that cares.

Leo on the Midheaven

Leo or the Sun conjunct the Midheaven like to be where they can shine, they admire personal confidence and those who can manage their lives. On a career level Leos expect to start at the top.

Unfortunately many are disappointed that their star quality is not always noticed immediately. So it is not surprising that a Leo Midheaven will eventually end up as department head, managing director or president of some company or other. Their star quality may take them into acting in a theatre rather than the movies as they love drama. They also get on very well with the younger members of the community through their association with the fifth house.

Virgo on the Midheaven

Virgo on the Midheaven or Mercury conjunct it admire people who have their lives in order, who are discriminating about their associations and who pay attention to important details. They may choose a career in which they can be of service to others, and they are often the valuable secretary behind a successful boss. Their communication talents often lie with the pen rather than the spoken word and they are more inclined to write a book than dig up information and report it to the Media. One of their talents is their ability to give constructive criticism so you may often find a theatre critic has a Virgo Midheaven.

Libra on the Midheaven

Libra on the Midheaven or Venus conjunct it admire diplomacy, they specialise in harmony and mediating between two warring factions. They are exceptional in careers that involve public relations, the diplomatic service, Prime Minister (Maggie Thatcher was a Libran) Counselling especially in the area of relationships. They may also be attracted to the beauty field such as hairdressing, modelling, make-up artists through the rulership of Venus. Librans more than any other sign are likely to go in to business with a partner.

Scorpio on the Midheaven

Scorpio on the Midheaven or Mars or Pluto conjunct it will put an enormous amount of energy into everything they do. Unless they can do it with passion then there is no point to it. Scorpio is the typical undercover agent, part of the secret service, the detective, the deep-sea diver, the muck-raker journalist, or on another level, they can be police divers, surgeons, psychologist, psychotherapist, psychiatrist; delving into the mind intrigues them. They have magnetism and can inspire others such as the evangelist Billy Graham. Scorpio can also be attracted to a Military career like Aries through their association with Mars.

Sagittarius on the Midheaven

Sagittarius and Jupiter conjunct the Midheaven are attracted to any career that doesn't seem like work, not that they are lazy, they are not, they just love to play. Sagittarians like to travel, to explore other cultures, to go to college and stay there for most of their lives. They are also attracted to any career concerning animals especially dogs or horses. They love to clown around and make people laugh. So they may choose to be a veterinary surgeon, a tourist guide, an explorer, a philosopher, a teacher of philosophical subjects, a sportsman, a clown or entertainer, and they are more likely than the other signs to do more than one job or have more than one vocation.

Capricorn on the Midheaven

Capricorn or Saturn on the Midheaven take everything seriously, they are often workaholics. They like structure and planning and building upon firm foundations. You are likely to find Capricorns as founder members of an organisation, as civil servants, as part of the structure of the police force, as President of a bank, property developers. They also have a strong sense of social responsibility so they make teachers, firefighters and ambulance drivers. Capricorns like to be at the top holding the reins as they survey their empires which are built on rock.

Aquarius on the Midheaven

Aquarius on the Midheaven or Saturn or Uranus conjunct it, are people who are going to go straight for anything that appears to be different or unusual in some way, not for them is the usual run-of-the-mill job. They want to express their individuality, they want freedom to come and go as they please, never ask these people to clock in or they will probably invent something that sends the mechanism haywire. Aquarians are likely to be attracted to careers that are connected to modern technology such as computers, earth sciences, Mathematicians, Astrology, Psychology, Social work, prison reform, trade unionist. They can also be fairly tricky characters that get a kick out of beating the system, or they make a career out of joining some well known cause, such as animal rights or Greenpeace.

Pisces on the Midheaven

Pisces on the Midheaven or Neptune or Jupiter conjunct it, are people who are artists, or poets or who write romantic novels. They are also attracted to the caring professions as they have very compassionate and sympathetic natures and strong healing qualities. They love music and dance and fantasy and are likely to be attracted to any career where they can develop these talents. Careers may be anything connected to the sea, music, dance, nursing, meditation, the church, counselling, clairvoyance and mediumship.

Chapter 22

Aspect Grid - Planetary Relationships

The Aspect Grid that follows is a guide towards helping you to understand the relationship between two planets that can be used in interpretation. Whilst using the grid the following points must be taken into consideration.

1.   This is only a guide and space limits a more complete interpretation.
2.   When looking at aspects remember that the sign containing the planets will have some considerable influence and the house will show the area of life where the aspect will manifest.
3.   Even with the easy aspects remember to weigh the nature of the planets. For example Moon/Pluto conjunction will not be as easy as the relatively harmless Moon/Venus conjunction and similarly for the opposition. Again Moon/Venus will not create as much internal discord as Moon/Pluto opposition.

Interpreting a birth chart requires a certain amount of skill which develops over the years as you begin to collect experience. Make your own notes when you begin interpreting so that you build up a reference of experience that will be invaluable as you continue on your journey.

Conj: = Conjunction (0⁰)   Oppos: = Opposition (180⁰)
Trine = Trine (120⁰)   Square = Square (90⁰)
Sext: = Sextile (60⁰)   Inconj: = Inconjunct (150⁰)

Sun/Moon Aspects

Conj: With the Sun/Moon conjunction you are born at the time of the new Moon, so your emotional life is well integrated with your personal goals. You are the one who initiates new schemes and ideas that can bring important areas of experience into your life. This will also be connected to the houses in which they are both in or the houses that they rule. It is difficult to separate the two so that your emotional life can affect your outer life.

Sext: This can be an aspect of friendship, because you are at ease with yourself you may find it easy to make other people feel comfortable. Your personal and emotional life is able to blend with your career or outer goals. You are not someone who makes waves but are fairly peaceable to be with.

Trine: With this position you have an inner serenity. You have a fairly balanced personality and are able to get along easily with others. People feel relaxed and at ease when they are with you. This can be a fairly creative aspect where you need to express your inner feelings in an artistic way. The biggest problem here may be lack of drive.

Square: This can be a fairly difficult aspect where there is always some tension between your outer goals and your personal life. It is a more stressful aspect than the opposition and you may always feel as though you are working at cross purposes to yourself and find it difficult to integrate your two separate needs and often have to sacrifice one for the other.

Inconj: This can indicate that certain relationships tend to be stressful which may have an effect on your health. You need to learn to relax away from the people that are putting stress on you, even though you feel under some sort of obligation to them. You may need periods of time away from 'work' to recover your energies.

Opp: With the Sun opposite the Moon you were born at the time of the full moon, and this can be a tense aspect. You may keep two sides of your life separate, so that your personal life is often hidden from your outer life. You may feel unable to bring them together because of conflict. There may always be some tension between your personal needs and your outer goals or your ambitions. Sometimes you may experience low energy levels through lack of purpose.

Sun/Mercury Aspects

Conj: With this conjunction you may have a fairly narrow viewpoint and are perfectly capable of being quite single minded over something. You have a restless and active mind, and enjoy communicating and tossing around ideas with someone else. Your opinions tend to be very subjective as you seem unable to take the broader viewpoint.

Oppos: An opposition between the Sun and Mercury is not astronomically possible as the Sun is never more than one sign away from Mercury.

Sun/Venus Aspects

Conj: This conjunction can often bestow an attractive personality. It may be someone who likes to please others and can use a great deal of charm when it suits them. Other people are drawn to you and like you with little or no effort on your part. You may be a romantic at heart and are often warm hearted and generous and are attracted towards music or the arts.

Oppos: An opposition between the Sun and Venus is not possible as the Sun is never more than two signs away from Venus.

Sun/Mars Aspects

Conj: This is a very positive aspect with a tremendous sense of self will. However, it can also be very aggressive, quick to take offence and jump into action. If you have this aspect you will have a tremendous amount of energy and need to use it, so your life will be one full of action and initiating new projects. Usually you will have a competitive temper- ament and may not make a good loser. You react to any outside stimulation impulsively and may need to learn how to relax. You can have a quick and volatile temper.

Sext: This is an aspect of energy and accomplishment. You are able to initiate new projects and have the energy to see them through. You are a very positive person with a strong will power and without effort opportunities just seem to come your way. It often conveys physical strength and good health. The tremendous enthusiasm and goodwill which accompanies this aspect takes away any of the more aggressive tendencies.

Trine: This aspect also contains energy but in a more relaxed way. It has leadership qualities and self confidence. You are competitive but do not take challenges so much to heart. You are not driven by anger or restlessness. You are driven by a desire to win, but not at all costs. You show enthusiasm and excitement for the task in hand. You enjoy helping others and are potentially very creative. You have an abundance of energy that will help you achieve your goals, also positive and self assertive you will challenge anyone who takes you for granted.

Square: There is the same amount of energy and excitement for a task as with the trine and conjunction but it is driven by a certain amount of tenseness. The energy tends to come from anger or aggressiveness rather than enthusiasm. This can be very competitive and you may feel constantly challenged, care needs to be taken that impulsiveness does not lead to accidents, as you may be careless and more accident prone. You are also inclined towards infections. You need to learn to relax and to channel your anger into more useful directions, which will help to relieve your tenseness.

Inconj: There is the same element of enthusiasm and desire to reach goals but there is an element of stress in everything that you do. Somehow it becomes more difficult to achieve your goals. You can never be truly relaxed and may feel that someone is secretly working against you most of the time. It is often difficult to harness your energies so that they fit into the pattern of your lifestyle. There may be lack of direction or assertiveness.

Oppos: This can be a fairly quarrelsome aspect that does result in a battle of wills between two people. There may be a lack of sensitivity and a need to work hard to learn consideration. There are strong desires involved here and there may be an inclination and indeed a positive joy in taking risks. There is a lack of patience and an inner restlessness that may be the cause of accidents. There is so much energy that a tendency to overwork is likely. You may need plenty of exercise to burn off your excess energy.

Sun/Jupiter Aspects

Conj: This conjunction bestows a positive and generous personality. You have an optimistic outlook and your general enthusiasm is able to motivate others. There is a tendency to go to extremes and you find it hard to hang on to your money. You have high aspirations, a good sense of humour and enjoy everything that you tackle. Your philosophical and easy going outlook makes you easy to be with.

Sext: With the sextile there may be quite a considerable intellectual ability and when opportunities comes your way you are not slow to take them up. You also have enough insight to know when something is worth the extra time to follow it through.

Trine: An easy flow of energy that brings honesty and enthusiasm and a far sighted optimism that leads you to make the right moves. Your philosophical outlook brings you many friends. Although this aspect can be deemed to be fortunate, it sometimes takes the easy or lazy way and lacks motivation. However, you do seem to attract wealth although it is not always the material kind.

Square: A tendency towards extravagance, money slides through the fingers whilst attempting to learn more control over desires. This is an aspect of extremes making a balance difficult, you are often over optimistic and possibly arrogant in your belief that nothing you do can fail. You restlessness and yearning for success can sometimes cause you to make foolish moves. You need to develop more self awareness.

Inconj: There may be a lack of confidence with this aspect with an effort made to please others. Strain caused by taking on too much, overextending yourself with too many responsibilities. In your attempt to alleviate stress you may need to watch over- indulgence with food and wine.

Opp. With the opposition there is a tendency towards greater extremes and a likelihood of promising more than you can actually produce. You may have a great deal of talent but are not quite so single-minded, so your talents can get lost along the path. You are not always one hundred percent reliable as you may not attach the same importance to tasks that others do. There may be a tendency for you to always take the easier path.

Sun/Saturn Aspects

Conj: Saturn sometimes holds down the power of the Sun and causes lack of energy and motivation so the person seems to lack confidence and fears failure. The tendency is to be more serious in nature and feel you have to work twice as hard as others to achieve your goals. However, there is the ability to conserve your energy and create a structured environment where you feel safe to pursue your objectives. Although you may have to work hard, achievements are greater, self discipline obtained will lead to personal fulfilment and greater rewards.

Sext: There are more opportunities for achievement with this aspect as you are generally practical and diligent and able to organise yourself and motivate others towards their goals.

Trine: You know how to use your energies wisely, this aspect confers practical and organisational abilities. You take responsibility easily and recognise opportunities when they come your way. You are well disciplined and work hard for success which never seems like a chore. You always conserve just enough of what you are doing so you are never caught out. You may not feel lucky but it may appear so to others as success is not difficult to achieve as you often seem to be in the right place at the right time.

Square: The square always seems to present obstacles in a persons life as though there is a barrier to success and you need to work twice as hard as others, but it is possible the sights are higher. There is a tendency for you to be extremely hard on yourself and there is often a lack of confidence, some very difficult lessons may be learned in the house of Saturn. Some favourable aspects linking the square could lessen the feeling of hardship and present more opportunities to overcome the negativity that could occur here. You need to have a more positive outlook.

Inconj: This aspect could cause stress through disorganisation and under achievement, the health could suffer if more care is not taken. You may find yourself going through unstable phases as stress increases.

Opp: There is a need to build up the self confidence or the self expression can suffer. One of the parents may be a burden or cause some difficulty in the life. You may feel you have a lot of opposition in life and that close or good friends are hard to come by. You need to love yourself a little more and not worry too much about what others think as this could block your progress. You need to find your own creativity and stop trying to compete with others and then you may find less obstacles in your path. Men find it hard to follow in fathers footsteps and women feel inadequate in some way

Sun/Uranus Aspects

Conj: You have a unique way of expressing yourself which could be considered eccentric by others. You dislike conformity, anything traditional or routine, you need to be free to follow your own path. You seek to live outside convention and are forever pursuing excitement or new ways of doing things that stimulate your ever active mind. You may not be considered to be reliable but unconventional and unpredictable never seeming to fit in with anyone else's pattern; you may feel you are isolated or a loner.

Sext: You are original and inventive and may find many opportunities in life to express these qualities. Others find you interesting and exciting and seek out your company. If you go into teaching you will be able to make your subject come alive, your enthusiasm is obvious.

Trine: Others are drawn to your personal magnetism as you are often exciting to be around. You have energy and enthusiasm and others are easily stimulated by your endless flow of ideas. Answers come easily to you and seemingly without effort, you are intuitive and have spiritual insight. You manage to find a more acceptable way of expressing your individualism. You can put your point of view across without offending the views of others. In other words, you rebel more efficiently.

Square: There is conflict and tension here within you, the desire to go beyond convention conflicts with the desire to stay within it. So you are likely to have moments of behaving in an erratic and unprincipled fashion if you do not allow for the desire to break free occasionally within your life style. If you remain conventional then it may affect your health especially your heart and nervous system. To release the tension you must give expression to both sides of your character.

Inconj: Learning to relax is important as there may be an inner restlessness that is hard to pinpoint. You need to find an occupation that allows you some freedom to express your thoughts or you will find yourself breaking out of the mould with dramatic effect.

Opp: This aspect can be more difficult than the conjunction as you appear to be pulled in two different directions and your behaviour can seem very erratic. You may appear anxious or highly strung in your efforts to balance the two extreme sides of your nature. Others may find you difficult as you can display extremely changeable behaviour. You have a strong purpose and can be very idealistic but you are more of a campaigner than a fighter, you organise and then retreat to let others do the fighting.

Sun/Neptune Aspects

Conj: This is a highly sensitive aspect of the mystic and clairvoyant. You pick up impressions from others and may easily lose your sense of identity. You need to develop techniques for grounding yourself as you may easily lose touch with reality. There is sometimes a strong need for escapism with the use of alcohol or the reading of romantic novels. You can be very creative especially if you focus on art, music or poetry. You will need to choose a career that allows full expression of your artistic and creative talents.

Sext: You are deeply aware of your creative potential and feel you have a lot to offer. Your outlet for expression could be through music, art or mysticism. You have the insight to know when a good opportunity is presented. You appear to have an unlimited source of inspiration that flows through you and will be freely given to others. Often a love of animals goes with this aspect.

Trine: You are able to express great empathy with others. Your intuition is highly developed and can be put to practical use. There is a warm emotional quality to your nature and you are always ready to listen to others in need, and are able to give them spiritual upliftment. You may be very artistically talented and should find space in your lives to give this the fullest expression. You have no great expectations of life and this gives you a quiet and easy confidence.

Square: There may be lack of confidence with this square as your faith in yourself early on in life may have been squashed by overly strict or exacting parents. There may be a tendency towards self deception as you struggle to separate the real from the unreal. There is an extraordinary imagination which goes beyond boundaries. As with most Neptune contacts there is a dislike of hurting others as the guilt can often be hard to take, so sometimes you choose deception rather than the truth.

Inconj: You are sensitive to the needs of others and may find it difficult to say no. You therefore may find yourself burdened by other peoples problems and unable to free your thoughts, there is an element of self sacrifice here. You need to establish your boundaries, what you are prepared to do and stick to it. Although you may find it difficult not to feel guilty when you say no.

Oppos: There may be confused ideals and lack of direction with the opposition. There is a lot of self doubt which sometimes causes you to back away from challenges rather than face them. You may be out of touch with reality which makes you easily deceived by others. You shy away from authority disliking any form of discipline or control. You need to establish boundaries and stay within them or you may easily be taken advantage of. At some time in your life you may find yourself seeking or giving spiritual guidance to others.

Sun/Pluto Aspects

Conj: You have a powerful ego and find it difficult to moderate your energies and desires. You may go to extremes as though you need to experience everything at the deepest level before you can finish with it. You must realise your power and your tendency to dominate all relationships, if you use this wisely there will be fulfilment and success but if it is used selfishly to further your own desires you will ultimately destroy yourselves.

Sext: This aspect has some of the capacity for regeneration as the trine, you can re-charge yourself when seizing an opportunity important to you. You are aware of your strength of will and use it in practical endeavours that will benefit all, like the trine you are interested in spiritual philosophy, meditation and yoga.

Trine: There is an inner vitality with this aspect that exudes an enormous amount of energy, these people express themselves with a fiery enthusiasm that can leave others breathless. A born leader in spiritual dimensions they can inspire others on to reach greater heights. You regenerate your energies quickly and effectively so are able to recover quickly from ailments. You are interested in all forms of self development which includes meditation and yoga. There is often some psychic and intuitive ability.

Square: This can be a wilful and forceful aspect seeking power over others which seems to follow a destructive path. This is the person who carries a chip on their shoulder and is always on the defensive which makes them attack first before they are attacked which can appear very aggressive. You are aware of the need to change but are afraid of endings. You may push others into making the changes you are afraid to make yourself. You need to concentrate more on your own transformation and let others make their own decisions, and ultimately you will achieve your dreams.

Inconj: There may be difficulties caused through inheritances or taxes and frustration in general concerning finances. You need to do things in moderation as there is a tendency to punish the body unnecessarily as you push yourself to the limit. You tend to invite conflict where none exists; you need to learn to relax.

Oppos: You may receive challenges rather aggressively as you take it as a personal affront to your abilities. You are used to exerting your influence over others and can get involved in serious conflict if they disagree. You find yourself going through great changes psycho-logically. A breakdown in your belief or support system could leave you totally demoralised and may need professional help to re-build. You need to find new ways to relax.

Moon/Mercury Aspects

Conj: With this conjunction the emotional nature affects the reasoning power so their feelings will always influence their thoughts. You are easy to get along with and always care about the feelings of others. You are likely to be very sensitive to personal criticism so therefore take a lot of care not to offend others. There will always be much concern for the family especially over health issues.

Sext: You are aware of the thoughts and feelings of others and give them consideration. You have a talent for communicating and can easily convey your meaning to others. You enjoy reading and talking and have a delightful sense of humour. You take up opportunities inside your home to expand your social circle.

Trine: This aspect often displays common sense as the energy flows easily between the mind and the feelings and is well balanced. You generally have a large circle of friends and enjoy a good social life, you are pleasant to be with as you don't dwell on negative thoughts. There is often some benefit from affairs concerning the third and fourth house, self expression comes easily where the feelings are concerned.

Square: There is a tendency to be influenced by past thoughts and experiences and you may hold on to negativity. Misunderstanding can occur due to being over sensitive to casual remarks. You may become pre-occupied with domestic issues which may often dominate your conversations. You only feel relaxed with those close to them and may have difficulty with strangers. Communication with your mother may have been strained or difficult in some way.

Inconj: A tendency to over react in any emotional issue, your thoughts can be irrational and you may have trouble sorting out personal problems. There may be communication problems with women in your life and tension may produce digestive problems. You need to learn how to manage stress and relax.

Oppos: Emotional difficulties will show in displays of nervousness and irritability. You find it hard to balance your thoughts and feelings and may often over react when something is said. You may go through phases of discussing your personal life with all whom you come into contact with, or equally they may remain silent and uncommunicative even when asked. You need to learn to balance these two extremes and then you will be more content.

Moon/Venus Aspects

Conj: This is a sensitive and affectionate placement and enables you to relate easily to others. You have a considerable amount of charm and will go out of your way not to hurt those around you. Your early years probably held pleasant memories and you may anticipate bringing the same harmony into your own home. You may have expensive tastes and there is a love of luxury.

Sext: There is a natural ease with relationships with this aspect, women tend to have all the feminine virtues and take to domesticity and men generally find they are able to empathise with the women in their life. They are likely to be extremely sociable and take up many opportunities to meet new people.

Trine: This aspect conveys a great deal of emotional and physical energy which can be applied to obtain maximum results in everything you take on. You will always find it easy to fight for what they believe in. You will put a lot of effort into their relationships so that you will be successful. You have a love of beauty and artistic talents which will benefit their homes.

Square: This is not a good aspect for relationships as it bestows a lot of tension, which perhaps developed in early childhood. Emotional problems come from not knowing what you want, a lack of calm and inner restlessness. Motherhood can bring emotional restlessness in a woman's chart and marriage can bring difficulties in a man's chart. Men may experience difficulty in settling down always believing that the grass is greener on the other side.

Inconj: Comfort may be taken by over indulging on sweet foods which could lead to health complications. You may always give in to the needs of others neglecting your own, so you need to build up their self esteem and learn to be assertive.

Oppos: There is likely to be some tension in your relationships, perhaps you are oversensitive and take offence easily over a careless remark. You find it hard to balance family responsibilities with your personal life as there is always some discord. You will need to learn to give space to your own personal needs as well as expressing your need to nurture and care for others. Your relationships with women may be strained.

Moon/Mars Aspects

Conj: This is a very fiery Moon which can tend to impatience and bursts of temper. There is a lot of energy attached to your feelings which are easily moved into action when emotionally aroused.

Actions are based on feelings rather than reason. There may have been a lot of anger surrounding you in your childhood, perhaps there were many arguments.

Sext: There is opportunity to channel the energy into a more positive mode with the sextile. This makes you a lively and energetic personality that will leap into action when challenged. There is also a tendency to react under emotional pressure but with less aggressiveness than the difficult aspects.

Trine: This aspect conveys a great deal of emotional and physical energy which can be applied to obtain maximum results in everything you take on. You will always find it easy to fight for what you believe in. You will put a lot of effort into your relationships so that they will be successful. You are likely to be healthy and robust and have an inclination towards dare-devil ventures.

Square: With many similarities to the opposition there is the same volatile nature but with more inner tension and more liability to emotional outburst. There is often arguments and disagreements on domestic issues and the inner tension this makes may lead to digestive problems, and difficulty in relaxing does not help. You are very competitive and need to succeed at all costs. You must allow others their views

Inconj: This is a restless and irritable aspect that may set you up for accidents if you do not exercise more caution. A lack of emotional control can make others wary of you. Digestive and intestinal disorders could be a problem unless you learn to channel the energies towards more positive outlets.

Oppos: Emotions can be fairly volatile with this aspect - it does not take much to move you into action either physically or verbally. You can get involved in disputes over quite trivial issues. You have an outgoing and lively personality and are quite impatient with the more cautious members of society. You need to curb the tendency towards irritability or you could lose friends.

Moon/Jupiter Aspects

Conj: The Moon conjunct Jupiter shows a fairly restless emotional nature and a need to have a certain amount of freedom within a relationship if you are going to make any sort of commitment. However, the nature is often very warm and generous and is very sociable and easy to be with. You have a good sense of humour and frequently act the clown.

Sext: The sextile bestows a cheerful and friendly nature with honesty and integrity and often considerable intellectual ability. You have strong emotional ties to the family and are able to instill them with enthusiasm, optimism and hope for the future. You have a fortunate knack of knowing when to grasp opportunities that will bring advancement.

Trine: Warm and generous personality that gives freely and easily of themselves. They are protective of their family and can give hope and optimism to all in trouble. You are a peace loving person who generally prefers an uncomplicated existence so will put a great deal of energy into solving problems.   Square: Some similarities to the opposition with a tendency towards emotional excesses. There is a greater tendency towards gambling and gaining credit with no means of repayment. You are overgenerous with funds you do not always have. You often take the easiest way out of difficult situations which often comes back on you.

Inconj: Your emotional life causes you some strain as you often take on other peoples problems. Health may suffer from over indulgence and you may find yourself involved at some time with legal problems especially connected to relationship or family difficulties that are not easily sorted out.

Oppos: There is a lack of moderation with this aspect, everything is taken to extremes. There may be over indulgence, a tendency towards extravagance and in some cases - gambling. However, you can be overly generous and especially to those who are under privileged, but the warning here is that you can be taken advantage of if you are not careful.

Moon/Satuяn Aspects

Conj: There is difficulty giving your emotions free expression, there is a tendency to attach yourself to material things as it feels safer. There is often a difficult relationship between your parents and you tend either to cut away from them early in life or you become enslaved to their needs through the latter years. With this aspect there is often lack of confidence, low self esteem and sometimes depression, but there is reliability due to the fear of letting others down.

Sext: You are patient and self disciplined and are able to make the most of opportunities when they come along. You spend time trying to understand how others are feeling and are willing to talk at length in attempts to solve emotional problems. You make a good teacher as you are able to give your knowledge in a clear and precise manner. You are ambitious and determined to make something of your life.

Trine: You are self disciplined, cautious and conservative, which probably stems from a stable and supportive background where you were taught that reliability and integrity were more important than fun. You probably have a great deal of common sense which makes up for any lack of imagination. You may not have a wide circle of friends but when you do form relationships you remain loyal and trustworthy and tend to carry on with the same friendships all through life.

Square: Similar to the opposition in that there is lack of confidence especially with the opposite sex. A tendency to cling to the past or childhood experiences as your family, especially mother is important to you and, even though you may blame mother for the way you feel, it is unlikely you will miss family events if you can help it. You rarely forget birthdays and anniversaries and you still feel you need parental support until quite late in life. You tend to work in fields that supply the same sort of support as a family.

Inconj: You may take on too many burdens that make your life dreary and stressful. You need to develop a more optimistic attitude than continually talk about how difficult life has been for you. Find ways to boost your self esteem rather than go through life feeling unworthy, or that you have nothing to offer a relationship. You need to be more positive, so that you can make achievements in life to be proud of.

Oppos: There is an emotional insecurity here which can lead to depression. A tendency to stick to past attitudes and hang on to unfulfilling relationships because it is safer to stick to the known than to explore the unknown. There is always a fear of rejection. A tendency to become a 'loner', self employment would suit you better than being responsible to others. Digestion will be a problem if you do not learn to relax or deal with the problems that cause you to worry.

Moon/Uranus Aspects

Conj: You have an unpredictable and exciting personality that is not always reliable, yet you draw people to you because they enjoy your company. Although more conservative individuals may be wary of your unpredictable emotional nature and will stay clear of any form of commitment. You are impatient with any form of restriction and will not form any personal ties that restrict your personal freedom. You may have a dislike of convention and refuse to conform to anyone else's ideals. There is a strong desire for independence and you will go to any extreme to ensure freedom.

Sext: You are eager to grasp new opportunities and deal with them in your own original way, you do things differently and always have, which may have stood you apart from others when you were younger. You are drawn to relationships that share intellectual stimulation as emotional support would not be sufficient to keep you together.

Trine: An unusual sparkling personality that captivates others, you generally mix in a wide circle of friends as variety keeps you interested. You function well in group situations where you will be a stimulating and positive member. You have an unusual imagination where ideas flow freely. Your family life seems to differ from the accepted norm in some way. You have a highly developed intuition which should be used carefully and with understanding. There may also be sudden changes of mood which creates less tension than the square.

Square: The square can show imagination and talent which are suitable for teaching or writing. Your nature tends to be erratic and impulsive and you are easily upset. Your emotions are so that you could be pursuing a different direction before others have the chance to realise that something is ending. Your impulsiveness may make you accident prone which could seem like carelessness. Partnerships are difficult for you as you expect and need plenty of freedom to express yourself in your own way. You need room to grow

Inconj: You may take on emotional burdens that commit you to a routine that is entirely unsuitable to your nature, the strain of these may lead to nervous problems. There is a restlessness about you that puts others on edge when in your company so you should endeavour to take adequate rest and relaxation.

Oppos: There are sudden and unpredictable mood changes with the opposition and this can be confusing and annoying to those close to you. Your unreliability may be so extreme that others will avoid including you in their schemes. You may have had an unusual family background. You could appear cold and remote as you find it difficult to express your true feelings. You may break relationships to fulfil your dream of pursuing excitement and adventure but very little lives up to that dream. You need to come down to earth and find other ways of making your life more exciting or you will end up lonely and bitter.

Moon/Neptune Aspects

Conj: You are a sensitive and impressionable personality with a vivid imagination. You have a strong psychic or mediumistic ability but it can be difficult to distinguish between a genuine talent and fantasy. You pick up impressions from others so easily that you need to be around positive people to avoid being pulled down as you may have a tendency towards depression. You are a romantic who loves to daydream with a strong urge to escape from some of the harsher realities of life.

Sext: There is much empathy for others and you are likely to work in a caring capacity where your strong intuition is very valuable. You are understanding of other peoples failings and handle your personal relationships with tact and warmth.

Trine: Your intuition is very keen and you express warmth and sincerity to all those who cross your path. You are imaginative and creative and put a lot of personal effort into your work. Family life is important and you have a close link to your own mother. You have a genuine compassion for those less fortunate than yourself and will go out of your way to help others.

Square: This has many similar manifestations to the opposition with more of a tendency to use drugs or alcohol as a way to avoid facing your confused emotions. Your psychic nature is less well developed and could cause you problems. Your early childhood conditioning did not prepare you to deal with the difficulties of life and you may feel you lacked parental support.

Inconj: You are sensitive and emotional and do not have a strong constitution that can take abuse. You therefore need to look after yourself by a good diet and exercise if you are not going to succumb to stress, which will ultimately affect your health.

Oppos: With the opposition you can be extremely creative and imaginative but there is some degree of emotional confusion. You create illusions in your mind and can lose touch with reality at times, there is a tendency to want to escape from reality to avoid coming to terms with your own emotional instability. Drugs or alcohol can be a means of escape but will only increase your problems. You are likely to be sensitive to all forms of medication so should take care not to exceed prescribed amounts.

Moon/Pluto Aspects

Conj: This is an intense emotional contact where you feel things deeply almost to the point of pain, 'if it does not hurt it is not real'. You have powerful feelings that can have a dramatic influence over others, but you can also be overbearing. You may be very idealistic which makes you difficult to live with. There is an attraction to spiritualism and the occult, a fascination for death, and reincarnation, with an awareness of those in spirit. You may spend much of your life alone looking for that perfect relationship that fulfils the craving to be loved by one who treads the same path.

Sext: There are more opportunities to succeed on a business and emotional level, because your feelings are more under control you are able to give more time to other things. You are a warm and caring person and others feel safe with you especially children who come under your protection.

Trine: This shows great depth of feeling and the ability to regenerate on an emotional level as well as being able to keep your feelings well under control. There is often psychic ability and you are intuitive when it comes to knowing how others are feeling. You give a strong image and people feel that you can be depended upon to care for and protect them.

Square: The square can show strong and intense feelings and a feeling of compulsiveness which makes others wary of them in a relationship. If things go wrong there is a tendency to cut off from the past which can in some ways be destructive. There is often a feeling of destiny, attack or be destroyed. Finding a balance would be helpful to avoid such extremes of behaviour.

Inconj: Difficulty letting go of the past and past habits and there is a tendency to judge the future by what happened in the past. You are sensitive to rejection and quickly feel disliked if anyone disagrees or criticises your way of doing things.

Oppos: You may be hard to get close to because of remembered pain from your past yet at the same time be possessive about those

219

you care for, there is also a strong manipulative quality. There may be an issue in your childhood that left scars and added to your insecurity. There may be considerable disharmony on a domestic level and disputes over money could cause anguish especially over inheritances. You can appear very emotional to others and very easily hurt by any hint of rejection. You need to learn to trust others in your personal relationships.

Mercury/Venus Aspects

Conj: You know how to be charming, and say the right thing at the right time, in other words you have all the social graces. You do have an easy going and gentle nature that tries to bring the best out of others. You could be very artistic and creative but generally on a literary level. Your self expression is imaginative and fresh and others find you easy to listen to, as you communicate with an easy fluency.

Sext: Similar skill to the conjunction with communication in all forms which include literary skills, you are often a pleasure to listen to with a good speaking voice and a calm and pleasant nature. There are many opportunities for success in these fields within the media.

Oppos: These planets can never form an aspect greater than 76^0 apart.

Mercury/Mars Aspects

Conj: This can convey a restless mind with a quick and sharp mentality. You are often one step ahead of everyone else and may irritate others by either interrupting or talking at the same time - but louder. You may need to learn consideration of other's viewpoints and also realise others too have something to say.

You may be curious and love to investigate mysteries. You may also come across as fairly aggressive and argumentative and you find it hard to believe you can be wrong. You enjoy being involved in conflicts and use your mind to win.

Sext: You are skilled in communicating and making yourself under-stood, you are able to get your point across in a clear and precise manner. Opportunities are found by talking to others and giving a clear indication of your needs. You are generally friendly and sociable but can be very sharp when crossed.

Trine: There is a lot of mental and creative energy with this aspect, so there is often talent but not necessarily the motivation to apply yourself, a good aspect from Saturn would be helpful here. You are quite a skilful communicator and enjoy this fact and it may sometimes be difficult for you to hold fire and enjoy some quiet moments. You can be very assertive and are unlikely to back down when challenged.

Square: This gives a similar argumentative nature as in the opposition but there is more tension involved here that makes others more wary of being involved in an argument. You may be easily aroused to anger by what others say. You need to learn to be more gracious if others disagree with you   rather than react in an aggressive and hurt manner, and remember they are also entitled to a viewpoint.

Inconj: This aspect may denote lack of judgement. You never seem to be able to say the correct thing, this can create a lot of nervous tension that can affect your health. You may easily get exhausted as you always try to do too much. You need to learn to relax and give more time to your thoughts before action.

Oppos: This is far more argumentative than the conjunction, you not only enjoy conflict but may get some satisfaction out of being antagonistic. You find it difficult to see the other persons point of view and may often change your own standpoint. You can be very talented and would be able to make the most of your talents if you were more diplomatic. You may have few friends and alienate others by not listening, being too sharp tongued and having a nervous and unreliable nature. Try to be more understanding.

Mercury/Jupiter Aspects

Conj: You have a good balance of reason and logic with an ongoing desire for knowledge so education is important to you. You are able to expand your ideas imaginatively and can put them across to others in a way that is easily understood. You are likely to find work in areas of education, philosophy or communication. At some time in your life you may also take the opportunity to advance your knowledge through travel. You have an optimistic quality and never look back, and never regret any experience that you feel has helped you grow.

Sext: A very restless mind that is always eager for new knowledge, you have foresight and judgement and excellent reasoning powers. There may be an aptitude for languages and public speaking would be a positive use of your talents as well as teaching, journalism and writing - especially connected to travel.

Trine: This is a fortunate aspect in that you absorb knowledge easily and are able to communicate in an easy and fluent fashion. You have a high integrity and are fond of the truth. You are optimistic and light hearted and are likely to have many friends as you keep them amused with your interesting and witty talent.

Square: There is a constant desire to improve the mind, you may seek one course after another. Always optimistic and striving for the ultimate, which is often unrealistic. You are always in a hurry to achieve and may lack judgement and common-sense. There may be some anxiety as you take on too much at a time.

Inconj: It may always seem difficult for you to express yourself in a way that is not mis-understood. You may experience a lot of frustration as you feel that your talents go unnoticed through lack of opportunity. Your generous nature makes you someone easily taken advantage of.

Oppos: With the opposition there is a tendency to go to extremes often promising more than you can hope to deliver. You expect too much of yourself and are often unaware of your limitations. Your thirst for knowledge is similar to the conjunction but with less motivation to pursue something through to the end thus leaving gaps in your knowledge that you may bluff your way through. You do have creative talents and if you learn to apply yourself there is more chance of success. You find it very difficult to stay in one place.

MeRcuRy/SatuRn Aspects

Conj: You are a hard worker and your thoughts tend to dwell on the more serious and practical side of life. Material things are important as they give you the sense of security you need. You work in a careful and exacting manner looking for perfection in all you do. There can also be a vast amount of tension with this aspect as you find it difficult to relax and unwind, you often see difficulties where there are none. Although there is a tendency to have a fairly logical mind, there are those with this conjunction who find the effort required is too great to achieve very real successes, in areas of education.

Sext: You are forever looking for opportunities that will enable you to make your mark in life. You are disciplined and conscientious enough to achieve success in your endeavours. Your logic gives you an aptitude towards maths and science. You are not always a social person and may at times find you are quite lonely. This may be an ideal aspect for a writer as you have the discipline and structure to finish a project.

Trine: You are well organised and able to plan ahead in a meticulous and methodical manner. You may be talented in practical ways such as skilled at making or repairing things. You are not a day dreamer, your mind is always active and constructive, everything you own must have a use. As you grow older you develop understanding and wisdom that will make you sought after for advise, and because of your reliability. Your concentration is excellent and you can be very ambitious, you have what it takes to make successful achievements in the business world. Your plans are well constructed and tend to run smoothly.

Square: You are a born worrier who lacks the scope of imagination to see beyond current difficulties. A tendency to dwell on petty trivia rather than the whole picture. If mentally depressed you will be afraid to experiment with your talents for rear of rejection. You may have experienced much criticism in your early years which has made you afraid to show exactly what you are capable of. There is much you can achieve if you adopt a more positive attitude to life and keep everything above board. Your earlier lack of encouragement may have driven you to be more underhand than you should be.

Inconj: You are over conscientious and may find yourself under a lot of strain by taking on too much. You may need to learn to say no. You feel unappreciated for your efforts and this may involve a lot of resentment when you feel that you work so hard. You need to work harder at getting more fun out of life, remember you need to regenerate your own personal energies.

Oppos: There is a tendency towards anxiety and depression always worrying about the future. There may however be considerable intellectual ability but this may not always be obvious due to lack of confidence. You can be very defensive and may be aggressive if someone criticises your ideas. You can be very rigid at times finding it difficult to let go of outworn ideas and opinions which can make you very narrow minded. The tendency towards negative thoughts may have to be consciously dealt with if you are to fulfil your potential. You need to develop flexibility.

Mercury/Uranus Aspects

Conj: You have an original if somewhat unusual mind, your thoughts are quick and changeable and others find you interesting and exciting. There is likely to be an interest in technology and science. You think objectively and rarely take sides for emotional reasons. You enjoy communication and the more bizarre the more enjoyable. There can often be a touch of genius with this conjunction as ideas flow fast and free.

Sext: Above average intelligence and a quick and active mind that is able to see an opportunity long before others. You seek knowledge and are able to impart it to others in a clear and easy to understand manner. You are attracted to the occult especially astrology and your intuition which comes in sudden flashes of inspiration makes you very talented in these fields.

Trine: There is a great deal of intuition with this aspect and a lot of original insight into the future. You have flashes of knowledge and instinctively know the right moves. There is an inner understanding of others and you make a good teacher or public speaker. You may be interested in the occult and especially astrology and you have an inner wisdom that helps you to understand these fields. You have original thoughts and ideas and are able to communicate them effectively to others. You should trust your intuition as it will help you towards a greater understanding.

Square: You have an original mind that craves stimulation and excitement. You can be an anxious or highly strung type who finds it difficult to relax. There is constant tension between the need to be active and to do things differently. Others could see you as rather eccentric or just mentally perverse - doing thing differently just for the sake of it. You may upset others through being rather sharp and abrupt and there is often a touch of arrogance when putting across your ideas. You are likely to be very talented and others find you exciting and enjoy having you around.

Inconj: You may be constantly on the go and likely to be under considerable strain through driving yourself too hard. Your enthusiasm and energy is not always consistent so you may suffer constant pangs of guilt through not finishing what you began. To ease the strain, you need to learn to conserve your energies.

Oppos: You have original ideas and may try to force them on to others so strong is your belief in yourself. You need to take care this does not appear to be arrogant in the eyes of others who may see your ideas as 'way out' or eccentric. You find it difficult conforming and may find group situations difficult as it is hard for you to not stand out in a crowd. There is a tendency for you to 'waste' energy and feel depleted.

MeRcuRy/Neptune Aspects

Conj: You are likely to be very sensitive and impressionable with a vivid imagination. There can be a tendency to daydream and live in your own fantasy world. You often find it hard to see the reality of a situation and can often deceive yourself as well as others.

You may possess unusual clairvoyant abilities and be very talented artistically. You may have exceptional creative and literary talents but suffer from confused ideals or uncertainty of life direction at various times in your life.

Sext: You can be very perceptive and use your intuition and insight to take up all opportunities that come along. You are warm and sociable and have much empathy with others. You should make use of your creative inspiration by writing or painting and seeking higher education so that you can channel your talents into more constructive areas.

Trine: You are a warm and friendly person who shows a great deal of empathy to those you are in close contact with. You may be extremely creative and artistically talented with a love of art, music and poetry. Your imagination is vivid and if it can be captured on paper it would be a successful outlet for your creative mind. Your sensitive mind shows you are easily hurt by others and feel very uncomfortable in discordant, sordid or harsh conditions.

Square: There is some tension between your thoughts and your dreams that makes your goals unrealistic. You are afraid of responsibility and when faced with the harsh realities of life, seek to escape. You may be susceptible to drugs that alter the mind or enable you to escape into fantasy. You are very creative and would do well to explore your artistic talents. Others may find you unreliable and erratic with your mind always away in the clouds, or following a new fantasy.

Inconj: You find it difficult to express your creative urges and feel under a constant strain to explore your potential. You have limited physical energy and must take care not to overdo things. You may easily deceive yourself in believing that you are doing the right thing, trust your intuition it is probably more accurate.

Oppos: Very imaginative and creative but can be deceitful and elusive. Others may find you hard to pin down and mistrust develops through your unreliability. You may be unrealistic about your goals. You may be seeking peace and tranquillity but this often eludes you as you get caught up in a web of confusion that is difficult to extricate yourself from. Do not get so involved in things you are unable to deal with, you can be very gullible and easily misled.

MeRcuRy/Pluto Aspects

Conj: You have a deep and penetrating mind that is curious to the extreme, you enjoy solving mysteries. You would make a good detective or private investigator. You can be mentally overpowering, try to avoid forcing your ideas or beliefs on to others. You can be very confident in your own beliefs and are able to pursue your objectives with great determination. If someone crosses you, you are likely to think long and hard of ways in which to take revenge.

Sext: You have a penetrating insight into business affairs and have a natural aptitude for handling finances. You have good timing and your intuition tells you when to make the right moves. You have a keen analytical mind which will uncover many clues to solve a problem or mystery, nothing baffles you for long. You are persistent and determined to succeed in all you do.

Trine: You have a powerful mind with good powers of concentration, this coupled with determination can be a very formidable formula to success. Your mind is particularly intuitive with a natural aptitude for psychology. You want to know how other peoples minds work. You love mysteries and could use your own special talents in writing, or perhaps medicine, engineering or as a financial advisor. You can be very persuasive in influencing the minds of others.

Square: There is a tension with the square and this can result in quite cutting or abrupt speech. There is a tendency to be rather suspicious of the motives of others and you may be permanently on guard ready to counter-act any adversary. You may find it difficult to concentrate or study, even more so when you were younger and schoolwork seemed rather tedious. You can sometimes be quite intolerant of others and seek to manipulate their lives to your own advantage.

Inconj: You are driven to succeed and in your efforts you put too much physical strain on your body and your mind. You must learn to take things more in your stride or you will become very anxious and your nervous system may let you down. Take some time to relax and have fun.

Oppos: There is often mental anxiety with this aspect, you may often find opposition to your ideas and feel you have to fight to achieve. You can be very arrogant when dealing with others as you are convinced of your own intellectual superiority. There may be problems in relationships if you refuse to compromise as others may get tired of your control. You may become argumentative when others disagree, you may have to learn to meet them halfway.

Venus/Mars Aspects

Conj: This aspect shows a strong desire nature that can at times be aggressive and demanding depending on whether Venus or Mars is stronger. The sexual side although passionate can show a lack of refinement. This aspect alone is not good for lasting relationships yet can be possessive while it lasts.

There is a certain amount of self centredness when Venus comes into contact with Mars or Aries, it does not necessarily show lack of consideration just an awareness of your own needs before others.

228

Sext: This aspect conveys lots of sex appeal, you are a warm and affectionate personality and create harmony within your relationships. You have a positive outlook and look for co-operation within your relationship.

Trine: You are a cheerful fun loving person who enjoys a 'good time'. You have lots of sex appeal and attract the opposite sex easily. There may be creative talents in either art or music which you will pursue as an interest. You are fairly flexible and easy going and need to be careful others do not take advantage of this.

Square: There may be some tension here with the way you use your energies as you tend to be very emotional within your relationships which causes friction. There is some difficulty in maintaining harmony as you do not always show others the same consideration you expect from them.

Inconj: There are sometimes difficulties in relationships, you seem to be attracted to people who are difficult for you to get along with, so there is much strain which can lead to health problems of a nervous nature.

Oppos: There is some similarity with the conjunction in that the desire nature is strong but there is more of a tendency to be hurt by others due to your emotional encounters. There seems to be a tendency to attract aggressive partners who draw you in to arguments concerning finances and sexual matters. You have a great deal of sex appeal yet find it difficult to include harmony in your relationship. There is often a discontentment that shows in your relationships. There is a tendency to argue or seek power over anyone who is involved with you.

Venus/Jupiter Aspects

Conj: In Taurus and Libra weight is often a problem. You are very sociable, you enjoy meeting people and are seen as someone who creates harmony and a pleasant atmosphere. There is a tendency to be a social-eater, the sign that this conjunction falls in will indicate the extreme to which the social-eating goes, in other words whether you have weight problems. You need material comforts and probably had an indulgent childhood and find it difficult not to go to excesses in everything you do including your love life.

Sext: There is much to gain through your relationships with others, opportunities come your way through the people you meet. There tends not to be any financial problems, generally your home is comfortable if not luxurious. Money is not one of your worries, as there are likely to be many financial opportunities.

Trine: A happy, cheerful and optimistic nature, also you have a talent for handling relationships, making people feel at ease and relaxed. You are the type who is always invited to parties because you are able to circulate and make everyone feel welcome. One of your best talents is dealing with the public with comparative ease as others find you very charming. There is still a likelihood of overindulgence especially when relaxed and in a lighter frame of mind.

Square: There is much of the opposition with this aspect such as self indulgence, vanity and laziness. There is an added tenseness to the situation which will make you more persistent in achieving as much as you can with as little effort as possible. There is a lot you can achieve as your nature can be very pleasant, you need to learn to put others first sometimes and be a little more sincere in your dealings. There may be a problem with your weight if you continue to be self indulgent.

Inconj: You tend to allow yourself to be taken advantage of by others as you are often defensive in your relationships. You use your energies unwisely and often feel exhausted, you need to build up your physical strength and learn to relax properly to avoid mental strain.

Oppos: You tend to seek approval from others for everything you do and are always seeking attention. You can be rather overindulgent in what you eat, and may also waste money on needless luxuries. You need to be more careful about sticking to the truth as you tend to exaggerate or bend the truth to fit your situation. There can be a certain amount of laziness and vanity with this aspect, you expect to use your charm and attractiveness to get others to do things for you. There is a likelihood of many love affairs.

Venus/Saturn Aspects

Conj: This can be an ambitious aspect where material achievements can take on great importance. There is often some difficulty with relationships and in a female chart there may be some problems with the father who may have been missing from their earlier life for one reason or another. Women may also be out of touch with their femininity and feel unloved or unappreciated. Men may display a rather aggressive or superior attitude to the women in their lives. However, this aspect can be fortunate for the artistic as Saturn gives structure and form to creativity, this can be helpful to artists and musicians.

Sext: With the sextile you often find the opportunity to express your creative skills. You know what you want from life and are able to go after it, however, you are often willing to give up your own happiness for the sake of someone else's. You shoulder responsibility well and like the trine you make a loyal and conscientious friend especially in times of trouble.

Trine: Any contact from Saturn to Venus can make you more serious and reserved but it also gives great loyalty and consideration to friendships. You are self disciplined and tolerant to the needs of others. You should always follow some creative pursuit as it is a way to enable you to relax and ease out the tension of daily living. There is a tendency to feel loneliness acutely even when you are with a crowd something seems to set you apart.

Square: There is a lot of tension with the square. You feel uncomfortable relating to others as you feel they judge you harshly. It is hard for you to relax and let go when with others and you may be seen as being cold and unyielding. There may be difficulty with authority figures as you may be too easy to push around, you need to learn to be more assertive. You may only feel secure with someone older than yourself especially one who is materially sound.

Inconj: Too many responsibilities can create a strain, especially as you take your relationships seriously expecting to put more in than others. Your low self esteem makes you feel others are more worthy. You need to learn to raise your self worth and be more assertive, remember you are worthy of being an equal partner, don't listen too much to others.

Oppos: This is a difficult aspect for relationships especially marriage, there is often an attraction to a vastly different age group which can have problems of its own. It is unlikely you will marry young as you may spend a large part of your youth being misunderstood which leads to emotional frustration. There is a tendency to under-value yourself and believe others find you lacking in some way. You need to build up your confidence by looking at your good qualities and pushing them forward. There may be some difficulties with the father later in life that needs to be overcome.

Venus/Uranus Aspects

Conj: This conjunction often makes for popularity as you have a bright sparkling personality that draws others to you, there is a quality of excitement around you that others want to share in. You are popular. You do have problems with commitment, you like variety and have a wide circle of friends, personal freedom is important to you. You would be unwise to involve yourself in routine or monotonous work as you need constant stimulation. There is a wilful side to your nature that enjoys taking risks for the fun of it.

Sext: This aspect also bestows sex appeal there is an unpredictable quality that the opposite sex will find exciting. You can be highly original on an artistic level, but you may also be interested in computers or other modern technology. You have a highly intuitive nature that is able to take advantage of any opportunities that come along.

Trine: You have an unusual zest for life, you enjoy surprises and unexpected situations and you can be a very surprising person yourself. You have a lot of sex appeal and have no trouble in attracting the opposite sex. You are sociable, optimistic and enjoy a wide circle of friends. There may be some degree of artistic talent that follows an unusual or original path. Romantic and sensitive you enjoy many and varied relationships. You are never short of ideas or things to do.

Square: Your emotions can be very changeable so that others are not sure where they stand with you, the strength of this depends upon the sign placement, as mutable signs tend towards more fickleness. You are very sociable and friendly but avoid commitment as you like a variety of different people and commitment to one person would not be stimulating enough. You can express a very nervous and anxious personality too restless to settle into any one task comfortably.

Inconj: You enjoy communicating with others but often feel taken advantage of, you can be very impulsive and erratic and often misread other peoples intentions. You need to learn to take things in your stride as you can become over anxious when things are not going according to plan.

Oppos: There is a greater unpredictable element with the opposition that can make others rather wary of you in that they are never certain how you will react. Your nature can often be very perverse or wilful, you often desire to create a reaction. You have a strong desire for personal freedom that makes partnerships very difficult and in some cases impossible. To establish a permanent relationship you will need to make compromises. If you are restricted or restrained too much you may become emotionally unstable.

Venus/Neptune Aspects

Conj: You are a romantic and very sensitive to undercurrents in your relationships. There is a deceptive quality here as you are so sensitive to hurting others that you are inclined either to bend the truth so you do not upset them, or become very evasive and make the avoidance of answering a question a work of art. You enjoy harmony and are very unsettled if you encounter bad feeling, because you are so easy going you may also invite deception as others will easily take advantage of you. Your idealism in relationships could lead to unhappiness.

Sext: You can be very intuitive and may also have a calming influence on those you come into contact with. You may be thought of as gentle and kindly in nature and always seeking to maintain a harmonious balance in relationships. You may have high expectations of a romantic nature and could be easily disappointed.

Trine: This aspect can show a lot of creative talent which may be particularly inspired by music and dance and occasionally art. You are a romantic who dislikes a sordid environment and who is not made for hard physical work. You have a gentle harmonious quality that soothes others. You have a great motivation towards leisure pursuits preferring pleasure to work. Can appear 'other-worldly'.

Square: You are very defensive and easily hurt by slights imagined or otherwise, you are not a particularly good judge of character and can be easily deceived. You have a strong urge to retreat into your own private fantasy world and are susceptible to addiction especially with drugs or alcohol. Positively you are very intuitive and have a strong creative ability that could be spiritually fulfilling for you.

Inconj: You are sensitive and vulnerable to the harsher aspects of life which can cause you a considerable amount of stress and strain. You are so eager to please and help others that you are easily taken advantage of. Use your creative talents which will make you more relaxed and in touch with yourself.

Oppos: You can be over idealistic with a vivid imagination that runs riot when under stress. You sometimes open yourself up to disappointment partly because of your unrealistically high expectations. Once someone has betrayed your trust you find it very difficult to believe in anyone again, mutual respect must build up slowly. You have a very sensitive nature that can look towards escapism when under stress. Drugs and alcohol should be steered clear of as it would be difficult for you to break a habit once begun.

234

Venus/Pluto Aspects

Conj: You tend to have very intense and passionate relationships, you have a great deal of charisma and others are attracted to you like a magnet. This can be a very dramatic conjunction and you enjoy playing out a drama through your relation-ships. You are always able to get a deep response from others and positively you can regenerate or breathe new life into a relationship. However, it is always possible that relationships can be short-lived so there may be many 'endings' in your life, but although this may be painful it is a learning process. Often you are the one to end things.

Sext: You may be very creative and you may use either art or drama as a way to express your creativity. You are very perceptive and alert to any opportunities that may come your way. When you are set on a project you follow it with great perseverance and determination.

Trine: There is a magnetic quality to your personality that is very attractive to others. When you fall in love it is with great passion and depth and you need a partner who can respond to you in the way that is fulfilling. There may be a tendency to psycho analyse everything as you always seem to be looking for reasons, this is okay as long as it doesn't become an obsession.

Square: Like the opposition there is a karmic or fated quality about your relationships. There is often some financial consideration to falling in love, you need security through Venus the natural ruler of Taurus. However, your emotions are deep and you have very intense desires. There may be a major upheaval in your life that leads to a spiritual regeneration in some way.

Inconj: The intensity of your relationships often puts you under stress and you may often need to get away and be alone to find out your true feelings. You are inclined to put yourself out for others and frequently end up disappointed by their lack of appreciation.

Oppos: There are likely to be very passionate sexual relationships in your life that can be quite devastating. In similarity to the conjunction there may be many endings but often with the opposition they can be more painful, as you always seem to be torn between two people or situations. You are intensely emotional and may attract partners who are wrong for you or who may simply be undesirable. There seems to be a karmic feel to all relationships in that they were 'meant' and in some way unavoidable where much is learnt through the contact.

Mars/Jupiter Aspects

Conj: There is a great deal of energy and enthusiasm with this aspect but there is a lack of moderation. You think big and are inclined to take on more tasks than most people would care to handle. You enjoy being recognised for what you do and will always endeavour to be in the public eye. You are positive and open and are quick to make decisions, but can tend to be rather reckless.

Sext: You are likely to be considerably talented, you are bright and resourceful and work hard to help those less fortunate. You communicate well and know how to assert yourself when the need arises. Your impulsiveness combined with the tactlessness of Jupiter can make you rather blunt at times but you respect the truth and tend to stick to it regardless of the consequences.

Trine: You are enthusiastic and optimistic about everything you do. Although you do not anticipate failure you have a philosophical nature that sees you through any adversity. You have a knack for being in the right place at the right time when opportunities are thick on the ground.

You may be deeply religious and can gain much wisdom and insight from your beliefs. You have a sense of freedom that inspires you to travel.

Square: There is much restlessness with the square that is looking for constant activity and stimulation, and there is always a great deal of tension and you can be extremely impatient. You like to be admired for your physical endeavours and can be reckless to the extreme if challenged. You are extremely competitive and can feel threatened by others who challenge you. Your disregard for safety can make you accident prone.

Inconj: There is some difficulty when dealing with others as your competitive nature always feels threatened by them. A high degree of nervous tension makes it difficult for others to feel easy when you are around. You may make a bad loser and be irritated by others who never seem to acknowledge failure.

Oppos: You enjoy a challenge and have enough physical energy to succeed at most tasks. However there is a tendency to go to extremes. You can be very extravagant to the point of being wasteful and may need to learn moderation in all things. You have a restless nature that may be expressed through travel where you can relinquish responsibility.

Mars/Saturn Aspects

Conj: You are able to conserve energy and use it constructively although at times you may not feel you are moving forward as fast as you would like to. You may have a rather rigid attitude to life tending to stick with earlier beliefs, it would be more beneficial on a health level if you learned to be more flexible. Life often seems quite difficult and you occasionally feel some resentment towards those who appear to have it easy. You may have been known to resort to physical violence when challenged or you may attract it towards yourself.

Sext: You have a great deal of discipline to achieve your goals, you apply your intellect with physical strength to get things done. You do things in a practical and efficient way using only meagre resources as any extravagance is alien to your nature.

Trine: You shoulder responsibility well and have good authority, people work well under you as you are fair and able to teach others to do things effectively without getting angry. You can be shrewd in business affairs and highly ambitious and your talents seem to know no limits. Others like you and you get along well with them as they respect your authority. You persevere with much strength in stressful situations. You are ambitious and work hard to achieve your goals.

Square: This can be similar to the opposition with much inner tension and you may feel that your way to success is constantly blocked which creates incredible frustration. This is not a particularly compassionate aspect as you are unlikely to give any assistance to others unless you are going to receive something in return. Work may often be dangerous and you need to be constantly alert to avoid injury or other hazards which affect your health.

Inconj: Relationships may be difficult as you are easily taken advantage of. You need to be more assertive and develop your own self esteem. Past accidents may give health problems later in life with bones or joints developing arthritic conditions.

Oppos: You have a challenging nature with a desire for personal freedom that makes you difficult to live with as you cannot fit into anyone else's order. You stick stubbornly to your own beliefs and refuse to listen to others. You want your own way and often use any means to achieve it. You may need to be wary of inviting violence when this aspect is triggered by transits. Your energy tends to fluctuate so that at times you can be extremely lethargic and at others full of vitality. You may hold anger in and find it difficult to release.

Mars/Uranus Aspects

Conj: You have an energy field that almost crackles, it is impossible for you to enter a room without others noticing. You are impulsive, quick moving with rather erratic swings of interest. Your attention span is fairly limited unless your interest is caught by something fairly unusual and innovative. You dislike rules and routine and find it impossible to stick to either. You often feel you stand outside the law. Accidents are likely through carelessness and lack of concern for safety.

Sext: You have a restless impulsive nature and find it hard to relax, you are always on edge awaiting the next opportunity. There may be some talent for mechanics or electronics and mathematical ability. You rebel against old systems and are forever finding new ways of doing things.

Trine: You are enthusiastic and resourceful in all you do your ideas may have a touch of genius and you always seem to be living on the verge of an exciting discovery. Freedom to follow your intuition is important to you as any restraints block your creativity. You are likely to be popular as friends find you exciting and interesting to be with.

Square: This can show a rather reckless nature that finds excitement pursuing dangerous sports. You enjoy a challenge and winning. You do have a stubborn and perverse side to your nature that often disagrees for the sake of it. You are impatient with those slower than yourself and may expect too much from others at times, not everyone has your energy.

Inconj: You always seem to be under pressure that causes strain in your life so that you never feel relaxed. You seem to be driven to prove yourself in some way. You dislike criticism and will go out of your way to prove others wrong.

Oppos: You have a challenging nature with a desire for personal freedom that makes you difficult to live with as you cannot fit into anyone else's order. You stick stubbornly to your own beliefs and refuse to listen to others. You want your own way and often use any means to achieve it. You may need to be wary of inviting violence or accidents when this aspect is triggered by transit. Try to use this energy positively when you can achieve a great deal.

Mars/Neptune Aspects

Conj: You are driven by impulses which may be unrealistic and this makes life more complicated. You are easily deceived by your own imagination as it is difficult for you to see a situation clearly.

You have a magnetic quality that draws others to you, yet you may often be hurt through your romantic entanglements. You do not often possess a large store of energy so, can often feel tired and listless if you don't take adequate rest. On the positive side you are very sensitive and intuitive.

Sext: You are sensitive and intuitive with a great deal of potential in bringing enjoyment and pleasure to others whether through the entertainment world or the caring profession. You are generally honest and know and accept your limitations, you have a social awareness and a sense of responsibility towards others.

Trine: You have a strong psychic energy which may be used for healing others. You are sympathetic and compassionate and much of your energy is used to help others. You are extremely sensitive to your surroundings and the moods of others. There is a dramatic side to your nature so you may seek the limelight at some time in your life. You have a fertile imagination and a sense of drama, you enjoy the theatre.

Square: There is some difficulty with keeping your energies consistent with the square, there may be intense activity followed by complete apathy which creates a lot of tension in your life. You find it hard to be assertive as you may have learnt that it was wrong during early childhood. You need to mix with positive people and avoid any negative influence which could evolve from misuse of drugs or alcohol.

Inconj: You find personal relationships difficult as it is hard for you to give too much commitment, you need personal and sexual freedom but this may also cause you guilt problems. There is much sensitivity and you may be particularly susceptible to infection, so take good care of yourself.

Oppos: There is a conflict of feelings with this aspect depending on the sign placements. There is an aggressive desire nature which is strongly emotional and a lot of your motivations can operate on an unconscious level. It is advisable to stay away from mind altering drugs and alcohol as it is easy for you to lose touch with reality and live in the world of illusions. You need to be open and honest in all your dealings as it is too easy to slip into deceptive ways or simply be misunderstood.

Mars/Pluto Aspects

Conj: This is an intense aspect with a lot of power and energy that would make you a force to reckon with. There can be more than one way of using this aspect, at its best it can show leadership qualities and a spiritual nature that could benefit all humanity. At its lowest level there may be violence towards others or drawn towards the self and possible criminal tendencies. Which ever level this operates on there is a fearless nature which can show great courage in the face of danger. However, there is an extremely strong emotional nature.

Sext: You have strong desires and are actively engaged in pursuing them. You strengthen the body by disciplining the mind and may be intolerant of the weakness in others. There will be many opportunities in life to use your physical talents.

Trine: You have remarkable control over your energies with the trine and you have the ability to regenerate and transform your energies so that you can become a dynamic force for change. You can be fearless in defending your rights and the rights of those unable to fend for themselves. There is a strong spiritual nature which enables you to survive most crises. You have plenty of confidence and work hard towards achievement on a personal level.

Square: You can be very forceful and direct but may have an obsession with controlling others which could turn to anger and aggression if someone goes against you. There is enormous frustration if things do not go right, there is a tendency to lack direction which adds to your disorganised life. You may be attracted to violence in that you are inclined to use it to prove a point. If you have a personal cause you are more inclined to use violence than intellect and friendly persuasion.

Inconj: You are constantly driven to satisfy your desires be they sexual or mental, you need to keep your body in good working order to keep up your pace. You need to learn to relax and take time out it will do wonders for your health.

Oppos: There is the possibility of attracting violence with this aspect especially if you fear your response to aggression. If other areas of your chart show control then you are one who will fight in defence and not back down from a challenge and may even find it exhilarating. You have an intense and dominating nature and can easily gain control over others, misuse of this or an obsession for power could bring about your downfall. However, positive use of these energies and adhering to a spiritual path could benefit all those you come in contact with.

Jupiter/Saturn Aspects

Conj: These two planets are diverse in nature and careful balance between the two is needed to get the best out of this conjunction. Jupiter is to do with expansion to the point of excess and Saturn is to do with limitation to the point of real restriction, depending on which planet is the stronger will show how this aspect will manifest. Positively there will be a good balance so these two planets compliment each other rather than counteract.

Sext: You use your carefully gathered knowledge to make the best use of all opportunities that come your way. You have good business qualities that are coupled with honesty and integrity in all your dealings and this commands respect. You are always willing to give help to others less fortunate but you do expect some measure of self help as you have little tolerance for laziness.

Trine: The trine shows on even balance of energies, you can be serious and disciplined at the right time yet understand the need for growth through new enterprises.

There may be a strong religious philosophy that sees you through difficult times. You use your energies carefully and wisely so you have a greater chance of success. There is a good business sense if used wisely, as careful planning can take you far.

Square: You may feel something is blocking your road to success as you seem to encounter many difficulties in your business or financial affairs. You may need to learn to be more flexible and avoid rigid or monotonous routine that kills your creativity and may lead to depression. Try pursuing more long term goals but with a more philosophical attitude towards success.

Inconj: You may take on too many responsibilities that become too much of a strain in your health and could lead to anxiety and digestive disturbances. You need to learn to value yourself more and not push yourself to prove your worth.

Oppos: You may at times feel a sense of inadequacy with this aspect, it is possible that it may have been difficult to achieve a satisfactory education which leaves you doubting your self worth. There may be problems with relationships, you can be irresponsible finding the burden of responsibility too limiting. There may also be difficulties with the law if all your dealings are not kept above board.

Jupiter/Uranus Aspects

Conj: You are interested in different schools of thought and can be quite philosophical but if your interest lies in religious philosophy then it is unlikely to be orthodox. You have a lively and restless mind that is continually changing and searching for new directions of thought.

Sext: This is a fairly positive aspect where you view the future with hope and optimism. You have a kindly and friendly nature that wins you a wide circle of friends, where you enjoy a meeting of the minds. You may experience sudden insights and periods of good fortune.

Trine: You are creative and imaginative and very talented in many ways. You must learn to trust in your intuition which can work in short flashes of inspired thought. You like to be free to follow your own train of thought and dislike any sort of personal restriction. You are a warm and generous person to whom travel will give an added fulfilment to your life.

Square: You may be enthusiastic in all you do but you can be very erratic and tend to lack structure. There is a wanderlust nature that leaves unfinished business in the urge to follow new adventures. Friends may be unpredictable and unreliable and you may be let down many times in your life before you learn not to leave others to finish your business.

Inconj: You have great expectations and tend to push yourself beyond the limits. You need to learn moderation so that your body can avoid the strain of doing everything to excess. Your hopes for the future may be unrealistic and difficult to attain.

Oppos: This is more of a restless aspect but with the same degree of enthusiasm and optimism. The restlessness may bring financial difficulties as you tend to lack moderation and staying power. You are attracted to groups that are unconventional in their philosophy.

Jupiter/Neptune Aspects

Conj: This is a very sensitive and idealistic aspect that does not necessarily indicate any practical aptitude or any common sense. You may be a little bit careless or a little bit scatty. You can be very impressionable and maybe a typical candidate for getting caught up in a religious cause where someone else does your thinking for you. This can be particularly attractive to you as you maintain a lot of trust and faith and belief in promises. However, you can be very creative and this would be beneficial to you if developed along a more structured path.

Sext: Like the trine you are imaginative and intuitive and you look for ways in which to express your creative side. Your imagination is such that you may consider writing for a living especially with a good aspect from Mercury. You have a tendency to believe in people and so may open yourself up to some form of deception.

Trine: This is a very sensitive and intuitive aspect where at some time in your life you are likely to be attracted towards a spiritual path. You have great compassion for others and may spend some time working amongst those less fortunate than yourself, in hospitals or institutions. You have a wonderful imagination and a talent for gathering knowledge. You have a philosophical or religious nature and a deep understanding of the mystical side of life. You are generally calm and reflective and believe in romance. The negative side of this aspect is an inclination to laziness, over indulgence and escapism.

Square: All aspects from Jupiter to Neptune seem to bestow impractical and undisciplined natures, but the square creates more tension with more difficulty to balance. So there seems to be more of a tendency to overdo everything, to go to extremes and over extend yourself and it may fluctuate with periods of laziness and self indulgence. You find it difficult to say no to others and may often be taken for granted. You have a kind and sympathetic nature and are always able to respond to one who is in trouble. You need to make extra effort to keep your feet on the ground.

Inconj: There is some difficulty between your thoughts and your feelings. You tend to take on too much for others that results in putting you under stress and because you are such an emotional person you feel your obligations deeply and you push yourself harder than most to fulfil them.

Oppos: The opposition finds you pulled in two different directions so that you often make promises that you cannot keep, but when made the intention is there. You are not particularly practical and may have rather scattered thoughts at times so it is not a favourable aspect for business or any financial involvement. There is more tendency to follow the mystical side of life with the opposition or to follow a spiritual path, although care must be taken that this is not used as a form of escapism. There is always a danger from drugs and alcohol.

Jupiter/Pluto Aspects

Conj: You are likely to be very talented but most importantly you will have determination and persistence to bring about any goals by concentration on achievement. You are likely to be interested in meditation, psycho-logy, clairvoyance and any other spiritual dimension. You are self motivated and eager for success and warmly attracted to other successful people. You have a lot of energy and can be very persuasive and influential. Make sure you use this power wisely.

Sext: Like the trine you should trust in your intuition which can give you penetrating insights into problematical situations. You may find many opportunities in the world of finance to express your creative energies. Your intuitive insights will help you in the business world to make a success. You have an unlimited reserve of inspiration and a philosophical attitude that keeps your feet on the ground.

Trine: This is a creative and powerful aspect that helps you to know instinctively what is wrong in any situation. You have an inner sense knowing the right path to take which give you excellent judgement in business situations. You have a good grasp of the abstract and may be interested in mysticism. You have a tremendous reserve of energy and are able to regenerate yourself with enthusiasm. Meditation may be a real source of inspiration for you. You have many opportunities to grow through the changes that life presents to you.

Square: With the square there is a tendency towards being rather rebellious, to go outside the laws of the land and be quite wilful in your determination to carry things out. You tend to see life on a rather grand scale, you are not one to be satisfied with small goals. Your biggest problems may be the tendency towards less than ethical dealings, you can be tempted by large financial rewards that require very little effort, and are less than legal. Your romantic interests may be connected to business but unless you learn to live life more honestly the future may hold an empty feel to it.

Inconj: There is a tendency to be rather self oriented with this aspect, not wishing to help others unless there is something in it for yourself. You are afraid of being taken for granted and may be overly aggressive or defensive which will cause some strain in your relationships.

Oppos: You have an instinctive desire to manage the lives of those around you however, there is a genuine desire to help others with their problems. But your difficulty is thinking that you know the answer to their problems better than they do themselves. Even if in some cases that may be right, others have the right to choose their own path. You could become quite a crusader for social injustices as you speak with confidence and command the respect of others.

Saturn/Uranus Aspects

Conj: This can give the ability to give form to your creative ideas and inspiration but the constructive use of this conjunction does depend upon other aspects in the chart as these two planets are very diverse in nature. If they conflict then the Saturn will curb the inspiration of Uranus, or Uranus may threaten the security of Saturn which can leave you feeling very uncomfortable indeed. Working in a balanced way this conjunction can give you a tremendous drive to succeed and make the best use of your talents.

Sext: You have a lot of self discipline and work efficiently towards your goals. You have the insight to know a good opportunity when it comes along and the discipline and structure to follow it through. You relate more easily to those who are interested in intellectual development and may enjoy working in a group situation.

Trine: Again like the conjunction you will make practical use of your inspirational ideas. The easy flow of energy between these two planets provides a good balance for innovative business. You have tremendous insight and the discipline to see it through. Areas where you can apply your talents are astrology, mathematics, science and research. Insight combined with practicality and common sense can be a very formidable force to success.

Square: The square always brings some inner conflict, in this area it is between your desire for freedom or more radical tendencies and the more traditional fanned conservative side. You may fear being stuck in a rut as you may also fear the lack of security. This creates a tension of indecision as you need to find an outlet where you can express both of these qualities. You may need to learn to flow with life more easily and go with the changes that will inevitably occur.

Inconj: Here you have the difficulty in knowing how to prioritise so you may find yourself resisting change however much you dislike being stuck in a rut. You need your freedom and yet you are afraid of change and this may make your life more stressful than it need be.

Oppos: The opposition is the more difficult of the Saturn Uranus contacts as these two qualities may pull you in two different directions. At one time needing or wanting freedom and on the other hand perhaps having to face up to responsibilities which ultimately makes it difficult to obtain any security in your life. There may be many irritable moods as you try to balance these two diverse natures. You need to find ways of counteracting the enormous frustration that could build up.

Saturn/Neptune Aspects

Conj: In general Saturn conjunct Neptune helps to give some construction to ideas and inspiration that come through Neptune. You will be able to develop your creative powers into more concrete expression which can be a very positive force. But if Saturn and Neptune have difficult aspects, depression and anxieties could arise; which could create rather fanciful imaginations that produce

248

a great deal of fear into the unknown or when dealing with unknown. It would be wise to avoid drugs or alcohol or any serious escapist tendencies when under any stress.

Sext: Like the trine you have ability to turn your inspired thought into a practical form. You have many talents and are good at seeking opportunities in which to express them. This is a particularly good aspect for career potential as you tend to be efficient and well organised and have a sixth sense for knowing which way to go.

Trine: This is a good aspect for meditation as it conveys concentration with imagination and inspiration. You can be skilful at using your intuition especially concerning business projects. You have the discipline to turn your imagination into the written word and you enjoy analysing mysteries. You can be very thorough and perceptive, and this talent can be used to your advantage not only in the business world but counselling and helping others less fortunate.

Square: With the square there may be a genuine fear of responsibility, perhaps due to a sense of inadequacy in dealing with situations. You tend to be over anxious about situations outside your control and you seem to attract those who work against you in secret. You need to learn to love yourself more and to look more carefully at why you fear failure. You are as talented and have as much potential as others but you must learn to relax and be less anxious about self expression.

Inconj: The fears and anxieties that you develop may contribute towards psychosomatic illnesses and difficult to diagnose problems. You need professional help and should not subject yourself to self diagnosis or self treatments. You should learn to relax to avoid becoming physically and mentally exhausted.

Oppos: With the opposition between Saturn and Neptune there is often a fear of letting go and a lack of trust in the unknown. You dislike competition even though you may be fairly ambitious. You need to be very careful not to deal in underhand methods but keep everything open and above board. You can be very suspicious of others which may create a strain on your relationships. You are susceptible to depressive moods with a tendency to suffer from illnesses that are difficult to diagnose or of a psychosomatic nature.

Saturn/Pluto Aspects

Conj: There is often a desire for power with this aspect but the tone of the chart will show whether it is used for the benefit of yourself or others. You are likely to be fairly ambitious and there is often a desire to be in a position of power. Your plans are often carefully structured and you have a good organising ability. You have the patience and the determination to take advantage of your own special talents.

Sext: The sextile gives good business acumen; the ability to organise and work systematically towards your goals. You tend to be ambitious and plan your path carefully and you may need to learn to be a bit more tolerant. Security may be important to you and there is tendency to work in financial situations.

Trine: The trine gives you a tremendous amount of will power and determination to pursue your objectives. You are considerate of other people and can work purposefully in the service of others. You may be attracted to positions that deal with finances or taxes. You eventually seek a position of power which may be in an advisory capacity to others for financial issues.

Square: There is much of the opposition in the square but with more tension surrounding it. You may also feel victimised and tend to be defensive as you lack security. You desire a more powerful position in life and can be envious of those who have had the things that you have been denied. You may resort to rather extreme measures to attain your goals.

Inconj: There is a sense of inadequacy with this aspect that may lead to periods of depression as you feel that some of your ambitions are blocked. You may feel taken advantage of in your personal relationships and go out of your way to avoid others dominating you.

Oppos: The opposition between Saturn and Pluto may have brought difficulties in earlier life, you may have received harsh treatment through no fault of your own. You may at times feel you are being victimised or there is no way out of your situation. You learn a lot from your earlier life and should be able to plan more carefully so that you lay more secure foundations for the future.

Uranus/Neptune Aspects

Conj: There is a period of about 171 years between the conjunctions of Uranus and Neptune. The one at the present time is in Capricorn and children born now will show us the influence of this particular conjunction. They may have imagination and originality but they will be able to put their plans together constructively. They may be more aware of social issues and have the emotional sensitivity to do something about it. These may be the children who in twenty years time begin to restore or repair the damage that has been done in past generations to the environment.

Sext: Like the trine this indicates a well developed intuition and an interest in mysticism. But with the sextile you may look to develop your interests so you may study it at a deeper level or perhaps write about it. You are not afraid to express your beliefs even in the face of opposition. You can be very creative and you will look for opportunities in which to express the artistic side of your nature.

Trine: The trine indicates great intuition and possible clairvoyant ability and there is likely to be much interest in mysticism, astrology, yoga and the occult. You need to trust in your intuition and develop it, so that it supports you through life. This is very much a generation aspect and may not have a significant impact in the individual. You have your own particular set of beliefs and spend much of your life time searching for the truth.

Square: Like the opposition there is strong psychic ability but you are also inclined to feel more tension and confusion and your abilities are likely to cause you a considerable amount of trouble. You find it difficult to stand up for your beliefs unless other areas in your chart show more courage. Freedom may be particularly important to you but you do need an exceptional amount of courage to fight for it. You may find it easier to relate on a group level than you do on a personal one to one.

Inconj: You may be very sensitive to the suffering of others and may feel that you are under some obligation to fight for the rights of others, so you may find yourself working for society as a whole. This aspect tends to give responsibility on a world level rather than a personal one.

Oppos: Here we have a sensitive and intuitive person who has a need for freedom but there is also a lack of awareness. You may be so used to following others that you are unaware of the ability to be free. There is often strong psychic ability but also the possibility of misuse. In your search for the truth there may be many times when you are disillusioned.

Uranus/Pluto Aspects

Conj: This is a generation aspect and occurs only once in approximately every 115 years. The aspect is rather revolutionary as both Uranus and Pluto seek to make changes on a social and world level. It can deal with regeneration and new beginnings. On a personal level it would have to be in a strong position but it will mean that you will seek every minute to preserve your freedom, and you may go through life making rather drastic changes to stop yourself getting caught in a rut. You have to take care that some of these changes are not destructive.

Sext: The sextile can show an interest in science or technology. There is also an inventive and intuitive nature and you search for opportunities on how to expand these talents. You are the person who hates being stuck, you have a restless nature and tend to seek change in every situation.

Trine: There is often the desire to instigate change that will bring about some form of transformation or social reform. It is less dynamic than the conjunction or the square. It means that you are willing to change and can make those changes fairly easily on a personal level. There is an interest in death and rebirth and in reincarnation. You seek the truth and prefer to choose your own ideologies rather than be told what to believe in by someone else.

Square: The strength and position of these planets that are in square are important as to whether you are part of a generation whose life has been disrupted by economic crisis or war or any other natural catastrophe, or whether you are an instigator for change. So if these planets are strong you will tend to be highly strung and restless, never feeling settled. You are intuitive and instinctive and you seem to know when danger is just round the corner.

Inconj: You may find that some of your aspirations are blocked through the ever changing environment that you live in. You may find yourself under stress because of your ineffectiveness to do anything about world affairs. Perhaps you should look on a more personal level and give your own world more structure.

Oppos: You live in an era or a generation where life is constantly changing and this can sometimes be reflected in your own life where you go through a lot of personal upheavals and changes. You adapt easily to different ways of life and different modes of thinking.

Neptune/Pluto Aspects

Conj: Neptune Pluto conjunction can sometimes indicate a new spiritual awareness on a personal level, and on a universal level a new spiritual philosophy and religious aspirations. The last conjunction was in the 1890's which showed an increasing interest in spiritualism and mediumship. This is a generation aspect and will only be important to you if Neptune or Pluto are strong in your chart, that is strongly aspected or placed on an angle, and in that particular instance there will be interest in mysticism, death and rebirth and reincarnation.

Sext: Neptune and Pluto were in sextile for a fairly long period of time and therefore is most likely to affect people on a generation level, although there is some indication that while Pluto was in Virgo it had produced those who become alternative healers, concerned with the environment and maybe healers of the planet.

Trine: This will not occur this century and therefore will not affect anyone living at this time.

Square: This aspect may be the person who lives in a time of social disruption, the strength and house position of these planets will show the part that you would have played in creating the changes. But as the last Neptune square to Pluto ended before 1825 this will not apply to anyone living now.

Inconj: This last aspect occurred before 1800 and would not apply to anyone living at this time.

Oppos: Again a generation aspect. Its most noticeable characteristic if strong in the chart of an individual would be psychic activities but these may cause stress and conflict and a desire to use these talents for power.

Chapter 23

Putting It All Together

Although it doesn't seem too difficult on the surface to be able to interpret various parts of a chart, this final chapter is, in fact, a very difficult area for most students. When you begin to look at charts for friends and family you may be able to tell them something about their Moon sign or the house that their Mercury is in but how do you synthesise this, how do you put it all together in a concise readable report, without being repetitive? There is no set pattern to this as every student eventually develops their own style, one that is easy for them to follow, but here are some guidelines that I hope will be helpful to you.

When you are beginning there is no quick or easy way to produce an analysis except to work your way systematically through the symbols of the birth chart, and to make this simpler you should begin with a fairly comprehensive set of notes. If the notes are set out in a clear and readable fashion then it makes your final report much easier to write in a fluent style.

One of the most effective ways that I have found, and most students seem to agree with, is to first write on a sheet of paper what you have chosen for your categories, the following suggestions may be helpful.

General Characteristics

Your Relationship
Emotions
Family
Childhood
Love and Marriage
Children

Your Creativity and Mentality
Spare time activities or Hobbies

Career

Health

Travel

The above are only suggested categories with some subheadings which could also be chosen as main headings, or you may come up with some more imaginative ideas of your own. The next step is to find yourself several sheets of A4 paper and write a selected heading at the top of a separate sheet. You should have in front of you several sheets each with a different category as a heading: draw in a wide 2" left hand margin where you will write your planetary significators. Also include a blank sheet to jot down your working checklist. Now you are ready to work methodically through your birth chart and for our example we will use the chart of Mary on page 140.

Take some time to study the chart and write on your blank sheet anything that you feel intuitively about the chart (this may come to you when you are actually drawing up the chart) that could be backed up with astrological facts later.

Also on your blank sheet note that Mary has the following points:

1. An over emphasis on fire

2. A lack of earth (Mercury in Taurus)

3. A lack of water (Uranus in Cancer)

4. A major configuration; A Grand Cross involving Sun/Neptune Mars/Uranus.

5. Ascendant in Scorpio and MC in Leo

6. Ascendant rulers are Mars in Aquarius and Pluto in Leo

7. Mars in the third house and aspects.

8. Pluto in the tenth house and aspects

9. The Sun in Aries in the sixth house and aspects

10. The Moon in Leo in the tenth house and aspects

11. Mercury in Taurus in the seventh house and aspects, remem bering that this is the only planet in the element of earth.

12. Venus in Gemini in the eighth house is very weakly aspected.

13. Mars has been dealt with in point 7.

14. Jupiter in Leo in the tenth house and aspects.

15. Saturn in Sagittarius in the second house and aspects.

16. Uranus in Cancer in the ninth house and aspects.

17. Neptune in Libra in the twelfth house and aspects.

18. Pluto is dealt with in point. 8.

Using the following points as a checklist begin to expand your notes by working through the checklist and writing all that you know on the over emphasis on the element of fire and writing it on the sheet under the category you feel is most fitting. For example you could write about the same aspect under the following headings in this way:

General Notes on Chart

Page 1

General Characteristics
Over-emphasis on Fire — A tendency towards aggressiveness and domi nating others, needs to develop more consider ation and patience. Likes   plenty of activity and needs to keep busy.

Page 2

Emotions
Over-emphasis on Fire — Needs to get in touch with feelings and express the emotional side of their nature. May lack consideration of others and could appear intimi dating to the more sensitive.

Page 3

Childhood
Over-emphasis son Fire — As a child you may have had difficulties expres ing how you feel. Needs to be a leader but may have problems with other children through being too domineering. Sport is a good outlet for releasing all your energy.

Page 4

Career
Over-emphasis on Fire — Your choice of career should involve something that keeps you physically active. You have a low boredom threshold so you will look for plenty of mental stimulation and challenge.

This shows how you can spread one aspect across several different categories. When you have worked methodically from the checklist and expanded your notes as far as you are able you then begin to write your final report.

The first page of your analysis should be a title sheet saying who the Astrological Report is for and who wrote it. The second page should be the 'Prologue'. The third page should be 'Notes on Chart' and the fourth page the hand drawn birthchart, as shown in the examples on the following pages. Students are entitled to copy and reproduce the Prologue and Notes on Chart for their own analyses if they wish.

In order for your completed analysis to look as professional as possible, the cover should reflect the quality of the contents, so it would be advisable to bear this in mind.

Remember, no matter how you write your first sheets of notes on the birthchart, the final analysis must be written with tact and diplomacy. It can be very stimulating and pleasurable to read about your good points and potential, but not so easy to read about the difficult or stressful areas of your personality. When you are stressing a difficult area it is always helpful to offer your client positive advice, never leave them with the understanding that they have a negative characteristic that cannot be changed or transformed.

Astrological Analysis for Mary

Date of birth: 19th April 1956

Time: 7.55 p.m.

Place: Gravesend, Kent

Latitude: 51°N27'

Longitude: 0°E22'

A. Astrologer
11.9.1994

Prologue

Dear Friend,

The purpose of Astrology is to give you an understanding not only of your place in the Universe but of the kind of energies that are flowing through you. The horoscope tends to act as a mirror to help us see more clearly our own potentials, strengths, weaknesses, and abilities, talents and conflicts, as we are all learning and growing. The path of growth includes making peace between the various conflicts that often exist within our psyches.

Astrology is not there to make up your mind for you but to provide you with information upon which you can make an intelligent decision.

Astrology is an art whereby a natal chart is studied in order to give insight into planetary influences. It is not a means of predicting the future and must not be considered as such.

It is impossible to forecast exact events and therefore you will find phrases such as "It is likely", or "There is a tendency", in your analysis.

A copy of the analysis and the reasons for my deductions will be kept by me should you wish to discuss it at any time.

Notes on Chart

In every birth chart the signs of the zodiac have a different emphasis according to the planets that are placed within them. Everyone knows their own Sun sign by knowing their date of birth but of equal importance is the sign on the horizon at the moment of their birth.

This is known as the Ascendant or rising sign, and the exact degree can only be computed by knowing the place of birth and the exact time, which makes this individual to each person for whom a chart is computed.

Your chart shows that:-

The sign ascending is **Scorpio**

The sign containing the Sun is **Aries**

Along with other features of your birth chart such as the other planetary positions and aspects, you are an intricate mixture of the characteristics observed in the above signs.

Technical astrological terminology will not be included in this analysis, but will be held on my files for future reference.

Glossary of Astrological Terms

Adjusted Calculation Date
This refers to the date in the ephemeris when the noon position of the planets coincide with the progressed position of the planets. This date is used to determine the precise time when the progressions are exact.

Afflicted
When a planet receives two or more difficult but no easy aspects from other planets it is said to be afflicted

Angles
The Ascendant/Descendant, MC and IC and corresponding houses.

Angular Houses
Houses 1,4,7,10. They correspond to the cardinal signs and represent activity in physical matters.

Applying Aspect
When two planets are forming an aspect to each other and the faster moving planet has not yet reached the exact degree of the slower moving planet, the faster planet is applying. This aspect is considered stronger because the planet has yet to reach culmination point.

Ascendant
The degree of the zodiac rising over the eastern horizon at the moment of birth, or the intersection of the horizon with the ecliptic. This marks the cusp of the First House and is one of the most quickly changing points in the chart since the degree on the horizon changes every 4 minutes.

Ascension. Long

The signs of long ascension in the northern hemisphere are those that require a longer time to rise over the horizon, i.e. Cancer, Leo, Virgo, Libra, Scorpio and Sagittarius. In the southern hemisphere these become the signs of short ascension.

Ascension. Short

The signs of short ascension in the northern hemisphere require less time to rise over the horizon than others i.e. Capricorn, Aquarius, Pisces, Aries, Taurus and Gemini. In the southern hemisphere these become the signs of long ascension.

Aspect

An aspect is the relationship between two or more planets. The number of degrees separating two planets or sensitive points in the chart. An aspect is based on the division of the circle by different numbers. For example dividing the circle by three establishes the trine aspect of 120^0. Thus two planets located 120^0 from each other are said to be in trine aspect. The aspects reflect the way in which two functions of the person co-operate or clash depending on the nature of the two planets involved.

Esoteric Astrology

A branch of astrology that deals with the degree of evolution of the individual whose chart is under consideration.

Locational Astrology

A branch of astrology which erects a chart for the place at which a person resides or the place where he is planning to reside, instead of the place of birth.

Medical Astrology

Branch of astrology that concerns health, physical strengths and weakness and areas of sensitivity in the body.

Mundane Astrology

Branch of astrology concerned with politics, that is charts of leaders, countries, important events and social and political cycles. Literally 'astrology of the world'.

Natal Astrology
The branch of astrology that deals with the moment of birth and the interpretation of the potential inherent in the birth chart.

Benefic
Term referring to planets which are considered helpful. Traditionally Jupiter and Venus are the two benefic planets.

Birthchart
A chart erected for the moment of birth showing a map of the planets and heavens in relation to the Earth and to the individual at a specific place on earth at a given time.

Cardinal Signs
These are the initiating signs and represent the four signs that begin each season. Aries - Spring. Cancer - Summer. Libra - Autumn. Capricorn - Winter.

Combust
Refers to a very close conjunction of the Sun with another planet, usually within 8º.

Composite Chart
A chart that is erected for a relationship, determining the nearest midpoint of pairs of planets and sensitive points of two individuals birthcharts. A composite chart represents the actual relationship.

Configuration
This refers to three or more planets that are connected to each other by aspects.

Conjunction
This refers to the moment when two planets or points in a chart are found in the same degree of the zodiac.

Culmination
A planet culminates or is at culmination point when it is located on or near the midheaven of the chart. Culmination also refers to the moment when an aspect between two planets becomes exact.

Cusps
The lines which separate the houses in a birthchart are known as cusps. It can also refer to the place where one sign ends and the next begins.

Declination
This refers to the distance of a planet north or south of the celestial equator. Planets having the same declination are said to be in parallel aspect to each other.

Descendant
This is the western horizon and the point opposite the ascendant, it is the cusp of the 7th house.

Detriment
When a planet is in its detriment it is located in the sign opposite the sign it rules. The planet has difficulty in expressing itself because of the contrary nature of the sign it is in.

Electional Astrology
A branch of astrology which attempts to find the best moment for any undertaking.

Exaltation
A planet is said to be exalted when it is in the sign in which it is able to express itself with the most ease.

Fall
A planet is in its fall when located in the sign opposite the sign of the planets exaltation.

Fixed Signs
The power signs of the zodiac, Taurus, Leo, Scorpio and Aquarius. These tend to have fixed opinions and ideas and find it difficult to make changes.

Fortune, Part of
One of the most well known Arabian Points in the chart. Its position by house in the birthchart shows how and where the person can find the most satisfaction.

Grand Cross or Karmic Cross
A planetary configuration in which there are two sets of planets in opposition to each other, creating four planets that are locked in to one another through 4 squares and 2 oppositions. See page 177

Grand Trine
A planetary configuration where there are 3 or more planets all forming trines to one another.

Hoary Astrology
A branch of astrology that casts a chart for the time a question is asked in order to find an answer to it.

Imum Coeli
One of the four angles. The opposite point to the Medium Coeli (Midheaven).

Ingress
This refers to a planets entrance into a sign or house and can also signify the Sun entering into the four cardinal signs commencing each of the four seasons, ie vernal ingress.

Luminaries
Another term for the Sun and Moon which are also referred to as the lights.

Lunar Return
The time each month when the Moon in its transit returns to the exact degree and minute it was located at the moment of birth.

Medium Coeli
The midheaven or highest point of the chart.

Midpoint
A point midway between 2 planets creating a sensitive point that is activated if a third planet is located at the same degree, or transits the point.

Mutable Signs
The sign when the seasons are changing. Gemini, Virgo, Sagittarius and Pisces. These people are the most adaptable to change.

Mutual Reception
This is a term used to describe the relationship between two planets located in the signs which one or the other rules.

Natural Chart
Positioning the first sign Aries on the ascendant.

Nodes of the Moon
Two points at which the orbit of the Moon crosses the ecliptic. The north node is called the dragon's head and the south node the dragon's tail. The north node represents characteristics and modes to cultivate, whereas the south is a symbol of the past.

Opposition
A major aspect occurring when two planets or points are 180^0 from each other.

Orb
Range of influence, the number of degrees allowed when a planet is in aspect with another planet within which the aspect operates most strongly. For example, a sextile means 2 planets are sixty degrees apart, the orb for a sextile is $5/6^0$so therefore if two planets are between 54^0-66* of each other they are within orb.

Progressions Secondary
A chart erected for the day that is as many days after the birth date as the individual is in years.

Quincunx Inconjunct
An aspect of 150^0 between 2 planets or bodies

Quintile
An aspect of 72^0 between 2 planets or bodies.

Radix
Natal chart.

Rectification
Method of determining the ascendant and house cusps of the birth when the precise moment of birth is unknown.

Retrograde Motion
Said of a planet that appears to move backwards through the zodiac. This is an illusion created by the altered position and motion of the earth and planets to one another.

Rising Planet
A planet which is on or near the ascendant is said to be rising.

Ruling Planet
The planet which rules the sign on the ascendant or 1st house cusp. It is the ruling planet and its position and placement in the chart is important.

Sensitive Points
Points in the chart that exert an influence similar to that of the planets such as the Ascendant, Descendant, MC and IC, Vertex and Nodes.

Separating Aspect
When a faster moving planet moves away from the exact degree of the aspect with another planet. The aspect is said to be separating

Solar Return
A chart erected for the moment each year that the sun returns to the exact degree and minute where it was found at birth. Said to represent the conditions of the coming year.

Solar Chart
A chart in which the degree of a persons Sun also becomes the degree of their Ascendant. This is employed when the birth moment is unclear, or for writing sun sign columns.

Square
A major aspect of 90^0.

Stationery
A planet appears to stand still when its motion is changing from direct to retrograde or vice versa.

Stellium
A conjunction involving three or more planets.

Synastry
A method of comparing the position of the planets and sensitive points in two people' charts in order to gain an insight into the nature of their relationship and its strengths and weaknesses.

Transit
The movement of a planet over a natal planet or sensitive point in the birthchart at any given time.

T. Square
A planetary configuration in which two planets are in opposition to each other (180^0 apart) and each is squared by a third planet (90^0 from the two opposing planets).

Vertex
Degree of the zodiac which is exactly due west of the person at the moment and location of birth. It represents karmic or a fateful situation, encounters and conditions with other people over which one seems to have no conscious control. Its house position shows the areas of experience which will be most significant to one's overall development and destiny.

Zodiac
An imaginary belt in the heavens divided up into 12 constellations, Aries - Pisces, which are the signs of the Zodiac. These form an encircling band along the ecliptic and each take up 30^0.

Glossary of Astronomy

Angles
The angles are the Ascendant/Descendant and the MC/IC. The Ascendant is the point of intersection of the ecliptic and the horizon and the Descendant is its opposite point. The Midheaven or MC (Medium Coeli) is the point of intersection of the ecliptic and the meridian and the IC is the opposite point. These are powerful energy points in a birth chart. A planet near the angles has added strength..

Aphelion
Aphelion is when the earth's orbit is furthest from the Sun and moving at its slowest, therefore the apparent speed of the Sun as seen from the earth varies at different times of the year. So any planet that is at Aphelion is a planet that is at its greatest distance from the Sun and moving at its slowest

Apogee
A planet (the Moon) is at its furthest distance from the earth at Apogee and its rate of motion is at its slowest.

Apsides
The progression of the line of Apsides is an effect causing the Moon's orbit to turn on itself once in approximately 9 years. This is the line that connects the two points of the Moon's perigee and apogee. The longest axis of the ellipse traced by the Moons orbit is the line of Apsides.

Arc
Part of the circumference of a circle. The cusps of houses are measured in degrees of Arc along the ecliptic.

Circle (Small)
A small circle is any circle, where its plane does not pass through the centre of the earth.

Comet
Comets are bodies which have an elliptic orbit around the Sun, they are easily recognised by an extended luminous tail which generally points away from the sun but is only visible when near the Sun.

Constellations
A constellation is a group of fixed stars which only appear to be fixed because of their immense distance from the earth.

Declination
The position of planets are measured in degrees and minutes either north or south of the equator.

Direct Motion
A planet is moving in Direct motion when it revolves around the Sun from west to east. The rotation is the spinning of a planet on its own axis which appears as if the whole sky appears to turn around the planet during one complete rotation. So a diurnal rotation is the rotation formed during a sidereal day.

Diurnal Rotation
A diurnal rotation is the rotation formed during a sidereal day. (see above).

Dragons Head/tail
The Dragons Head is the North Node and it is where the Moons orbit crosses the ecliptic from south to north. The South Node which is known as the Dragons Tail is where the Moons orbit crosses the ecliptic from north to south. The nodal line is an imaginary line which links these two points and is where the plane of the earth's path intersects with that of the Moons path.

Ecliptic
The ecliptic is the apparent path of the Sun around the earth and is a Great Circle. It takes the Sun a year to follow its journey around the earth, completing one cycle of the Ecliptic. In reality it is the earth that orbits the Sun so the Ecliptic is not exactly an imaginary Great Circle in the heavens, it is the line of the earth's orbit.

271

Elongation
If a planet is at Elongation it means that the planet is at its maximum angular distance during its revolution of the Sun.

Equator
The Equator is a Great Circle midway between the north and south poles and is around the earth's largest circumference. If the plane of the terrestrial equator was projected beyond the earth then this extended plane would be called the Celestial Equator. It is used as a circle of reference for fixing the planets position in the sky.

First Point of Aries
There are two intersections of the Ecliptic and the Equator. The first being the First Point of Aries and the second being the First Point of Libra. Both intersections are spoken of as equinoctial points and have day and night of equal length.

Fixed Stars
Fixed Stars are so called because of their enormous distance from the earth. They do not appear to shift their positions over many centuries and appear to be fixed in the sky, and the Sun and planets are plotted against the background of the Fixed Stars.

Galaxy
We call the system to which the Sun and the planets belong the Galaxy and this is one of the largest known Galaxies. Its structure is spiral and appears to bulge in the centre and taper off towards the ends and it contains at least 100,000,000 stars.

Geocentric
Geocentric is placing the earth as the central point of reference for planets which appear to be going around it. So in astrology we use a Geocentric viewpoint.

Heliacal Rising and Setting
This is the rising or setting of the star at the same time as the Sun: in other words when a Sun and star rise and set at the same time.

Heliocentric
Heliocentric is the Sun being the central point of reference from which to locate the positions of planets in orbit around it.

Horizon
The Horizon is a Great Circle and the four cardinal points can be traced along it from north to east and from south to west. It is called the rational or true Horizon. If you extend this circle to meet the heavens then this is called the Celestial Horizon. With reference to the astrological chart the function of the Horizon is that it's eastern point of intersection with the Ecliptic, (the apparent path of the Sun around the earth), determines the rising degree or Ascendant for any given time and place. As the earth continuously rotates on its axis a different degree will rise above the eastern horizon approximately every four minutes and on average every two hours a new zodiacal sign will be rising. (See signs of long or short ascendant).

Houses
The houses in a chart are numbered anti-clockwise from one to twelve beginning on the left hand east side of the chart at the ascending point. The signs from Aries to Pisces are also listed anti-clockwise. Standing on the earth facing south the earth moves in an anti-clockwise direction on its orbit, therefore causing the houses to be numbered in an anti-clockwise direction. Rising planets move in a clockwise direction because the Earth on its axis spins at a greater speed than the moving planets, causing them to appear to go backwards.

Ingress
Ingress is simply the entry of a body or a planet into the disc or area of another body. In astrology an Ingress indicates the entry of a planet into a sign or a house. When the Sun enters into Aries it is called the Vernal Ingress and when it enters Libra it is the Autumnal Ingress.

Light Year
A Light Year is the distance measured by the speed that light travels in one year from one place to another.

Lunar Eclipse
A Lunar Eclipse occurs at a full Moon when the earth is between the Sun and the Moon and the shadow of the earth falls on the Moon.

Long and Short Ascension
In the mid-latitudes some signs take longer to rise above the horizon than others. This is due to the ecliptic lying at an oblique angle to the equator. In the Northern hemisphere the signs Cancer to Sagittarius are the signs of long ascension and Capricorn to Gemini are the signs of short ascension. You will notice this when you are looking in the table of houses to find the ascendant.

Medium Coeli
This is the Latin name for Midheaven which is the point where the sun crosses the meridian at noon. It is the point where the Ecliptic intersects the Great Circle of the Meridian.

Meridian
The Meridian is a great circle that passes through the zenith and the nadir and the north and south poles of the equator. (see the celestial sphere on page 186)

Occultation
An occultation occurs when one celestial body is hidden or eclipsed by another, so this can only occur when two bodies are in the same degree of longitude and declination.

Parallel of Declination
When planets are in the same degree north or south they are said to be parallel which can be seen as a weak conjunction. If one planet is north and the other south but in the same degree then they are counter parallel which can be seen as a weak opposition.

Perigee
The Moon's rate of motion is at its fastest and at its nearest point to earth. At perigee the tides are also 20% higher than at apogee the Moon's furthest point from earth.

Perihelion
This is when a planet is at its nearest point in orbit to the sun and is moving at its fastest speed.

Polar Elevation
The height of the pole above the horizon at any given place is equal to the latitude to the said given place or its angular distance from the equator.

Poles
The poles (north and south) are the points where the axis of the earth's rotation meets the earth's surface.

Precession of the Equinoxes
About 2,000 years ago a displacement of the earth's axis was discovered by Hipparchus. At this time the vernal equinox fell in the constellation of Aries and due to the retrograde cycle of equinoctial points it is at this present time in the constellation of Pisces, about to move into Aquarius. The precession is caused by the influence of the Sun and the Moon on the protuberant matter at the earth's equator. Precession is a slow swinging motion of the earth's' axis of rotation, rather like a spinning top when it is slowing down. The swinging motion is produced because the earth's axis is tilted and produces an angle between the plane of the equator and the plane of the ecliptic which is referred to as the obliquity of the ecliptic. Due to the precession the earth rotates obliquely upon itself and is seen as a gradual retrograde motion of the equinoctial points along the ecliptic, and against the background of the stars. The equinoctial points advance each year by a mean velocity of 50 seconds of arc from west to east. The complete retrograde cycle takes approximately 25,800 years (A Great Year).

Prime Vertical
This great circle is sometimes called the east to west great circle as it is a vertical circle passing through the east and west points of the horizon. It also passes through the zenith and nadir but its contact with the east and west points make it distinct from other circles passing through the zenith and nadir.

Quadrant
It is a quarter of a circle (a fourth part) the angle is 90⁰·

Retrograde Motion
The orbit of a planet around the Sun is from west to east which is termed as Direct Motion. However due to the different speeds of the orbiting Planet, from an observers point on earth, if the Earth is moving faster than the observed planet, then the planet appears to be slowing down and moving backwards. This is termed as Retrograde motion. A planet that appears to be motionless is termed as Stationery.

Solar Eclipse
A Solar Eclipse occurs at a New Moon when the Moon passes between the Sun and the earth blocking the light of the Sun from the earth.

Synodic Period
This is the time taken by a planet or a satellite (the Moon) to return to the same position with respect to the Sun and the Earth.

Synodic Month
This is the interval between consecutive conjunctions of the Sun and the Moon as seen from earth, the length of the synodic month varies by as much as 13 hours due to the eccentricity of the moons orbit of the earth.

Syzygy
When the Moon is in conjunction or in opposition to the sun it is said to be in syzygy.

Time (Equation)
Due to the varied speed of the Sun in its apparent path around the earth, we need to make various additions and subtraction's to convert apparent solar time into mean solar time.

Time (Sidereal)
Sidereal time is in effect 'Star Time'. A Sidereal day begins at the first point of Aries and each day falls short of the 24hr day as we know it by 3' 56" . By looking in the ephemeris you can see that the

sidereal time at noon increases each day by approximately 4 minutes. We therefore have to make a series of calculations to find the local sidereal time for a given birthplace and a given birth time.

Time (Solar)
Apparent solar time is time reckoned by the Sun and its apparent speed of motion around the earth.

Learn Astrology

Using This Text Book

as a

Step-by-Step Guide

For further details contact:-

Student Enrolment Secretary
Astrological Institute
163 Hever Avenue
West Kingsdown
Kent TN15 6DU

Tel: 01474 854955